# THE AUTHORISED ILLUSTRATED
# BIOGRAPHY
## OF
# WILL CARLING

## David Norrie

HEADLINE

First published in 1995
by HEADLINE BOOK PUBLISHING

10 9 8 7 6 5 4 3 2 1

British Library Cataloguing in Publication Data

Norrie, David
Will Carling: Authorised Illustrated
Biography. – 2 Rev. ed
I. Title
796.333092

ISBN 0–7472–1691–6

Typeset by Keyboard Services, Luton, Beds
Design and page make-up by Penny Mills

Printed and bound in Great Britain by
Mackays of Chatham PLC, Chatham, Kent

HEADLINE BOOK PUBLISHING
A division of Hodder Headline PLC
338 Euston Road
London NWI 3BH

# CONTENTS

Introduction: The Price of Fame                              5

1. 'Old Farts' Blown Away – 1995                             9

2. Growing Pains of a Rugby Superstar – 1965–87            16

3. Army Halts Carling's Charge – 1988                       31

4. Cooke Promotes the Will to Win – 1988–89                 42

5. Grand Slam Calamity – Murrayfield, 1990                  54

6. Winners at Last – Grand Slam 1991                        67

7. World Cup Winners and Losers – 1991                      83

8. National Anthem for Twickenham Faithful – 1992           98

9. Captain Carling in Doubt – 1993                         112

10. Rising from the Lions Mire – 1993                      124

11. Rowell Enters the Comfort Zone – 1994                  136

12. Hat-trick of Twickenham Grand Slams – 1995             147

13. Lomu Looms Large – 1995 World Cup                      162

14. Packer, Diana and the Wind of Change – 1995           180

Carling's Career Statistics                               191

# NEWS OF THE WORLD

### BRITAIN'S MOST POPULAR NEWSPAPER

AUGUST 6, 1995    LAST WEEK'S SALE: 4,581,527    Price 55p    No.7901

# ♛ TWO ROYAL SCOOPS ♛

**EDWARD: Ready to wed**

## Edward to wed Sophie

### EXCLUSIVE

By RAY LEVINE and CLIVE GOODMAN

PRINCE Edward has finally decided to marry his sweetheart Sophie Rhys-Jones, friends revealed last night.

The couple were celebrating aboard the Royal Yacht Britannia at Portsmouth before a cruise of Scotland's Western Isles.

Their decision comes after weeks of pressure on Edward to end speculation about Sophie's role in his life.

"Both the Queen and the Duke of Edinburgh are very happy with the relationship. But they want it to move on," confided a family friend.

Another close friend said: "I'm expecting to hear something official sooner rather than later."

**SOPHIE: Royal favourite**

# DI'S SECRET TRYSTS WITH CARLING

**SPORTS DI: Princess and Captain Will**

### EXCLUSIVE

By DENNA ALLEN

TODAY the News of the World can reveal the extraordinary relationship between Princess Diana and England rugby captain Will Carling.

Married Carling has been slipping quietly into Kensington Palace up to three times a week.

They swap nicknames and intimate gifts. Carling, 34, has a special phone to take Di's calls. She has given him her private number.

His ex-personal assistant Hilary Ryan revealed: "He's been running round after her like a puppy."

*FULL STORY: Pages 2,3,4,5*

---

### EXCLUSIVE — PALS CLAIM BARRYMORE HAD GAY FLINGS: PAGES 16 & 17

# THE PRICE OF FAME

Will Carling is the symbol of England's recent rugby success – three Grand Slams and a World Cup final. For the majority of England's rugby fans, the story begins and ends there. Yet, crucially, England's rugby captain is also the symbol of modern rugby – glamorous, commercial and high profile. Two incidents in 1995 proved that Carling is now the most famous sporting face in the land, as well as demonstrating the benefits and drawbacks that come with such fame. When Carling was sacked by the RFU as England captain after his remark about '57 old farts' in early May, the nation rallied to his cause, astonished that Twickenham could dismiss the most successful captain in rugby history a few days before England headed for the World Cup in South Africa. Carling was reinstated two days later after a furore unlike any other in English sport. Carling returned to the front pages in early August when his close friendship with Princess Diana was made public. Carling, married for just over a year, had naively believed that time spent with the wife of the future King at the Harbour Club gym and Kensington Palace would not be misinterpreted. Neither the Princess of Wales nor the England rugby captain are free agents. Charles and Diana may lead separate lives, but the revelations put a serious strain on Carling's marriage to Julia.

Carling has been portrayed as the 'golden boy' of English rugby, the man born with the 'silver spoon' in his mouth. The reality does not bear this out. England's success on the rugby field since he took over as captain in late 1988 has been played out to a background of money wrangles, clashes with officialdom and increasing problems of rugby's growing professionalism and commercialisation. Carling has been dragged to Twickenham on charges of having breached his amateur status. His captaincy has been regularly criticised, along with England's style of play. He was blamed for England's defeat in the 1990 Grand Slam showdown against Scotland, for the 'player power' that led to England's silence after winning in Cardiff for the first time in 28 years in 1991 and for the tactics that cost England the World Cup final against Australia later that year. His aloofness and coldness were given as the reasons that Gavin Hastings was made the 1993 British Lions captain instead. On that tour Carling was dropped for the first time in his rugby career and found himself among the midweek 'dirt-trackers'. When Geoff Cooke resigned in early 1994, many predicted that England's captain would follow without his protector. New coach Jack Rowell retained Carling for the 1995 World Cup, but lost his skipper when president Dennis Easby decided Carling's criticism of the RFU could not

OPPOSITE: The front page of the *News of the World* on the day that Carling's friendship with Princess Diana hit the headlines.

be tolerated. Carling was in charge for the World Cup, but England were squashed by Jonah Lomu and the All Blacks in the semi-final. Then Carling returned to the negotiating table with the RFU as Kerry Packer threatened a rugby revolution, but the Princess Diana revelations intervened to ensure that Carling's 1995–96 season was going to be as hectic and closely scrutinised as all the rest. The Will Carling story has been one of battles, many unknown, as well as of unparalleled success.

The battles make his achievements all the more remarkable. This is not just a story of a great rugby player, but a great team. It is a team that has included Geoff Cooke, Roger Uttley, Dick Best and Jack Rowell. Carling's England should really have been known as Cooke's England. He was the dominant influence from Carling's debut until his resignation in 1994. Since then Rowell has been the guiding hand on England's direction. Many have found England's success difficult to deal with, on and off the field. England have been the team to beat, and the side to beat with a big stick. That is strange because the national soccer and cricket teams have given their supporters much less to cheer about in recent times. England have lost to just one visiting Five Nations side at Twickenham since Carling took over in 1988. The newly built stadium has surpassed the Parc des Princes as the most intimidating rugby venue in the northern hemisphere. The purists may complain, yet Carling's England delivers. To a whole generation of the Twickenham faithful, rugby is Carling, Rob Andrew, Brian Moore, Rory Underwood, Dean Richards and Jerry Guscott. They are the inspirations to the thousands of youngsters who are taking up the game.

The Rugby Football Union have seen it differently; they have been happy to build spanking new stands on the back of England's sell-out achievements. Yet the same authorities have seen Carling's squad as the biggest threat to the future of the game. However, the arrival of Tony Hallett in the summer of 1995 has given many, not just the players, hope for the future, even after the collapse of the Packer Circus. The feeble leadership of the International Board has led to inconsistency and chaos in the rugby world. In Australia, South Africa and New Zealand, the players are king. In England, he is a pauper where the committeeman rules. The announcement by the IB just before the start of the 1995–96 season that rugby union would be totally 'professional' was long overdue.

The authorities not only mistrusted the players – views reinforced by the part played by some senior England stars in the Packer saga – many resented them. The 'no player is bigger than the game' view was countered by John Arlott years ago: 'The game is the players.' The basic problem is that rugby is still ruled by committees, full of negative thoughts, anxious to maintain the status quo and in some cases the perks of their job. It's a gravy train that has sprouted wings. Officials who have spoken out for the players are accused of siding with those trying to destroy the very fabric of rugby. If you are not for us, you must be against us.

Will Carling has been through the mill, as have most modern sporting stars. The sacrifices, in terms of time, effort, privacy and the rest of his life, are the price for competing at the highest level these days. Carling has been dedicated to the job of being an international centre and an England captain for seven years now. He has learnt to appreciate there is a national hang-up with success. He has been accused of being arrogant, of not caring about the grass-roots of the game, of trying to turn rugby professional and of reaching the top on the back of a successful team. Yet Carling has never denied or played down the efforts of his team-mates, even those like Jeff Probyn who have stuck the knife in since retiring. Nor has he denied that he is a 'lucky' person with the knack of being in the right place at the right time. And he appreciates that his reign as captain would have not lasted more than a couple of years in any other era of English rugby. Carling has never been bothered by personal records or land-marks. He understands that while some are jealous of his success, many more have little comprehension of the demands on current players and, especially, the England rugby captain.

Carling has made his mistakes. Plenty of them. He has never professed to being perfect. The Princess Diana headlines proved he is going to have to be more careful than ever. It was the final signal that England's rugby captain has little or no life of his own. Even former rugby legends like Bill Beaumont or Gareth Edwards did not have to cope with such intrusions. The fame brings its rewards, financial and otherwise. Carling is a popular face for endorsing products in TV and newspaper advertisements. The Carlings featured together on TV promoting Quorn, with England's rugby captain looking every inch the 'new man'. But such deals mean that the couple have to maintain a 'happy families' image at all times. The public has an impression of Carling as a serious young man because he takes his job as England captain so seriously. In fact, his schoolboy sense of humour is never far away. His appearance with Mr Blobby was one of the highlights of that series, with Carling kicking, pushing and abusing his way around the studio. But such behaviour does not go with the job of England captain when he is on duty.

Carling has always been guarded about his private life, though that has become increasingly impossible. What hurt him most when details of his friendship with Princess Diana were made public was that a close employee should betray his trust. Even skilled interviewers rarely managed to do more than scratch the surface. Carling came across as fairly one-dimensional on Sue Lawley's 'Desert Island Discs'. Even his luxury item, a flotation tank, was rather predictable. But such high-profile appearances are resented by the rugby Establishment.

Colin Herridge, the former Harlequins secretary, has provided valuable support for Carling since he came into the England team. It was to Herridge's house that Carling went when he was sacked by the RFU and from whom he sought advice in the middle of the Princess Diana storm. The remarkable thing about their friendship is that Herridge is an RFU committeeman. Yet he is respected by the players, which is why he was made England media liaison man during the 1995 World Cup. 'Will tries to promote English rugby in the best way possible. I believe he has done more for rugby in this country than anyone else to promote the spread of the game. As a role model, he has done a few things wrong. Sadly, he is never going to win with certain members of the committee. Will has already made a great success of his life and will continue to do so. They feel that rugby has given him that fame and fortune. The truth is the other way around. Will Carling's England have brought fame and fortune to rugby. The officials are happy enough to bask in that glory.'

Rugby union is the game that Carling fell in love with aged six. Yet, even at school and university, he was a player apart. That continued when Carling was handed the England captaincy at 22. It has been a lonely life since then, and an increasingly turbulent one, despite England's and Carling's record-breaking achievements. The wonder is that Carling is still around, and still smiling. The reason for that is simple: the buzz. The buzz of three days of preparations, the buzz of running out in front of a packed Twickenham, the buzz of winning and the buzz of celebrating a job well done. As long as that buzz continues to ring in his ear, William David Charles Carling will find expression and relief on the rugby field. When it stops, so will he.

# CHAPTER 1

# 'OLD FARTS' BLOWN AWAY – 1995

Will Carling was a budding rugby star when he made the big phone call to Geoff Cooke in his parents' kitchen. His hands were trembling as he wrote a note to his Mum and brother while carrying on the conversation: 'I am the captain.' That was October 1988.

The next time Carling put the phone down in a kitchen in a similar state was in his own home near Barnes Common in May 1995. Carling exclaimed: 'Shit!' His wife, Julia, looked at him. 'I am an ex-captain.' Carling had just been sacked as England's World Cup skipper, 10 days before the squad was due to fly off to South Africa. Carling had been speaking to Dennis Easby, the RFU president and a member of the committee whom Carling had described on TV a few days earlier as '57 old farts'.

Carling's 'old farts' remark sparked off one of the most sensational sporting weekends in recent times. The rugby authorities tried to bury Carling. They succeeded only in making him a martyr. The whole of England rallied to his cause and the RFU were forced to make a humiliating climbdown. The most astonishing part of the whole ridiculous affair was that the 'old farts' thought they could get away with sacking the most successful leader in rugby history.

Carling's words had been recorded during an interview before the Calcutta Cup and Grand Slam clash with Scotland in March. They were used over the closing credits of a programme in the *Fair Game* series which looked at the changing rugby world. Jon Holmes, Carling's agent, had seen a draft version before it was broadcast. He claimed the comments were not included at that stage, an allegation disputed by Yorkshire Television, who made the programme for Channel Four. 'I think I am sufficiently astute that I would have noticed it and I would have said to Will, "I think we have a problem here because it could be taken out of context."'

Had Channel Four not used Carling's off-camera remarks to promote the programme in a press release, they would probably have passed unnoticed. The press release alerted the media, who were on the trail of a bust-up before the programme had been broadcast. The whole affair was a storm in a teacup. It should have been treated as such, or as a joke. The best response came from Sandy Herridge, wife of England's media liaison officer Colin, another member of the RFU committee: 'What Will says is absolutely true. My daughters have been calling Colin an old fart for years.' That was the most sensible statement of those that emanated from an RFU source over the next three days. Most extended their stepladders and prepared to mount their high horses. Yorkshire's representative Roy Manock was first off the blocks with the condescending official line: 'Youth would be an ideal state if it came later in life and was accompanied by a bit of common sense. Committee members – the same old farts he goes on about – have not just given hours but days and years of their free time to provide the very opportunity for the Will Carlings of this world to get where they are.' The pre-publicity meant the RFU president faced a rough ride at the Norwich Rugby Dinner the night the programme was shown. The diehards in this hotbed of rugby demanded that Carling be put in his place. 'The ordinary rank-and-file people there thought it was quite improper,' Easby explained.

There is little doubt that Easby believed ignoring Carling's remarks would be perceived as weakness. It's doubtful that he intended to relieve Carling of the captaincy at the outset. However, Easby started a fire that one or two others were only too eager to stoke. The part played by retiring RFU secretary Dudley Wood will never be fully revealed. He had been in attendance at the meeting where the decision was taken as an observer only – though certainly not an impartial one. Wood helped assemble a bunch of senior RFU officials who, Bill Bishop apart, had been waiting to show the players, especially Carling, who was boss. Ian Beer was a former president, John Richardson was a vice-president, John Motum was the assistant honorary treasurer and the late Peter Bromage was the treasurer who was about to become chairman of the newly created RFU Executive Committee. Bishop was the vice-president who took over from Easby. Bromage and Richardson were in contact by phone; the rest were at the East India Club with Wood, who was taking notes. That was where the deed was done.

Initially the firing squad had two major problems. Jack Rowell could not be involved in the decision-making process. If he were to threaten to resign as manager, that would end any moves to sack Carling. How could they remove the captain without involving the coach? They presented him with a *fait accompli* and emphasised that he could not abandon the squad in their hour of need just before the World Cup. The other concern was timing. They could not wait to announce Carling's sacking. Once Rowell and others knew, the pressures would begin to postpone or abandon the idea. There were even doubts about whether this kangaroo court could act as it was doing. They wanted Carling out. And out quickly. The small matter of the Pilkington Cup final, the sponsor's biggest day of the season, was ignored.

Rowell was told on Friday night. Carling had already got wind that the knives were out. A planned apology in his Sunday newspaper column was brought forward and released late on Friday. It was fairly grovelling. 'The comment was not made to camera and was not a quote I would like to be remembered for. I hope the members of the committee will not take offence.

But, if I have offended any member, I apologise unreservedly and would like them to know I will not allow myself to be put in that situation again.' The journalists, who had got wind of the trouble Carling was in, read it wrong. No one believed that the RFU would sack the most successful captain in rugby history just before the World Cup, especially as he had held his hands up. Carling rang Easby on Saturday morning. England's captain could tell from the president's tone that the threat was to be carried out. Carling then called Herridge, who explained there was still hope. But a call from the *News of the World*'s rugby correspondent, myself, ended that. I read out to Carling the statement that the RFU had released at 11.30 that Saturday morning. 'It has been decided with regret that Will Carling's captaincy of the team will be terminated forthwith and an announcement concerning his replacement will be made shortly. In the light of the views Will Carling has expressed regarding administrators, it is considered inappropriate for him to continue to represent as the England captain, the Rugby Football Union, England and indeed English sport.' That was it, after seven years and 47 internationals in charge.

It was the biggest bombshell that has ever hit British sport. The Pilkington final became a sideshow as Twickenham and the rest of England went into shock. Politicians looked on enviously. None of them had ever united the country the way Easby had done. There was total condemnation for an act of utter folly. The RFU, normally guaranteed to raise a titter, had become a laughing-stock.

## WILL CARLING

The first thing about the whole affair is that I don't remember saying it. I'm not denying I said it. I just don't remember. If I had said it to camera, I would have remembered. I've been in hot water before. I would have thought: 'Hang on. That might not sound too good.' It was Thursday when the office got a call from the *Sun*, alerted by the press release. They wanted publicity for the programme. I'm sure they got it. I had a word with Jon [Holmes]. We didn't think it was too serious. I was playing golf on the Friday with Jon and Gary [Lineker]. I got calls on the mobile from Colin Herridge and Tony Hallett. I knew it was getting serious. It certainly put me off my game. Gary said: 'Don't worry. Even they would never be that stupid.' I spoke to Colin after the round and he told me to get my apology out that night. I sent a copy to the president at the East India Club and tried to ring him there. I couldn't get hold of him.

Then I rang Jack [Rowell]. As ever, he was to the point. 'You prat!' He told me to speak to Colin. That night Julia and I went out for dinner with Hugh Laurie and his wife. Hugh had a great time making toasts. 'Just think, I was there on your last night as captain, Will.' I was trying to step back from the hysteria and think logically. I expected, whatever happened, that I would be allowed my say. 'Before we pass sentence on you, Mr Carling, have you anything to say in your defence?' In this day and age, even the RFU wouldn't try to get away by condemning me without a trial, fair or otherwise. We've all said stupid things, even Dudley Wood. He had been plastered all over the papers after less than politic remarks about coloured athletes in this country the previous year. My comments paled into insignificance compared to that. I had no problems sleeping that Friday night.

I thought I'd better get up early the next morning and ring the president, apologise once again and ask if my public words of remorse were enough. As soon as he came to the phone, I knew I was history. The tone of his voice was like a funeral march. 'William, thank you for ringing. You are no longer captain of England. We have had a meeting. You will be allowed to go to South Africa as a player. Thank you for all you've done. Sorry to tell you this news.' I put the phone down in the kitchen. 'Shit.' Julia looked at me. 'I'm an ex-captain.'

I rang up Colin, who knew what I'd been told. He told me not to worry. 'This is not the end of it. We are trying to persuade them to change their minds. Don't say anything. Don't talk to anyone.' He headed off to Twickenham. Then you rang on behalf of the *News of the World*. I was history, officially.

Players arriving for the Pilkington final were stunned. Bath skipper John Hall was the first to talk about a players' revolt. Reaction from round the country and round the sporting world was unanimous. The Rugby Football Union was stark raving bonkers. The punishment bore no relation to the crime. The English are traditionally a difficult lot to get moving. Once roused, though, they can move mountains. And mountains were moved over the next couple of days. The backdrop of the Pilkington final helped Carling. So many of the protagonists were in one place and could not avoid answering probing questions or making defiant statements. Easby, Rowell and Wood were all at Twickenham. Wood made two statements that were thrown back in his face. The first was that Rowell had been consulted. The second was that the RFU Executive had made the decision. Certain members of the Executive had. Some of the Executive knew nothing about it. Rowell had been asked to come up with an alternative captain, so that the appointment could be approved by the president. Few had realised the strength of the tie between the president and the national rugby captain. Easby has described the captaincy as 'a gift from the president' to be granted and removed as the president saw fit.

No one believes for a minute that Easby took the decision lightly. But he was totally unprepared for the furore it caused. Others assured him the hue and cry would quickly die down. It was apparent by Saturday night that it would not. The full force of Fleet Street hit Easby on Sunday morning. The RFU president was on the front and back pages, hailed as the most famous and loathed 'old

Dudley Wood, recently retired secretary of the Rugby Football Union, needed police protection after the Pilkington Cup final when the Twickenham crowd became aware of Carling's sacking. *(Colorsport)*

fart' in the country. The media camped on his doorstep and he was filmed and photographed mowing his lawn. Wood, in his King Canute role, ignored the water lapping round his shoulders, and commented: 'We discussed everything from sacking him from the team to leaving a decision until after the World Cup. Quite a few members of the committee would have taken the most severe action of all. They would have kicked Will out of the team and out of the World Cup. We have had a lot of letters and phone calls from all over the country asking for him to be removed from the team. As of yet we have not had one message of support for Will.'

Easby's first big problem was finding a new captain. Dean Richards was the man the meeting thought should take charge. Richards turned it down. His words were the death knell to Easby's plans. 'I would not accept the captaincy in these circumstances, even if pressed by Jack Rowell.' Andrew also said he would decline. The players united behind Carling. Their manner and statements were not confrontational. They thought the RFU had got it wrong and asked them to reconsider. That was the sensible approach. As early as Saturday night, some of the more aware members of the RFU were looking for a way out of this problem, for a compromise that would allow Carling to lead the squad to South Africa. It would have been disastrous if the players had backed Easby and the RFU into a corner. The one man who might have done that, Brian Moore, was away for the weekend in Yorkshire and missed all the fun.

WILL CARLING

My sacking showed no concern for me or the team. I couldn't believe the statement after all my time in charge. I was devastated. At least I was going to South Africa. I had been worried I might be out altogether. I can't deny I was in shock. All the planning, all the hard work, gone for a few careless words. I lay on the floor watching the Pilkington final on Sky. Despite my situation, I remember thinking: 'How could they do this to one of their major sponsors?' My dismissal completely obliterated their final. I could hear this chanting through the game. I kept wondering what it was. It didn't sound like Wasps or Bath. After the game Rob rang me and told me they were chanting my name and that Dudley needed a police escort at the end. Suddenly, half the world's media were outside my door. They would follow me if I went down the road for milk. They told me they were there for the weekend. That Saturday has to be the weirdest day of my life. Dean rang me and said: 'This is a joke.' Rob said the news had ruined the cup final and put him off his game. Everyone who came to my door was interrogated by the press. The media weren't that bad. After all, they were being supportive. God knows what it's like if you've done something wrong. I've never seen anything like the papers on Sunday. It was everywhere. I know it was a big thing in my life, but I couldn't believe the space the editors felt it merited. I got in touch with Colin and went round there for Sunday lunch and my first full day as an ex-England captain.

The breakthrough came on Sunday afternoon. It involved a live radio link between Carling's agent Jon Holmes and Easby. Holmes explained the background to the comments being made. Easby was on the back foot because Carling had not been given the opportunity to put his side of the story. A retired solicitor, Easby could not ignore the rules that had governed all his professional life. Easby took a deep breath. He and Holmes had a private chat after the programme. The result was that Carling phoned Easby and a meeting was arranged for the following day. On Sunday morning, Easby had declared: 'I stand by it and there is no chance whatsoever that it might be reversed.' A few hours later Easby explained: 'In the light of what Will said to me on the phone, I am meeting him tomorrow to discuss the situation. It is feasible that he could be given back the captaincy.' The tide had turned. Easby had been shocked and overwhelmed by the public outrage and support for Carling. That alone, however, would not have forced him into a turnaround. Easby's legal brain told him that he had acted in haste and without full possession of the facts.

The world waited to see how the RFU president would eat his humble pie – in small pieces or one large gulp. In the event, England's squad session at

Dennis Easby, president of the Rugby Football Union, shakes the hand of peace with Carling after reinstating him as England captain. *(Express Newspapers)*

Marlow that Monday night meant Easby had to eat it all down in one sitting. Carling was back as England captain. It was a triumph for the players, it was a triumph for Jon Holmes, it was a triumph for the entire population of England – apart from 57 'old farts'. Easby's climbdown was simple: 'Will and I had a very good meeting at Twickenham. He gave me all the assurances I needed and I am delighted to be able to ask him to take on the captaincy for the World Cup. I regret what happened, but Will's original apology was not quite sufficient.'

England's Grand Slam squad had been without a captain from Saturday lunch-time to Monday afternoon. Now the man under threat was Easby. 'I will not be resigning.' He was as good as his word and travelled to the World Cup with the England squad. He is still the most famous 'old fart' in the land and will be for evermore. Yet Easby was big enough to correct his mistake. More often than not, the English Establishment compound one mistake with an even bigger one. Easby was big enough to face the music, and face the players.

WILL CARLING
That radio link-up was the first glimmer of hope. I knew nothing about it. Jon rang up and said he'd just been on radio with the president. 'Ring him in an hour.' Jon was so excited. I had to wait till he calmed down so he could explain what had happened. I rang Dennis and we arranged a meeting. I had no hesitation in wanting the captaincy back. I felt I knew who had

orchestrated my sacking. I'd never thought of the captaincy as a gift. Often it has been a burden. I can never say enough about the support I received, especially from the team. I wasn't flattered they were behind me as a person, but as a leader. You can't quantify that support. I'm pretty sure I would not have got that level of support in 1993. A lot changed on the Lions tour. Not too much had gone wrong for me before. If I had been sacked in 1993, I would have been out. There would have been no way back.

When I rang the president, his tone was different. Once a meeting was fixed I was hopeful of getting the captaincy back. I didn't see the point in getting together if I wasn't going to be reinstated. Dennis had said that if we could come to an understanding and apology, then we could put this behind us.

It was the most bizarre weekend of my life. I met Dennis on the Monday afternoon. We sat in an office and talked it through. I admire him for holding his hands up and taking the blame, for the way he was in the World Cup. No one else stood behind him. I don't believe he was the instigator. He accepted a lot of what I said. It was a private discussion. It will remain that way.

From a PR point of view, it couldn't have gone better for the players. Or worse for the RFU. We had a mad rush from Twickenham to Marlow with the mass media on our tail. I knew there wasn't a problem with the squad when I arrived. 'Good God, Will, they haven't given you the job back! How did you talk your way out of that one?' I think the officials were staggered by the hostility and it made them realise the support for the players there was throughout the country, especially when all their fax numbers were published. I have seen copies of some three or four hundred letters sent to Twickenham. That was only a few of the total. Some of them were less than polite.

It does seem to me that one comment off camera, however stupid it was, can't have been the sole reason for what happened. It was about me, the players and their grievances with the RFU. It really amounted to a last desperate stand against professionalism. It is very fortunate that we have a new secretary. Tony Hallett will take a more realistic, progressive view. He'll do a far better job. Dudley saw everything from his traditional viewpoint. He would fight his corner, but that approach is the reason the relationship between the players and the committee got as bad as it did.

I don't believe that my sacking and the aftermath had a detrimental effect on our World Cup. It was resolved so quickly and was over by the time the squad got together. Basically, it disturbed a few people's weekend and disrupted the Pilkington Cup final. It hadn't really sunk in that I had lost the captaincy. It was over before it had begun, like I was waking up after a bad dream. And really, once it had happened, it was never really mentioned again by the players. It was not a big issue and was quickly forgotten. There was far more interest in the media who carried it forward. The only memento I have is a bottle of 'Old Fart English Gin' in my office.

# CHAPTER 2

# GROWING PAINS OF A RUGBY SUPERSTAR – 1965–87

Those searching for the secrets of Will Carling and his success have spent much time delving into his background. Plenty has been made of Carling's upbringing – how the Army background and the boarding public-school life moulded a character of privilege and arrogance, a leader with a stiff upper lip and aloofness. Carling has never denied it was a privilege to attend such a famous rugby nursery as Sedbergh. As for those lonely nights when he cried unheard in the dorm at his abandoned state, they simply did not exist. Neglect is not the way of the Carling family. Will and his elder brother, Marcus, are members of a close-knit, affectionate family. That family has continued to provide Will with valuable support and refuge during times of strain, but he did not find separations from his parents an ordeal.

Carling's love affair with rugby began at the Terra Nova prep school. Even then he was a player of distinction, a player with a future. Success at school, as elsewhere, came at a price. At Sedbergh, Carling's ability took him ahead of his classmates and into sides above his age group. His classmates were not his team-mates, and vice versa. Carling learnt to live a rugby life alone. That role is not alien to his nature; he is perfectly comfortable as the man apart.

Unfamiliar surroundings were a regular part of Carling's childhood. His father, Bill, was a lieutenant-colonel in the Air Corps. He had also been a burly prop who gave sterling service to Cardiff, Bath, Blackheath and Cornwall and earned an England trial. Tours of duty, mainly to Hong Kong and the Far East, meant the Carlings averaged an address a year for his 25 years in the service. Bill was stationed at Warminster when the two boys were born. Marcus and Will were born in the same maternity bed in Bradford-on-Avon in Wiltshire. The future England captain – William David Charles – arrived 19 months after his brother, weighing 7 lb 15 oz. The younger Carling ate and slept. Ate and slept. His mother, Pam, was not unhappy with that. 'William was incredibly placid. I used to forget about him. It would be the middle of the afternoon and I'd suddenly realise that I'd forgotten to give him lunch. He would never remind me by screaming or crying. As you can see by the photographs, he was a baby who liked his lunch.'

Carling's first three school years were spent at Montgomery Infants in Colchester. When his father was posted abroad, he joined his brother at Terra Nova School in Cheshire, a location chosen because their grandparents lived

LEFT: The Carling boys at a Sergeants' Mess function, Gravesend, 1968.

RIGHT: William the Conqueror, Christmas 1970, with Marcus less than happy.

Carling (left) with elder brother Marcus. At two years old, he looked more likely to end up as a front-row colleague of Brian Moore's.

nearby. By the time Carling left there in 1979 his sporting career was up and running. He was a crack shot in the rifle team, an off-spinner and hard-hitting middle-order batsman, a record-breaking long jumper and runner. On the rugby field, as the puppy fat vanished, the young Carling moved from hooker back through the scrum to the comparative safety of the backs where he eventually developed into a sniping fly half. The competitive edge was apparent from an early age – rather too much so. His father remembered the turning point: 'Pam was watching him in a prep school cricket match. Willie was given out. He was not happy and stormed off in a fury making a scene. His bat was hurled away in anger. I was away. But Pam was having none of that. She went straight into the pavilion. It took a clump around the ear to quieten him down. He never did it again.' There were other lessons to be learnt outside the classroom. Carling got a reputation for being a bully.

WILL CARLING
It's not pleasant to look back upon. You wonder why you do it. I had been beaten up by my own brother, so I thought it was about time I got my own back. I wasn't into the protection-racket business. Money didn't pass hands. It was more 'Do this – or I'll beat you up.' Not much of a difference I suppose. I suddenly stopped one day. I turned on someone and made my usual threat. I saw this look of fear in his eye. I realised that this was not the way to treat people. My fondest memories of Terra Nova are the rugby and the Danish matrons. When a maths teacher ran off with one of them, I was distraught.

His Terra Nova headmaster Andrew Keith said goodbye with a warning: 'He has dominated much of Terra Nova life for a fair amount of time. Much of our sporting and artistic success is due to him. I hope that William can make the adjustment from being master of all he surveys to being just another lowly new boy with the right degree of humour and humility.'

Carling arrived at Sedbergh as the school celebrated 100 years of rugby. It was an impressive century. Eleven former pupils, including captains Wavell Wakefield and John Spencer, had played for England, sixteen for Scotland and two for Ireland. Sedbergh's 'brown shirts' are no less famous or feared than Oswald Mosley's. With the jersey came the brown blazer. Carling went into the Sedbergh record books when his entry into the first XV as a fifth former meant no place for an established 'Brown Blazer'. For his final two years, W. D. C. Carling was a regular in the England Schools team, leading them in his final season. For this reason, Carling's week tended to revolve around rugby, although he did manage A levels in geography, economics and English.

WILL CARLING
We trained on Mondays and Tuesdays. Wednesday was a practice game.

LEFT: Carling (right) on his way to open the innings for Terra Nova.

RIGHT: The Terra Nova rifle team were into big trophies. Will is at the left end of the back row, with Marcus at the front on the left.

Will Carling was captain and fly half of the Terra Nova 1st XV in 1978. The side lost one match, scoring 229 points against 30.

Another short session followed on Thursday. Friday was spent getting ready. I cleaned my boots and stuffed them with newspaper – the *Telegraph* was all we were allowed to read – and polished them. That's how I spent my five years, with a little work fitted in.

LEFT: Carling in the famous 'brown' jersey of the Sedbergh 1st XV.

Carling's softer side manifested itself in his poetry and sketching at school. He had arrived at Sedbergh on an art scholarship. His poetry was a passing phase, although a couple – 'Love' and 'Mutual Evolution' – made the school magazine. Carling would rather they stayed there. Sketching is still an important part of his relaxation. He claims no special skill or insight, just enjoyment and, occasionally, the satisfaction of a job well done.

RIGHT: Carling, outside Winder House, enjoying life in the sixth form at Sedbergh.

Carling's first year at Sedbergh was spent in a dormitory. After that he moved to Winder House, where his brother was domiciled, and his own room. Marcus was something of a rebel at school. There had been talk of keeping the Carling brothers apart, but this did not happen. Carling was head of Winder House in his final year, but the place had one drawback: it is the furthest house away from the centre of school – two-thirds of a mile, a journey that had to be made six times a day. Carling remembers how bleak the Yorkshire moors could be in the middle of winter. On one camping trip, when he was 14, Carling's trust in his own instinct for self-preservation was reinforced.

LEFT: Carling, 14, up to his neck in it during a holiday in Pipione, Italy.

RIGHT: A moody Carling, 15, at the family's chalet in Gruyere, Switzerland.

Carling receives the *Rugby World* School Team of the Month pennant for November 1983 from former England captain John Spencer, himself a Sedbergh old boy.

## WILL CARLING

Half a dozen of us were on the moors, getting from A to B with the help of maps. Suddenly, this blizzard came down and all the landmarks disappeared. We had no master with us. We had to decide quickly which was the way to safety. After a discussion, we chose a route. I wasn't happy. It didn't feel right. I knew we would be going in the wrong direction. The lads said that we had taken a majority decision. 'Fair enough, but I'm going this way.' I didn't storm off into the storm. I explained the reasons for my doubt. They agreed and we were back safely within half an hour. Two of the group already had hypothermia. I've never been so cold in my life. We lost all our equipment. I would have gone off on my own if I hadn't persuaded them. I trust my instincts.

Carling's rugby ability singled him out at Sedbergh, even in an outstanding side. Every school year has its sporting stars, but Carling was a star outside his year. Richard Mowbray, master in charge of the Colts, made this assessment: 'The success of the XV this term has been largely due to Carling's great maturity. As a player with impressive individual skills, particularly in his timing and awareness of space around him, his own performances have been outstanding. However, it has been his character which has most impressed me this term. Despite their record, the XV are not a team of world-beaters. William's leadership, encouragement and example have brought the best out of the players around him. Their respect for him is considerable. It has been a genuine pleasure to work with such a gifted but self-effacing young man. People like William make education such a pleasure.'

Carling moved to full back and took over the goal-kicking duties in his final year, scoring 13 tries and over a century of points. His achievements brought him representative honours and trips with Yorkshire, the North and England. Carling led Yorkshire to Zimbabwe in July 1984 when they beat the national school side and the Under-19s. Brooke Dawse, who taught Carling Classics in the fourth form, was a Yorkshire Schools selector and managed his first tour as captain.

BROOKE DAWSE
The first time I really noticed him at Sedbergh was when he made a superb break against Blackrock College. Opposite him that day was Brendan Mullin, who went on to play for Ireland and the British Lions. The first XV was outstanding in his final year. We held a buffet lunch for parents before the Loretto match. We turned up a few minutes late. Sedbergh were already leading 24–0. I remember thinking John Spencer and Alistair Biggar were quite good. I thought the same about Will Carling. You are never quite sure how they will do in the outside world. At his first Yorkshire trial, one of the other selectors approached me: 'Is there really something to this lad?' Yes, there was. The interesting thing about Will was the bigger the challenge, the better he got.

I was very impressed with him as captain in Zimbabwe. We had one problem. He sorted it out very quickly. The lads went on a Booze Cruise when we visited Victoria Falls. It's a floating bar. Some drank too much.

There was some damage, about ten pounds' worth. Will sorted it out, got the money to pay for the repairs and I gave them a two-minute lecture. Will was super. He backed me up a hundred per cent. Will was nearly in tears when we lost our only game to a late dropped goal. I had to remind him that he had just taken part in a marvellous game of rugby.

Carling led England Schools before he captained Sedbergh. His first season with England Schools saw him alongside the skipper, Kevin Simms. The pair were together again when Carling made his debut for the senior side in 1988. Now, seven years before the Murrayfield heartbreak, Carling was about to endure his first Grand Slam failure. Having beaten Ireland, France and Scotland, England lost to Wales 13–12, with Carling denied a last-minute try when Robert Jones, later a Lions team-mate, tackled him into the corner flag. Carling was made captain of England Schools in 1984. He was not ready for another defeat by Wales. Given permission to take the squad to the pictures, Carling took them to a pub instead – not for a piss-up, but to try to build some team spirit. His diligence paid off: England won 18–0. Defeat in Belfast followed, then Carling scored in the final minute for victory in France.

The sixth former had taken his responsibilities seriously, but thought little more of it. He felt this leadership experience might be of use when he went into the Army, following on in the family's military tradition. However, he was made captain of Sedbergh for only two matches in his final Lent term, both of which ended in defeat. Those two losses were to be the last time he was put in charge of a rugby XV in England until he led the national side out at Twickenham in 1988.

Carling remembers his time at Terra Nova and Sedbergh with great affection. He enjoyed the outdoor life. As with most people, school exposed and corrected certain sides of his character. The bullying stopped without any outside influence. That display of petulance on the cricket field was dealt with effectively by his mother. His intolerance of others has lived on, but he has learnt to control and hide his annoyance. As for the arrogant and aloof schoolboy, his success on the sports field ahead of his year dictated a low-key approach. John Morris, his tutor at Sedbergh, was in charge of cricket and the assistant at rugby.

JOHN MORRIS

Will was a very good cricketer and was in the first XI for three years. It was always obvious that rugby would win the battle for his attention. I always found him a great man for the team, who enjoyed the success of others. That's very important. Marcus was a joker, very amusing. Any chink in a master's armour and Marcus would find it. That made him something of a nuisance. Any worries that Marcus might lead Will astray were soon gone. Will went his own way. It was Marcus who rather lived in the shadow of his younger brother. That's never easy. There were and are certain contradictions about Will. He is very sensitive, rather shy. But he is a very confident sportsman. I remember a TV close-up of him in the tunnel before coming out for his first England cap in Paris. He certainly didn't give the impression this was going to be a nerve-racking experience. Will just wanted to get out there and play. He was lucky that he found some kindred spirits at Sedbergh. Will's group were all very gifted. I think he still feels secure here. He came up with his girl-friend and stayed for a week after the World Cup in 1991. The school is certainly proud of the image he projects.

Carling's final rugby report, written by the master in charge, Kerry Weld, stated: 'A captain's contribution often sets the tone for the rest of the team. And William must take much of the credit for the thoroughly pleasant and level-headed atmosphere to be found around Buskholme. It is difficult to weigh his value to us except to say that his freshness and enthusiasm and sheer class have been watched and enjoyed by a lot of youngsters and, hopefully, new standards have been set for the years ahead. On a more personal level, I have been impressed by his increasing maturity and sound judgement, both in rugby matters and elsewhere. I am not surprised that both Yorkshire and England have recognised his qualities. He will need to steel himself for a carefully organised few months ahead, so that he can move on to Durham with some respectable grades and his head high.'

Carling's Army future was more in focus than his rugby career when he left Sedbergh. Like Marcus, who took a year off before heading for Lancaster University, he headed off round the world before continuing his studies. Before leaving, Carling appeared before the Regular Commissions Board. Like his father and brother, Carling was destined for the Royal Regiment of Wales. His grandparents provided him with the round-the-world ticket, plus £100 of spending money. His journey took him to Hong Kong, Singapore, Australia, New Zealand, Hawaii, Los Angeles and New York. Carling connections, family and school, meant the teenager arrived in most spots with a friendly contact or address. The country he enjoyed most was Australia, a place that has played a major part in Carling's sporting career since. He watched the 1984 England–Australia match in Perth, and later that night bumped into a Scotsman, who told him his brothers were going to play international rugby. The names Gavin and Scott Hastings did not mean too much to him at the time. Carling worked as a welder and driver in Perth, sold paintings in Sydney and served in a sandwich shop in Melbourne. Then he hitch-hiked around New Zealand before flying off to the States.

WILL CARLING
I worked in the Australian desert at Moomba, near Alice Springs, as a surveyor of pipe corrosion. It was a male-only refinery. The money was

LEFT: Carling had a few years to go before he could properly fill his dad's Army uniform.

RIGHT: A typical Pom, sticking up for the Old Country in Moomba.

fantastic – over £100 a day. The locals were classic Aussies, real Crocodile Dundees. And I was a typical Pom. There wasn't too much to do, except play cards and drink. Poker and pontoon were the games. It was just as well I was paid a lot because I lost a lot. I've never eaten so much in my life. With the heat, all you could do was eat, sometimes five steaks a day. When I came back from the trip I was over fourteen and a half stone. In the school environment, I was the top dog. Now I was just a young, immature lad. Nobody knew who I was. It was great. I didn't play one game of rugby. I did nothing at all in that year off.

Carling, on an Army scholarship, was destined for Hatfield College, which was then an all-male, sporting institution at Durham University. Newcomers are allocated rooms to share with another student. His first room-mate, Will Fawcett, was worried when he saw Carling's Army boots dumped in the room: was he shacking up with a skinhead? But his concerns were unfounded. The first year was a happy time for Carling. He had the status of a minor celebrity. The rugby club had a healthy reputation, on and off the park. It was also a close-knit community. Even today, most of Carling's small circle of friends come from school and university. Andrew Harle and Alex Hambly were with him at both. These friends remain fiercely loyal. If there was a disappointment in those early university months, it was that he felt his rugby career was going nowhere.

## WILL CARLING

That first season was spent at full back, where I had played my final year at Sedbergh. I hated every minute of it at Durham. When the ball came to me, our coach Ted Wood told me to kick, not to run. It used to drive me mad. I had Chris Oti on one wing. I had come from the idealistic world of schools rugby, where you run all the time. Suddenly, I was stuck at full back. All I got was high balls and Blaydon rugby club kicking nine bells out of me because I was a student. University rugby is all about getting hammered up front, then try to run the feet off them in the backs. But Ted Wood was having none of that. At the end of the first season, I thought if this is senior rugby, then you can keep it. I didn't train all summer. I went back to Sedbergh to play in an old boys' game. I really enjoyed myself, so I thought I'd give it another go. I'm not saying I would have quit, but I was seriously hacked off. For me it was a serious problem at the time.

All the advice I got was 'Bide your time. Don't stop. Enjoy it. Play for fun.' I had a lot of success at schoolboy level. Probably I was expecting too much to happen to me in that first year. I was frustrated. My England Schools partner Kevin Simms had been capped during my year abroad. I was just waiting for the same thing to happen to me. I wasn't going anywhere stuck in a kicking role at full back in the Durham University XV. Should I be playing for the university at all? Would I be better off at a club, trying to get into a county and divisional side? I've had a few words with Ted Wood since. He's never given me any explanation other than: 'That made you what you are today' I had no objection to playing full back. You can't expect to walk into sides. But being required to kick the ball every time I got it was heart-breaking. I can't say I relish standing under the high ball. After two years at full back, I thought it was much better to stick with what I knew.

Carling's rugby career was put right back on track after an outstanding performance for Durham against Lancashire in the County Championship at West Hartlepool in the autumn of 1986. Durham lost by a point. Carling certainly made his. North selectors Dave Robinson and Geoff Cooke were in attendance. They decided that Carling's talent would serve the divisional side well. Carling's frustration from the previous winter then exploded in a series of devastating displays that helped the North to the Thorn-EMI title. In less than a month Carling went from nowhere to the fringe of the England team.

## GEOFF COOKE

I had first heard his name mentioned when he was playing for Yorkshire and England Schools. He was billed as a 'lad who's a bit special'. I hadn't heard

Carling came to national attention with an outstanding Divisional Championship for the North in December 1986. Behind him is Kevin Simms, whom he partnered on his England debut in Paris the following season

anything that marked him above being just a 'good prospect'. The first time I met him I was dining with Ted Wood. Will came by. 'Hello' was the extent of our conversation. A very quiet guy. He obviously had ability and an outward confidence in that ability. Really, though, he was just a young player with stars in his eyes. But when I saw him for Durham County, I had the same feeling as when I saw Rory Underwood for the first time. The guy had it. I didn't need any further proof that here was someone the North should be promoting.

Stephen Jones of the *Sunday Times* saw his divisional debut. The headline read: 'Carling Turns Into North Ace Of Clubs.' The report added: 'The North also discovered a meteor in Will Carling, their young centre.' Mike Weston, then chairman of the England selectors, was impressed. 'He obviously made a favourable impact against the South West. I will be interested to see if he can build on that. His emergence shows that, in forward-dominated games, the opportunities are there for eager young backs to show their worth.' The North's backs were full of running. Fly half Rob Andrew had already played for England, along with Carling's three-quarter colleagues Rory Underwood, Mike Harrison and Kevin Simms. The North finished their campaign with a six-try demolition of London.

Higher honours were calling for Carling. Worryingly for England, they came from over the Severn Bridge. Because of his father's playing days with Cardiff, the youngster on a Royal Regiment of Wales scholarship had been in touch with London Welsh and planned to play for them in the Christmas holidays. The Welsh were keen to emphasise his eligibility for Wales, so England moved fast. A fortnight later, Carling was picked as one of the centres in the final England trial. December finished with Carling a new Barbarian. A week later, he was named William Younger Rugby Player of the Month.

ROB ANDREW
I first got to know him when he was picked for the Divisional Championship in 1986. He was rather quiet. That surprised me. The word had gone round that Will Carling was going to be the greatest thing since sliced bread. Will didn't blow his own trumpet, though. There was a steely determination. He didn't feel the need to shout from the rooftops. Straight away, we could see why he was brought in – his power and pace. He didn't have the electrifying burst of the Underwoods or Jerry Guscott, but he had the power to break through tackles. The divisional side is half-way to an England cap. I had little doubt that Will would be an England player before too long. Several of us were in the squad already. He was just like the rest of us. A young bloke who enjoyed playing rugby.

Weston advised Carling that it was time for a change. Carling listened carefully. Weston had dangled a very big carrot in front of the young centre – a place in the England squad for the first-ever rugby World Cup in Australia and New Zealand that summer. Weston told him that club experience was essential; and that did not mean London Welsh. There was one small drawback: the club suggested was not exactly on Carling's doorstep. It was the Harlequins, the famous London club that played and trained a mere 250 miles plus down the road from his Durham University base. Carling was in no position to argue. Nor has he ever asked why it was necessary for him to travel the length of England several times a week in search of a first England cap. Carling would leave Durham at three o'clock in the afternoon and arrive back on the last train at three o'clock in the morning. Not surprisingly, that was the end of Carling's serious university studies. He also disappeared from the mainstream of university life.

WILL CARLING
My season took off after that Durham game at West Hartlepool. I made three or four outside breaks. I didn't even know the North selectors were watching. It was the right game at the right time. That's down to luck. I'm not even sure they had seen me before. It was a crucial breakthrough, especially as I'd been considering packing it in a few months earlier. I'd felt my rugby career had been in limbo for a couple of seasons. The year travelling abroad had been my own decision. The year at full back had been a waste of

time. Quitting was not the answer. I knew deep down that I still wanted to play rugby. A few months later I was lining up for a final trial at Twickenham with the best rugby players in England. Playing for England had always been my long-term ambition. I had allowed myself to be distracted. It was a valuable lesson so early on.

Simon Halliday and Jamie Salmon were the senior centres in the England trial, although Kevin Simms partnered Salmon in the Five Nations before being replaced by Halliday in the final game against Scotland. Mike Harrison was the new England captain for the Calcutta Cup, which England won to deny Scotland the Triple Crown. Richard Hill, the previous leader, had been banned for one game, along with Graham Dawe, Wade Dooley and Gareth Chilcott, after a violent afternoon in Cardiff. That Scotland victory saved England from a championship whitewash and gave them renewed hope as they set off for the World Cup. Carling was still in the frame. Durham won the UAU championship at Twickenham and four days later Carling was back with the Army. His four Barbarians appearances included the traditional Easter Saturday clash with Cardiff, one of his earliest televised matches. Carling linked well with Martin Offiah, shortly to be a rugby league star, in their only match together, and then partnered Fran Clough as England B beat France B 22–9 at Bath. The World Cup call would have crowned a tremendous season. It never came. The selectors went for Salmon, Simms and Clough.

WILL CARLING
I really believed I was going to the World Cup. I know I had not played for England, but all the signs were promising. When the chairman gives you the nod, you tend to accept it. It was a shock when my name was missing. Nobody said anything. I had to go searching for an explanation. They said I was too tired! I couldn't argue with that. The main reason being that they had asked me to travel around 1,500 miles a week in my spare time. It was a real kick in the teeth. Players have been treated far worse than that. But it was my first contact with the England set-up. No wonder players moan about selectors. But when I stood back, I had to confess I was much happier about my rugby future than I had been a year earlier.

CHAPTER 3

# ARMY HALTS CARLING'S CHARGE – 1988

England's dismal defeat in the 1987 World Cup quarter-final catapulted Geoff Cooke into the team manager's position. At that stage no single person had ever been entrusted with such responsibility for the national rugby side. Roger Uttley's appointment as coach gave Cooke a valuable right-hand man, a former world-class forward with England and the British Lions. Any thoughts that Uttley would be in charge were quickly dispelled by Cooke. The team manager has the final word in selection, although the pair were united in their determination to get English rugby back on course.

Carling spent part of that summer on exercises with the Army in Germany. Final exams were looming at Durham, but this psychology student had lost interest; and the tedious train trips from Durham to London no longer had the attraction of a possible World Cup place. December brought some relief with the Divisional Championship reducing travelling time. Carling partnered John Buckton in the centre as the North took the title again. His reward was a centre place alongside Kevin Simms for the junior side in the England trial. That international call came much sooner than expected when Buckton and Simon Halliday, the senior centres, were ruled out through injury. Carling was selected to make his England debut in the 1988 Five Nations opener in Paris. He was enjoying his Christmas vacation at home when the news came through.

WILL CARLING

The trial meant I was in the frame. But English rugby is littered with players, even those who've played for the senior side, who've got that far and no further. I was getting close, that's all. So the news did come as a shock. France was going to be tough and often the selectors recall a player with experience if the first choice drops out. It was great for the family. I knew it meant so much to them. Of course, there were the customary celebrations and over-indulgence.

Carling was now the object of the media gaze for the first time. Little was known about him. It quickly became obvious that the newcomer was not totally at ease talking about himself. Some thought him quiet and unassuming, others felt he was cold and reserved. Those arguments continue today. Jeff Probyn and Micky Skinner were the other new caps. Only six survived from the Welsh

World Cup quarter-final defeat. Nigel Melville returned at scrum half, while Mike Harrison retained the captaincy.

England were given little chance in Paris. The French had reached the World Cup final and were rarely troubled by the Home Countries at the Parc des Princes. Carling was determined to enjoy himself. Even Uttley was surprised by the newcomer's confidence.

### ROGER UTTLEY

My first recollection of Will came when I was coaching London. The North came down to play us at Wasps and blitzed us. I had heard about Will through the grapevine. The view was that this strong centre was destined to play for England sooner rather than later. After watching him, I had to agree. Even among England's best, he stood out.

Normally, the newcomers in the side make a special journey into Paris on the Friday to have a close look at the Parc des Princes. There's no more intimidating venue on the rugby circuit and it helps to be prepared. Will came along, but was only there for a couple of minutes. After a cursory glance round, he disappeared into the city to see a friend. That level of confidence before a first cap was very striking.

### GEOFF COOKE

Our biggest problem was also our top priority – lack of confidence. The World Cup defeat by Wales had been devastating. This was England's first game back and the team flew to France as no-hopers. They were written off. The only discussion was how many points France would score. What amazed me was the way the players were looking to the management for guidance. I remember saying to Roger: 'These guys are unhappy because nobody is telling them how to play.' Well, 'these guys' were England's very best. I could not believe or understand the complete lack of confidence.

Before the game, Roger and I made sure there was no reference to the negative side. Being in France, there was no problem with English papers or TV. The players tend to spend a lot of time together, so we insisted the talk about the game was positive. Roger and I immediately noticed a strong feeling of 'them and us'. Roger and I worked hard that season to break that down. Rather naïvely, perhaps, I had expected the players to realise that we were all on the same side.

France, as expected, won. Carling's international career had begun in defeat. Yet the result was a travesty. The England pack dominated up front and should have been home and dry, rather than 9–3 up with ten minutes remaining. A frantic French finish ruined Carling's big day, as France scraped home 10–9. The new centre had been holding the ball when the final whistle went. It was immediately wrenched away by French flanker Eric Champ. Carling

Carling on his debut in Paris in 1988, with a youthful-looking Rory Underwood in the background, although the RAF flier had already been in the England side for four years. *(Colorsport)*

finished up with Philippe Sella's jersey instead, as a souvenir of the game, after swapping in the tunnel.

Since the pundits had been predicting doom and gloom, England's display was praised to the rafters; but Uttley was not satisfied. It was yet another example of England winning the ball, but not the match. John Orwin, the pack leader, was distraught: 'I've never been so disappointed in my life. We certainly put the effort in up front. We managed to get sufficient ball for the backs to use. If you don't score the points, you don't win the game.'

Paris had its compensations. Just because England had been beaten, Carling was not going to miss out on the delights that the Paris nightlife has to offer. Another benefit of winning his first cap abroad was that it allowed him a further debut at Twickenham. Carling had three weeks to wait for the visit of Wales. Here he saw a lot less of the ball than he had done in Paris. The scoreboard was bare at half-time, but then two tries from Adrian Hadley separated the sides as Carling suffered another international defeat. This 11–3 setback hit him a lot harder than Paris. Carling felt dejected walking off after his first championship match at HQ with the Welsh cheers ringing in his ears.

Two defeats in a row was a much more serious threat to Cooke's master plan than to Carling's future. The heat was on. Carling's new partner for the Scotland trip was Halliday, with Melville replacing Harrison as captain and Oti taking over from him on the wing. Rob Andrew returned at fly half in place of Les Cusworth. Those changes showed that Cooke and Uttley placed the blame for the two losses firmly on the England backs. Scotland was not much of an improvement; but, to England's relief, two Webb penalties and an Andrew dropped goal gave them a 9–6 victory in one of the drabbest, dullest games in years, even by Calcutta Cup standards. Carling, understandably, refused to worry beyond the result.

WILL CARLING

It was such a fantastic feeling. My first England victory. I couldn't argue that it was a boring spectacle and a close match. But my first two outings in an England jersey had ended in defeat. I was bubbling when I reached the dressing-room. I was greeted by the sight of a depressed Rory Underwood. 'That was terrible.'

'Rory, hang on. This is my first international win.' Now I understand his feelings. If I played in a game like that today, I would probably not be satisfied. But then – wow, Edinburgh, watch out! Edinburgh that year is the only time I've ever seen Geoff Cooke lose it. Geoff is one of the most level-headed people I've met. But it's remarkable what losing the first couple of Five Nations matches can do. Suddenly, the vultures gathered as others began to distance themselves from an England management that looked like failing. Geoff's judgement and ability were being questioned seriously. The backs were going through their drills in training. We were making a right mess of it. Even with five attackers on two defenders, balls were being dropped and knocked on. It was pathetic and Geoff really blew his top. I couldn't blame him. It wasn't his style, though. The pressure had got to him. As we left the field, I turned back and saw him standing alone. I couldn't believe Geoff, of all people, was so uptight.

Ireland came to Twickenham to complete the Five Nations campaign. It was another slow start. The scores at half-time against Wales and Scotland had been 0–0. This time England were 0–3 down – and the situation was worse because the England captain was stretchered off at the interval with an ankle injury that effectively finished Nigel Melville's career. Richard Harding took over at scrum half with Orwin as the new skipper. No one can say what Melville would have done in that final 40 minutes, but surely it could have been no more than Harding, who set England's backs running at last. England scored six tries – five to wings Oti (three) and Underwood (two) as Ireland were crushed 35–3. Even more significantly, the Twickenham crowd followed the England backs and cast aside its inhibitions and found its voice as the strains of 'Swing Low, Sweet Chariot' echoed around HQ for the first time.

Carling congratulates Rory Underwood on scoring his second try in the 35–3 trouncing of Ireland on 19 March 1988. *(Colorsport)*

## GEOFF COOKE

I hadn't really known what to expect when I took over. The lack of basic skills astonished me almost as much as the lack of confidence. That sort of coaching should be finished by the time you get to international level. Yet there were so many things the England players couldn't do. Roger and I shouldn't have been wasting valuable session time teaching basic skills. I was also disappointed to find out there was no rugby thinking to any great depth.

We had to win at Murrayfield. As simple as that. I make no excuses for our dour performance. Two down with two to play in the championship leaves you with no alternative. And at half-time in the Ireland game, I had no idea that we would finish on such a high note. As ever, the dividing line is wafer-thin and matches can turn on a little thing. The Irish started the second half by kicking the ball straight into touch. We won the scrum and Harding's first touch was to get the backline moving. Rory sped away for Gary Rees to score. The injury to Nigel worked for us. Corky [Richard Harding] released the emotion everyone felt for Nigel. We started running. It was spontaneous, just like the crowd singing 'Sweet Chariot'.

England's clash had been the supporting act that afternoon to Cardiff, where France's 10–9 win denied the Principality its first Grand Slam for ten years. Yet this was a vitally important day for England, Cooke and Carling. The disappointments of the early championship matches were forgotten and England made it an Irish double when they travelled to Dublin for the Millennium match. Carling's real problems began after that match when hosts Paul Dean and Michael Kiernan entertained the youngster to such an extent that he still has no idea where he went, what he did and when he finished.

That extra international, plus the Harlequins' cup run and the Inter-Services tournament, played havoc with his university studies. Carling was forced to make concessions to those responsibilities after he was picked to tour Australia. A request to delay sitting his exams until after the tour was denied, despite representations from the RFU on his behalf. Academic obligations had to be fulfilled before he was allowed to fly out after the first Test. His late arrival allowed Simon Halliday, who had been unavailable for the whole tour, to go for the first Test.

Carling's winning season continued. The Army beat the RAF at Twickenham to take their first Inter-Services title for five years. Another trophy came Carling's way when Harlequins became the first London club to win the cup, overcoming Bristol 28–22 in a thrilling John Player Special final, as Carling set the seal on a remarkable first full season of senior rugby with two tries in the final.

WILL CARLING

The final was just an extension of my dream season. Everything seemed to be going my way. England finished with three wins. The Quins were going well, too. In the final we went out there to run, to counter-attack, and run again. Conditions were ideal, and it worked. There are times when the ball just runs your way. This was one of them.

Carling's good fortune was to vanish on his arrival in Australia. That was not his fault. By that stage the England tour had fallen apart. Uttley was unavailable for the visit. His replacements were the England B coaches, Alan Davies and David Robinson. The tour did little for their England futures. Had the press reported all the goings-on, Cooke might not have survived. The tourists spent the first week in Mackay, Queensland. When John Bentley refused to pay his fine at one of the players' traditional courts, he was tied to a palm tree, told to drink and sing a song by Charles Aznavour. Although most of the players were rather the worse for wear, nobody could quite believe it when the England captain, John Orwin, appeared from behind the tree and relieved himself over the helpless Bentley. It was just as well Bentley's knots were securely tied. On his return to England, Bentley signed on the dotted line and sought sanctuary among the supposedly less civilised folk from rugby league.

England lost the first Test 22–16 after leading by 13 points. Carling arrived two days later to regain his international jersey. His winning sequence came to an abrupt end as England were well beaten 28–8 in the second Test. Cooke came home a worried man. The Test defeats were bad enough, but he had never expected the spirit and progress made in the second half of the championship to disappear and disintegrate in a matter of weeks. England moved on to Fiji, where the Test was won 25–12 with Richard Harding as captain. Orwin was originally picked for the side, but withdrew with a calf strain.

TONY ROCHE, *TODAY*
After John Orwin told us that he was pulling out of the Test team with a calf injury, we not unnaturally asked him which leg was the problem. We were astonished when he shouted at Cooke, who was some distance away: 'Which leg was it again, Geoff?' Draw your own conclusions from that.

GEOFF COOKE
That tour was hard. Visits to the southern hemisphere always are. You face different attitudes and different referees. That tour was where I started to identify a core. We were certainly still 'iffy'. It was a patchwork tour. Will came out late, Halliday went home early and Webbie flew back to get married. All this reflected the modern demands of international rugby. The other big shock in my first year was the extent of the media attention. I had only been involved at a regional level before. This was a whole new ball game. Dealing with committees was hard work, too – and time-consuming. You can't forget or ignore the powers that be. If you want to change the system, then you have to get involved. You must have the committee on your side. You need their support to get things through. It's no good wishing the committee wasn't there. You have to get on with it, but that side of things was far more demanding than I envisaged.

Back at Harrow School, where he taught, Roger Uttley was keeping a close eye on proceedings.

ROGER UTTLEY
After the early results, I thought England had a good chance of winning the first Test. Australia were awarded a try that wasn't grounded properly. That tipped the balance. The Test was lost and the wheels came off. It was disconcerting reading the newspapers. We had thought of John Orwin as a Bill Beaumont-type of leader, but you have to lead from the front for that. I was very concerned because it was going to be me who had to pick up the pieces before Australia arrived in England in the autumn.

Those concerns were not yet Carling's. Yet even such a new member of the side could not fail to pick up the bad vibes.

WILL CARLING

When I arrived, I noticed a tremendous division between the forwards and the backs. There was a lack of respect between the two. That is not healthy. Unless there is humour underpinning the traditional hostility between the two, there can be trouble. Orwin publicly criticised the backs. I couldn't believe it. Orwin set no captaincy standards for me. I must admit that I did not take in a lot from the other captains in my first year with England. I felt I was just struggling to stay afloat. Both Nigel [Melville] and Mike [Harrison] were good guys. I called Mike 'Dad' because he was so old.

Carling's own future was rather vague. His university exams had not been a great success. That did not particularly bother him. More alarming to his prospects was that a major stumbling block had appeared in his path. Carling had to make a decision that had not been on the agenda: he had to choose between the Army and his England career. The Army had just made it painfully obvious that the two were not compatible for at least a year while he underwent his initial training.

The Army had been as much a part of Carling's upbringing as rugby. His father, Bill, had combined his love of that sport with a professional career in the forces. His brother, Marcus, had made his way to Sandhurst, and Will planned to follow him. His Army future had been set in motion before he set off on his round-the-world trip, when Carling had appeared before the Regular Commissions Board and gained an Army scholarship to Durham University. Carling has always had a fascination with war and those who are prepared to fight. His father's helicopter-flying career was only part of the attraction; the mental battle intrigued him just as much as the physical one.

WILL CARLING

I've always enjoyed biographies and historical books. I tend not to read fiction now, although *The Hobbit* was my favourite when I was growing up. I remember reading books on Churchill and General Slim. I didn't see them as war heroes. I was interested in how they reacted to extreme situations. I've never been a hero type. I was more into the mind games. Just how much could people take? How they performed when exhausted and under intense stress. That was my thesis at university. It was the one part of my university course I enjoyed and about the only serious bit of work I did in my three years.

Carling's compensation for not going to the 1987 World Cup was an Army exercise in Germany. He had not been one for playing soldiers, and Carling had left the cadet corps at school when attendance was no longer compulsory. He went to Germany as a private.

WILL CARLING

I was just one of the lads. Members of my squad had been in the Army for two to twenty years. I'm still bound by the Official Secrets Act and can only reveal that we tramped up and down the German countryside. The ranks lead very disciplined lives. I admire them. They have got a real idea of what's important in life and what is not. I think I amused them and was adopted as the squad mascot.

The Services have always had a great rugby tradition. It continued in the 1980s with Rory Underwood and John Orwin. The image of Underwood, the flying rugby wing and fighter pilot, was a perfect one for the RAF, and his prominence among England's sporting heroes has provided the Air Force with masses of free publicity. Although it was still early days in Carling's sporting rise, there was little doubt that he could do the same for the Army. Not that the young England centre was looking for a free ride: Carling genuinely believed that he could combine his rugby and Army careers. Why not? The Army had led him to conclude that they thought his rugby was as important as he did.

WILL CARLING

I met the General of the Land Forces after an Army game at Twickenham. Outside the dressing-room, he told me: 'We are delighted with your rugby. Don't worry about it.' I had already spoken to my Dad about whether he thought there was going to be a problem. I was about to go to Sandhurst. Would they let me play rugby for England? Dad made some enquiries and the word came back that it wasn't going to be a problem. So, when the General made his comments to me, I took that as official confirmation.

While I was in Australia, Dad heard on the grapevine that life was not going to be that simple. Basically, Sandhurst had changed its mind. I was not going to get any time off during my initial training. As that ran from September through to March, I would have to give up international rugby for a season. I went to see Colonel Charles at Sandhurst to find out if there was any room for manoeuvre. There wasn't. The decision had come from the Commandant. I retreated in some shock.

It was no contest. I wasn't going to let someone have my England place for a year. I didn't feel I could talk to Geoff Cooke about my dilemma, to make sure I was actually part of his plans for the coming season. I had to make this decision for myself although I sought out my Dad's opinion. So, I told the Army: 'Thank you, but no thank you.' It was towards the end of my school days that I decided that I wanted to go into the Army. I was always interested in soldiering. It was an occupation which would allow me to pursue my sporting ambitions. I never saw the Army as a career.

Buying yourself out is not that expensive. They just tell you what it costs. It was a lot of money to me at the time – £8,000, payable over five years. But that's the best investment I've ever made. I've heard stories that my father bought me out and cleared the debt. Not true, but it fits the image of the privileged youngster.

Turning my back on the Army meant my carefully mapped out future for the next four years had vanished. I had to confess that I had never given a single thought to life beyond the Army.

Had Carling realised that he was about to enter a commercial world which was starting a recession, he might have been more studious at Durham. His treatment of the degree course had been most un-Carling like. That methodical, thorough, attention-to-all-detail style which was to become his trademark was missing. Carling was bored with studying. Believing that his rugby/Army future would not be harmed by his failure as a student, Carling got further and further behind in his work.

WILL CARLING
The thesis on stress was my only piece of written work. I was happy reading at Durham. Unfortunately, only a few of the books were relevant to my course. I lost interest as the work became more scientific. Statistics was not my favourite subject. People and their behaviour was what I wanted to study. I was expected to come to a conclusion about why 75 out of 100 rats in a cage learnt how to work a lever. I wanted to know why people react differently to situations. Why is Brian Moore the way he is?

Even today, Carling is shamefaced about skipping one of his final exams. The work had not been done, so he saw little point in turning up. Carling left Durham with a degree in psychology – just: England's future captain was given a 'recommended pass', the lowest grade to qualify for a Bachelor of Arts degree.

Carling sat down with Harlequins officials, Colin Herridge and Roger Looker, to discuss alternatives to the Army. When he was asked what he wanted to do, he replied: 'I don't know.' But Carling did at least realise that he wanted a career, not something to fill in the time while he travelled the rugby world. Suggestions were made about the legal profession, marketing or accountancy. Carling was definite on one thing: no more exams. Being a practical person, collecting more diplomas was not his game. Eventually, he decided on a marketing job with Mobil.

WILL CARLING
I know I could pass exams. I simply lost interest in my course at Durham. That's not an excuse. Most exams are just a test of your memory. Nobody has ever failed the psychology course. I believe I was the first student to receive anything less than a 2:2. I'm quite proud of that. Mum wasn't. She

felt I had let myself down. I didn't know if marketing was going to be for me. I was buying time. I needed some experience and to see how the big business world worked. I already suspected I wasn't a 'big company' man, but I did enjoy my two years with Mobil. I learnt that I was not into routine. The timing was perfect. I had job security when I needed it. I joined Mobil at the start of October 1988. By the end of the month, I was captain of England. I have never regretted the decision I took. I was sad about missing the Army, but there's no way I could have been captain of England and combined it with a military career.

# CHAPTER 4

# COOKE PROMOTES THE WILL TO WIN – 1988–89

Will Carling faced an agonising 48 hours after Cooke offered him the England captaincy. Accepting the job that Thursday night was not the problem. His difficulties arose because England's new leader was sworn to secrecy. His identity would not be announced to the team until two nights later – 30 October – and the world at large would not find out until the following morning. Carling was stunned by Cooke's decision, and knew the players and public would be just as astonished. The players were his main concern. How would veteran warriors like Wade Dooley, Paul Rendall and Dean Richards react to this young upstart being put in charge? The good-looking Harlequin three-quarter with a university education was still wet behind the ears. The youngest England captain for over half a century was an international novice.

Merely naming Carling as England captain was enough to shock the rugby world. Nobody saw it coming. But it was Cooke's admission that Carling would lead England in the 1991 World Cup, still three years away, that indicated that Cooke's and Carling's careers were on the line together. Cooke added a proviso about Carling maintaining his form, but such was the effect of the announcement that that get-out clause got lost in the wash. It was a giant step into the unknown.

Cooke and Uttley were determined to bring stability to the England set-up, yet finding the right leader had proved almost impossible. Much of Cooke's reputation up north had been built on player loyalty. Yet, after six months of 1988, Cooke had a credibility problem. After less than a year in the job, his first four attempts at picking an England captain had ended in failure. He could not afford another mistake with number five.

GEOFF COOKE
Nigel Melville was my long-term choice. He lasted one and a half games before that serious leg injury. John Orwin took over at half-time and did enough to justify getting the job for the summer tour. I was buying time. I needed time to identify the man who could lead England into the next World Cup. Suggestions that Will was always lined up for the job are way off the mark. So are remarks that I turned to him because the Australian trip went so wrong. For me, he stood out. I didn't consider Brian Moore or Simon Halliday as serious contenders, Peter Winterbottom was not playing

for England at the time, Wade Dooley was not a captain and Dean Richards would not have been comfortable with the job. It boiled down to Will or Rob Andrew. Rob was the more obvious choice, but he had just returned to the side and was having enough trouble with his own game. I couldn't give him that extra pressure.

Will had precocious talent, and so much confidence. I believed there was a good chance he would grow into the job. But I had doubts, lots of them. Talented and confident, but also young and inexperienced. I was about to offer him one of the most demanding jobs in sport. Was I going to ruin one of the best young sportsmen in the country? He wasn't going to be an instant success. I told him to concentrate on his own performances as a player. Captaincy, I said, was a collective effort. Will knew he wasn't on a match-by-match trial. The opportunity was there to grow into the job.

ROGER UTTLEY
Geoff phoned me. 'What about Will?' I didn't have to ask what for. The captaincy was our big crisis after the summer tour. We could not duck the problem. Time had run out. Once Geoff had set his criteria – automatic selection, good attitude – there was only one choice for me. There was no guarantee Rob [Andrew] would hang on to his place. If it had been a year later, I'm sure Rob would have got the job. Rob was much closer to Geoff than Will. Rob would certainly have been easier to get along with. Will, for better or worse, had the facility to make me feel uncomfortable. Still, he was definitely the man for the job in 1988. I had no doubts about him coping. Will was the one man in the England side at the time who would relish the challenge.

Carling was oblivious to all this thinking. A month after tackling his own immediate career problems and leaving the Army, Carling was named England's rugby captain, still two months short of his 23rd birthday. He was the youngest skipper for 57 years and the 10th leader since Bill Beaumont retired on medical grounds in 1982 after what was then a record 21 times in charge.

Carling was well aware of the debate over who should be the new England captain. It was just that he never dreamed that Cooke would turn to him. His life changed for ever the night he visited his parents' house and was told that Cooke had called. Normally, that was not a good sign. Uttley was the man in the England set-up who told you the good news. But, if it was bad, Cooke took it upon himself to speak to the player. Maybe leaving the Army was not such a good idea after all. Maybe his first England season was not as promising as he thought. England were well served for centres and the need to find a new leader might see an outsider returning. All these thoughts were suddenly racing around in Carling's head, but he did not hang about. He phoned Cooke straight away and braced himself for the worst moment of his sporting life.

Minutes later, Carling was scribbling a message, in disbelief rather than relief, for his mother and brother to read. 'I am the captain.' But that was about as far as he could communicate the news for the next 48 hours. It was not easy. He did at least resist the temptation to make a fortune on the very favourable odds being offered on his being named the next England captain.

Carling's first test came in the players' room on Saturday night. They knew the new captain had been told of his elevation, but he was keeping quiet. It was an early sign that Cooke had chosen well. Rory Underwood remembers audible gasps going round the room as Will Carling's name was mentioned. Rob Andrew had been top of most players' guess list that night.

## ROB ANDREW

It was a brave decision by Geoff. Will hadn't been around long, but he was an established member of the side. Nobody doubted his right to be there. With Nigel Melville gone, Geoff plumped for Will because of what he'd seen of his character and the strength of that character. Geoff could mould a side round Will. I was still finding my feet. There was no dissent. I'm sure many there felt 'rather him than me'. Will had our full backing. He had seized most of the rugby chances that had already come his way. Why should the captaincy be any different?

## WILL CARLING

It was a hell of a shock. I had just started playing for England. I've kept the cards from friends who congratulated me on the England selectors losing their senses. Lining me up for the 1991 World Cup was even more stagger-ing. I didn't feel an established member of the side or an integral part of the set-up. Had I stayed with the Army, I wouldn't have been offered the cap-taincy. That's why I think I'm a lucky person. One day when all my rugby is behind me, I'm going to sit down with Geoff and, after the right influence of alcohol, I'm going to get a straight answer to the question that's puzzled me ever since: 'Why the hell did you pick me, Geoff?'

By and large, my whole rugby career has been a bed of roses. I've so often seemed to be in the right place at the right time. It's been very easy. People said I was mad to give up the Army when there were no rugby guarantees. I believe you have got to be positive. I was going to stay in the England side. Problems are there to be confronted, not ignored. I did struggle to keep it quiet. I went to watch the Quins play at Richmond. Everyone was talking about who the new England captain would be. Our forwards went through the card, with one exception – me!

I'd been waiting two days for the England squad's reaction when the news came out. But I just stared at the floor. There was certainly a heavy silence. They all came offering congratulations. I don't know whether a few thought I'd been given the short straw. Getting the job was about the

quickest way of going out of the side at the time. I thought I had the potential to do the job and I was looking forward to being involved in the
process. I felt I had nothing to lose. If I was kicked out in a couple of games,
what the hell. I'd have given it my best shot. The World Cup was not in my
game plan that weekend. I felt my entire rugby future was tied up in that
Australian game, which was less than a week away.

The rugby press, who pride themselves on their ability to tap the RFU's jungle
telegraph, were even more ignorant of Cooke's plans than the players. Steve
Jones, the rugby correspondent of the *Sunday Times*, did not attend the press
conference that revealed Carling's elevation, and it took him 13 guesses to come
up with Carling's name.

Cooke's brave new captain caught the mood of the moment. Three of the four
divisional sides had inflicted defeat on the Australians. London started the ball
rolling with a 21–10 victory at Twickenham, and four days later the North won
15–9 at Otley, with Carling's run setting up the winning try by Dewi Morris.
Cooke's selection of Morris for the Test epitomised England's bold approach.
London's Andrew Harriman and lock Paul Ackford displayed the pace and
quality that had exposed Australia. The trio of new caps had something else in
common: none had been born in England. To many, Welsh-born Morris had
seemed to come from nowhere. He had sprung to the fore after Richard Hill
was sent off in a club game at Twickenham. In a spectacular two months,
Morris went from junior to senior rugby, playing for the North, England B and
the full national side. Cooke made seven changes from the team that beat Fiji in
the summer. Out went Harding, Chilcott, Barrie Evans, Barley, Barnes, Redman
and Rees.

Carling was careful to make his first public utterance as skipper as positive and
thoughtful as possible. 'Although we have three new caps in the side, there is a lot
of experience. I have to see we gel and get it mentally right. I'm not getting carried
away because we have not seen the full Australian Test team yet. They are dangerous and they must win the international to make their tour a success. But I think
we will win. They look very vulnerable when you run the ball at them.' The media
made much of Carling's officer class. John Orwin, England's leader in Australia,
was a corporal in the RAF. Most of the Carling headlines in the week leading up to
the match were of a military nature. Cooke's bold decision was applauded. The
judgement on Carling was put on hold. Quite rightly, they concluded that Cooke
would be calling the shots anyway.

GEOFF COOKE
Will didn't try to impose himself. There was no 'I am the captain – we're
doing it this way.' One of Will's strengths is that he can relate to different
people. He adopted a low-key approach straight away. He asked senior
players 'what do you think?' I was amazed by the way he handled it.

Cooke need not have worried. England carried on from where the divisional sides left off. The Twickenham crowd, so often reserved and inhibited, were seduced by the emotion of the national rugby side's adventure. Seven years later, that one-night stand has become a full-blown affair and Twickenham is now the most intimidating stadium in the northern hemisphere. That development can be traced back to Guy Fawkes Day, 1988.

'Did England deliver – did they ever!' was the *Sunday Times'* verdict. Carling, virtually unknown the week before, had become a national hero. The new captain was given a rousing ovation when forced off near the end with concussion. His final act had been to make the game safe, putting Simon Halliday clear before being taken out by a late tackle. Carling did not want to go, but eventually the RFU doctor Ben Gilfeather led him away.

England had trailed twice, the second time early in the second half when a David Campese try put the Australians 13–9 ahead. Two tries from Rory Underwood put England back in front before the tourists reduced the deficit to three points. The Halliday converted try sealed this pulsating contest. England's gambles and bold approach paid off. Crucially, the side showed character and held its nerve.

Uttley missed the match, having left the England squad two hours before it started. As a schoolmaster, his first loyalty was to Harrow School. However, his mind was not totally on his first XV performance against Wellington. A small transistor in his anorak kept him in touch with events at Twickenham.

## ROGER UTTLEY

It was the most bizarre afternoon of my life. It was so important for us to win the game in the way we did. We shattered the myth of antipodean invincibility. The way the boys dealt with the pressure gave everyone a boost. We didn't beat them by that much. But it's the wins that are important – not the quality. England came through in the final quarter. That's the sign of a good side.

## GEOFF COOKE

At last we believed we had begun to turn the corner. Now we could start the next phase. We had planned carefully and you could see the benefit of the collective approach. We gave the Aussies a hard time in England. They were apprehensive and we took our chances. Three years later in the World Cup final we didn't. That's why we lost. This first game was an important start for Will. He played a full part and the Twickenham crowd had a captain to identify with for the first time since Bill Beaumont.

The television coverage of the match helped make Carling one of the most famous faces in the land. But the cameras missed one important moment. Carling gathered his team under the posts after Campese's interception try.

OPPOSITE: An historic moment as Carling takes the field for the very first time as England's rugby captain – Guy Fawkes Day in 1988. *(Colorsport)*

Carling, concussed, being led from the field by RFU doctor Ben Gilfeather a few seconds before England marked Carling's captaincy debut with a 28–19 victory over Australia at Twickenham. *(Colorsport)*

WILL CARLING

I told them not to panic. I reminded them that we had agreed beforehand that we were going to play an expansive game. Things might go wrong. We were disappointed, but I felt it would come. We had to keep our cool and keep on attacking. I wasn't reading the riot act as might have appeared. It's just that you've got to make your points pretty forcibly in the middle of a rugby international if you want to have any impact.

Cooke warned everyone not to get carried away by the result. The press, of course, went over the top. The *Daily Mail*'s Terry O'Connor was one who didn't hold back: 'England conjured up more movement than I've seen in 40 years of rugby. Skipper Will Carling symbolised the new adventurous spirit of English rugby when he smashed aside two defenders to create a final try before being floored by a later tackle at the climax of a magical Twickenham autumn day.' After less than a week in the job, Will Carling had become everyone's darling.

Carling was looking forward to his first championship in charge, although the captain had two worries. The first was predictable. Expectations were now high that England would sweep the board in the 1989 Five Nations and that the Grand Slam was a formality. Carling was not the first to perceive that such views are the kiss of death. His other problem concerned his own fitness. Shin splints were diagnosed on his left leg and rest was the recommended cure. Cooke was beginning to think the England captaincy was jinxed. The decision was taken to try to carry on playing. The management played down his condition when he was unable to take a full part in the squad session before the Calcutta Cup.

England had sat out the first weekend of the championship. They were still favourites, despite Scotland's 23–7 win over Wales. There is no love lost between England and Scotland on the rugby field. Now the officials of both Unions were at each other's throats after the Calcutta Cup had been battered round the streets of Edinburgh the year before. Dean Richards had missed the Millennium game as a punishment, while John Jeffrey's participation in the affair kept him out of Scotland's summer tour.

England hung on to the repaired Calcutta Cup for another year. The 12–12 result was a great disappointment as Scotland frustrated England's tactics, not for the first or last time. 'They did what they came to do – not a lot,' was Cooke's verdict. Although French referee Guy Maurette missed a blatant offside when Jeffrey hacked on for the game's only try, England had only themselves to blame. Scotland were punished by the referee, but Andrew and Webb missed seven kicks at goal out of 11. England's inability to raise the game out of the mire to overcome Scotland's negative tactics showed Cooke and Uttley that there was still much work to do. There would be no Triple Crown or Grand Slam in Carling's first season in charge. Painfully, his honeymoon period as captain had ended as abruptly as it had begun.

WILL CARLING

The media really got behind us after the Australian performance. They felt English rugby was going somewhere at last. I was staggered how all that changed after one poor match. We were given the full treatment after the Calcutta Cup. Before the next game in Dublin, I told them that I thought some of the criticism was harsh. Nobody said a word and they wandered off. The *Standard*'s rugby correspondent Chris Jones stayed behind:

'Big mistake, Will.'

'What?'

'Criticising the press.'

'I hardly call that criticism.'

'They won't take kindly to it.'

'Chris, they criticise players in front of millions and we have to take it. I'm just passing on some thoughts.'

'I'm just telling you how it is.'

Chris was right, of course. You can't win. They have the final word. That was when I learnt my first lesson as captain.

That was the first of three hard lessons for Carling in Ireland. The second came the night before the game as the backs relaxed.

ROB ANDREW

Us backs often behave a bit childishly. It's our way of easing the tension. Will's usually in the middle of the shaving-foam or talc fights. That's him. Sometimes he finds it hard to suppress those instincts. Being boisterous can lead to conflict before a big match. We tend to be less keyed up than the forwards who are preparing for the big battle. Will received a terrible rollocking from Dean Richards, our pack leader in Dublin, for messing about.

Carling showed more authority at Lansdowne Road as England came away with an impressive 16–3 win. The game turned when England took a tap penalty midway through the second half and Brian Moore scored. That was an important moment for the captain. Another followed that evening as Carling discovered his life had changed for ever.

WILL CARLING

Rob wanted to kick that penalty, but I felt the forwards were coming on to their game and it was better to run it. It worked. Beating Australia had been like a dream, especially after suffering concussion. This win was for real. After the bad Scottish experience, it was a great relief to go to Dublin and win. I felt I had arrived as an international captain. I was going to celebrate and really got hammered at the dinner that night. My speech was a complete disaster. I could hardly speak, but I didn't care. I could see the rest of the lads laughing. A few days later I had lunch with Rob.

'The lads were really surprised at your behaviour on Saturday night. You were out of your box.'

'So were they.'

'That's not the point, Will. You're their captain.'

I was stunned, probably more than when I was made captain. Now I was expected to behave in a certain way. I couldn't let go. I was on show all the time. There was a demarcation line between me and the players. Not them and us. But me and them. Whatever they might say, the players expected me to be different. I couldn't be one of the boys any more. That was a terrible realisation for one so young.

France were the next visitors to Twickenham. Pierre Berbizier's side had won their opening two matches, which included recovering from a 15-point deficit in Dublin and a record victory over Wales. The French got no change out of England, though, as the home side produced their most disciplined display under the new regime. The England pack controlled the match and their tempers. Serge Blanco was reduced to scrapping. Morris had a bustling day behind the scrum, although it was not his best work which provided Carling with a special moment: his first international try.

## WILL CARLING

The try came from a planned move. The ball would go along the backline quickly, so I could feed Chris Oti coming inside on the crash. That was the

Carling's first England try. A planned move went so badly that the confused French defence allowed Carling a clear run to the line in 1989. *(Colorsport)*

grand plan. Actually it went something like this. Dewi lobbed the ball to Rob at two miles an hour and Rob passed it on at about the same speed. Chris was coming on the inside, but there was no way I could give him the ball. Everything was happening in slow motion, except the speed at which the French tacklers were approaching. I turned and braced myself to get thumped. Nothing happened. Lafond, Sella and Mesnel converged on Oti, obviously thinking the laborious passing was part of a grand plan. Amazingly the French line had opened up for me. I wasn't going to get many gifts like this and I dived over. I got to my feet immediately, trying to be super-cool, only to fall over again – very stylish.

I must say it was a very satisfying moment to score my first England try. It's a relief. It takes the pressure off. If you've been in the team for a couple of seasons and not broken your duck, there's a fair amount of ribbing, especially if you're outside the scrum. Rob got wound up when he didn't score for 30-odd matches. Being a try-scorer has never bothered me that much. I don't see it as a major part of my job. Anyway, I'd rather create them. That gives me much more pleasure – making the break, going through the gap to put someone else away.

England were now favourites for the Five Nations, with five points out of six and a trip to Cardiff to come. 'If England don't beat us down in Cardiff this year, they never will,' was the view of former Welsh captain Jeff Squire. Neath's supremo Brian Thomas had other ideas. 'The English are mentally inferior, rugby-wise and as a race. Whenever I played against England, I knew Wales were mentally the better side. That can still happen – it's all a question of strength and will.'

England did lack the strength and will that day. Mike Teague was clobbered from the kick-off and his departure disrupted England's forward strategy. England's lineout was exploited by Bob Norster, not for the first time. Carling has always insisted that Cardiff holds no terrors for his generation. That was not obvious that afternoon. The final margin was 12–9, but Wales were always in control. The decisive moment came after the interval when Rory Underwood's intended back-pass missed Webb and was pounced upon by Mike Hall. Robert Jones's narrow-side kicking kept England on the defensive for the rest of the match and the visitors could find no way out.

GEOFF COOKE
Our defence had been excellent against France, so we went to Wales with high hopes. Unfortunately, in Cardiff we showed a lack of coolness, of understanding, under pressure. We did not have the capability of finding a way out of their stranglehold. It was obvious that Roger and I still had a lot of work to do on the mental side. We were only just making inroads on the confidence problem. In some ways our defeat was predictable. The fact

England hadn't won in Cardiff for 26 years got on top of them. They couldn't believe they could do it. It felt like a backward step. It was our last game of the season and there was no way for us to redeem the situation.

ROGER UTTLEY

We didn't have the mental edge to withstand the Welsh pressure. Our short-term aim was to achieve stability. We had done that. The medium-term goal was to win the championship. We should have done that in our first year in Cardiff. It eventually took us three years – a nightmare. We had no answer to their tactics. Our only alternative was to kick the ball off the park. So there would be another lineout on our 10 metre line and the whole process started again. Norster jumped, passed to Jones, who kicked it back down our line. Our boys couldn't work it out. They allowed themselves to get locked into that game.

Nevertheless, Carling's first shot at the captaincy had gone well. He was the first to admit his mistakes. England had made genuine progress. To avenge the Australian summer defeat, to challenge for the championship and not to be satisfied with second best was a big step forward for England's national rugby side in six months. The new skipper's performance was all the more creditable because his shin splints injury had worsened through the championship campaign. Carling was an automatic choice for the British Lions on their tour of Australia that summer. But he was forced to withdraw from the squad and England's game in Romania in May. Exhaustive medical tests discovered a stress fracture of the lower left tibia. Three months' rest was the recommended cure.

His misfortune promoted a large cloud with a bountiful silver lining. Jerry Guscott not only scored three tries on his England debut in Bucharest, with Andrew as captain, but took Carling's place on the Lions tour. In Australia, Guscott, with his match-winning try in the second Test, established himself as rugby's newest superstar.

# CHAPTER 5

# GRAND SLAM CALAMITY – MURRAYFIELD, 1990

England's Lions forwards came back heroes. The pack provided the tourists with the power to recover from a 1–0 deficit in the three-Test series. The five Englishmen who had played in those final two winning Tests were now battle-hardened veterans. Paul Ackford, untested a year earlier, was now ranked as a world-class front jumper. Ackford played in all three Tests, as did Brian Moore and Dean Richards. Wade Dooley and Mike Teague, who was named Man of the Series, played in the two wins. England received another boost in the backs with Rob Andrew's assured displays in those two victories, while Jerry Guscott's moments of genius and Rory Underwood's clinical finishing were further pluses. Alongside those five forwards, England had Andy Robinson, Gareth Chilcott, Jeff Probyn, Paul Rendall, Peter Winterbottom, David Egerton and Micky Skinner to choose from. Small wonder Cooke and Uttley were licking their lips.

Carling had enjoyed a summer away from the spotlight, although he would have preferred to have played his part in the most successful British Lions tour for 15 years. Two tries in the final of the Monte Carlo Sevens in August at least convinced him he was on the way back.

As the new season approached, Carling and Andrew gave up their allegiance to the North. There was nothing more sinister about the switch than the fact that both were living and working in London. Carling explained: 'The North set out a training schedule that would have meant six days off work for those of us in the south. Both Rob and I have England commitments. On top of that Harlequins train three nights a week, while Rob is captain of Wasps. And don't forget, we've got careers as well.'

Such hectic schedules mean that injuries can often be a blessing in disguise. Carling was concussed again, against London Irish. The compulsory three-week rest kept him from taking an active part in the squad session before the Fiji visit. Carling and his more experienced squad took a bigger part in the preparations now, with Carling and Moore in charge of the Friday sessions. Uttley regarded the change as inevitable: 'When the players go on the field, they have to be accountable for their own actions. By that stage, the coaches had spent three days with them, not to mention the previous two years. They didn't need any spoon feeding. We can only be advisers, anyway. They play the game.'

Rory Underwood shared the headlines with Fijians Tevita Vonolagi and Noa Nadruku after England's 58–23 victory. Underwood's five tries equalled Daniel Lambert's England record in a match and Cyril Lowe's career record of 18. The two Fijians were given their marching orders by Irish referee Brian Stirling for reckless tackles.

Carling's injury problems continued the following week at Bristol when he limped off. Not that he got much sympathy from his Harlequin team-mates: he was in their bad books after making the draw for the next round of the Pilkington Cup, which resulted in Quins travelling to face the cup holders Bath.

Carling felt much more relaxed and confident entering his second championship as captain. Approaching the opening match, against Ireland at Twickenham, the skipper felt able to take a more long-term view of England's aspirations. 'We are slightly more sure about our style of play and better acquainted with each other than at this time last year. We have tried to work out the situations we are likely to be faced with and impose our own style upon them. Last year we slipped up against Scotland and Wales, who probably read the situation on the day better than we did. There were times when we wanted to play an expansive game, but it was too wet to do so all the time. I am confident that we are only a handful of games away from producing the 15-man game we want.'

England were closer than that, although for most of the Irish game it was the same old story. The Irish scrum was taking a pasting, but England could not capitalise and only held a 7–0 lead with eight minutes remaining; then late tries from Egerton, Rory Underwood and Guscott transformed the scoreline and wiped away all negative thoughts. England had set their standards for the season. Carling, after last year's failure to build on the Australian victory, was determined this was not going to be another false start. A month later his England team was being hailed as one of the greatest of all time after two staggering performances against, traditionally, their toughest opponents.

Paris was the next stop. England had enjoyed more success there than any Home Country side, but the Parc des Princes was still the most difficult visiting venue in the Five Nations. Ireland and Scotland (until 1995) had never won there; Wales's only success had come in 1975, while England had won twice, in 1980 and 1982. Carling's team made it a hat-trick in 1990. This win was different, though. For the first time ever, the French were played off the park. The visitors, playing into an atrocious wind, led 13–0 at the interval. That advantage was down to inch-perfect kicking with Rob Andrew's boot setting up a try for Rory Underwood, and Simon Hodgkinson subduing the wind and France with three inspiring penalties. Any hopes of a French revival were dashed at the start of the second half as Denis Carvet's kick through bounced off Carling. Guscott hacked away and finally gathered for the decisive score. Carling joined the try-scorers in the dying minutes when he left French captain Serge Blanco struggling to complete the 26–7 rout. Peter Winterbottom, the only survivor of

Carling dives over the French line again, this time at the Parc des Princes, to seal England's conclusive victory in 1990. (*Colorsport*)

the 1982 victory in Paris, gave his verdict: 'This is a much better team than the one eight years ago.'

The *Sunday Times*' Stephen Jones summed up the damage: 'England were so good they even robbed the occasion of some of its drama.'

## WILL CARLING

Suddenly, we were billed as world-beaters. The Grand Slam, so we were told, was a formality, probably two before we went on to win the World Cup. That was the mood and those were the predictions. My whole attitude to life and sport is about being positive, however desperate the situation, but this was ridiculous. Ironically, after reading that we were the greatest team in the world, it was only a few days later that we were told that England would once again succumb to the psychological hold the Welsh had over us. More rubbish.

Carling and his team emphatically proved that Welsh ghosts held no fear for them, at Twickenham at least. It was more than a day to remember for the Twickenham crowd, who had seen their national side humiliated by Wales on repeated occasions over the previous 20 years. For the Twickenham faithful, it was an even more significant afternoon than for a relatively new England side.

Carling touches down, despite Mark Titley's despairing tackle and Andy Allen's late arrival, for the first of England's four tries. *(Colorsport)*

Wales had claimed Irish refereeing bias in the England victories of 1974 and 1980 at Twickenham. Not this time. England's 34-6 was a record victory. Carling set the ball rolling with his best international try as he wove through five Welsh tackles after a quarter of an hour. No wonder the fans cheered. This was England's first try against the Principality for five years and 478 minutes. England added three more. Roger Uttley could not hold back: 'That was the most outstanding performance that any of us have witnessed from an England side of any era. It had the stamp of greatness and there is still more to come. Even the 1980 side would have had great difficulty living with England today.'

The *Sunday Times* was not the only paper struggling for more superlatives just two weeks after Paris. 'It strains the credibility when you see two once-in-a-lifetime performances produced within a fortnight. But there were aspects of England's seethingly glorious victory which rendered the demolition of France a fortnight ago a failure.'

Ten years on, Carling's team had followed the exact pattern of the last England side to win a Grand Slam with wins over Ireland, France and Wales. Now, as they did a decade earlier, England took a month off before travelling to Murrayfield. Nothing, it seemed, could stop Carling emulating the 1980 achievements of Bill Beaumont's England.

There was a significant difference, though. Two weeks before the 1990

Calcutta Cup game, Scotland won in Cardiff. Unlike their predecessors ten years earlier, David Sole's Scots were after a Grand Slam of their own.

Scotland v England, Murrayfield, 17 March 1990 has become 'The Match' for more than one generation of rugby supporters. For the first time ever, the Five Nations Championship, the Home Championship, the Grand Slam, the Triple Crown, not forgetting the trophy donated by the Calcutta Cricket and Rugby Club, were all up for grabs in one single afternoon of rugby passion. Rugby history was only part of it. This was the Red Rose versus the Thistle, Bannockburn against Culloden, and passion over power. Forget about winning. This was one rugby match that you could not contemplate losing.

Even Scotsmen were paying ridiculous prices for tickets for what was being billed the rugby match of the century. Certainly this clash had caught the public imagination like no other in recent times. The Scottish Rugby Union, with its traditional fervour, investigated the resale of tickets. Secretary Bill Hogg admitted to being 'horrified' by some prices being obtained on the black market – £1,000 a pair. 'It is entirely out of proportion for a game of rugby,' declared Hogg. Quite correct. Those prices were dirt cheap. A week later a pair of £14 tickets were fetching £3,000. England were firm favourites, 4–1 on, with the Scots 11–4 against.

Carling felt the full force of the media machine. These were his last few days as a rugby innocent. England's young captain was rarely off the feature pages. 'Captain Carling's a Darling' was typical, as were pictures of him draped in a St George's flag. Nothing could stop the Carling rollercoaster celebrating Grand Slam glory.

WILL CARLING

I was determined not to get caught up in all the hype. It was easy to become distracted. We had a good session on the Friday morning, probably too good. We didn't drop a ball in 45 minutes of work. I knew why the Scots were determined that we should be seen as overwhelming favourites. No scenario suits them better than being outsiders in their own backyard against the English. Countering the Scottish passion was something that we could not ignore. I told the players that they had to be strong enough to shut the Scottish noise and antagonism out of their system. But I'd be lying if I said I didn't have premonitions. A fortnight before the match, I didn't think the Scots would be able to withstand our overflowing confidence. But the night before, I sensed that they would be harder to dominate than the teams we had already beaten. I told the team that this was their chance to establish themselves as a great side. I didn't need to spell out the consequences if we lost.

Disaster. As Carling feared, it was the Scots who took their chance to establish themselves as a great side. From the moment David Sole walked out slowly and defiantly at the head of his Scottish army, England were on the defensive.

The slow march was a master-stroke from the Scot the English feared most, coach Ian McGeechan. England's Paul Ackford saw it coming. 'Ian is such a brilliant coach, as many of the English players discovered on last year's Lions tour, that he is certain to have thought up something original to make our task more difficult,' predicted England's lock the day before the match. That was not all. The Scots had arranged for two verses, not just the one, of 'Flower of Scotland' to be sung before the kick-off.

The match was notable for its defence and intensity. England, playing into the wind, countered Craig Chalmers' two early penalties when Carling went round Scott Hastings and Guscott dummied his brother, Gavin, to score a spectacular try. Another Chalmers penalty left England trailing 9–4 as they turned to feel the wind on their backs. England had other scoring chances in the first half, but the confidence of those wins over France and Wales encouraged them to ignore penalty points and go for tries. As England went for a pushover try, the scrum collapsed. Despite England protests, no penalty try was awarded.

Those wasted points were brought sharply into focus at the start of the second half when Scotland scored a try. Gavin Hastings kicked ahead to

Carling is held by the Scots during 'That Match' at Murrayfield in 1990. England's captain looks for support from Wade Dooley, Brian Moore and Micky Skinner, but David Sole's (No. 1) Tartan Army are there in force.
*(Colorsport)*

New Zealand referee David Bishop signals the try that stunned England at the start of the second half. Scorer Tony Stanger (facing camera) celebrates with Chris Gray while Rory Underwood, outjumped for the try, is grounded in resignation. *(Colorsport)*

Scotland's line, where the bounce was kind to the home side. It eluded Rory Underwood's outstretched arms as Tony Stanger leapt to gather and score. The impossible was about to happen. There was time for England to recover, but the capacity Murrayfield crowd sensed this was Scotland's day. Simon Hodgkinson kicked a penalty to bring the visitors to within a score, but Scotland withstood a fierce late flurry to take the spoils, 13–7.

The inquests began as soon as the final whistle sounded. They rage today. No questions were asked in the dressing-room. Even a wily old campaigner like Uttley, a member of the 1980 Grand Slam winning side, had never witnessed such desolation. This Grand Slam was only part of a bigger objective, winning the 1991 World Cup. Yet, now that it was lost, it became the most important thing in the world. The pain was intense. No matter what was achieved in the future, the 1990 Grand Slam had gone to Scotland and England were going to have to live with the gloating and failure. Even now, after three Grand Slams and a World Cup final, Carling's England are still the side who lost the biggest game in rugby history.

WILL CARLING

Murrayfield was a big turning point for me as captain. I asked a number of players during the game if they thought we were capable of beating the Scots in a certain way. They said 'yes'. It just didn't work. I will never blame anyone for that. At the end of the day, I'm the one who lives or dies by those decisions. I have to decide the way it's going to be. I didn't assert myself enough at Murrayfield.

It wasn't what happened on the field that changed me. It was afterwards when I sat down and thought: 'What more could I have done?' I realised that we had to be more ruthless and professional in our approach. I don't believe we lost that game. The Scots won. David Sole's team got it right on the day. I will never say that we lost to a better side that afternoon. But they did beat us and that's different to saying we lost it. I don't suppose we had considered losing hard enough. We had been playing so well. It came out of the blue. After that we considered losing in far more depth, how to cope. Losing at Murrayfield was a hell of a shock. It's five years now, but the bitter memories are still there and will never leave me. What really got me were the faces in the dressing-room. I know England's supporters were devastated, too, but my responsibility was to the squad. They are the ones who put in all the effort. I know it was a sad day for the fans. They were looking forward to a Grand Slam. It's great to achieve things and see the fans enjoy them. They didn't that day. It meant a lot to them and we got it wrong.

That was the public perception, too. For the very first time Carling's leadership came under intense scrutiny.

GEOFF COOKE

I was angry that Will was singled out as responsible for the failure. Murrayfield was the day we really let ourselves down and Will took a lot of flak for that. Certainly, it was the lowest point of our time together. It hit us hard. We were the better side, but we didn't come to terms with what the Scots were doing. Ultimately, we made a nonsense of it. Will took a lot of hammer. I felt fairly protective towards him. He was just one guy. There were more experienced guys around in England shirts that afternoon. The failure was a collective one. No one person was responsible for our defeat.

ROGER UTTLEY

For the second year running, we had blown the Five Nations because of our ineptitude on the field. Will was part of that. When you're the captain, you have to take responsibility for what happens out there. There were definite signs of a lack of decision-making. You can't lead by committee in the middle of a Grand Slam game at Murrayfield with the Scots rampaging around. It was a nightmare being in Edinburgh that night. We were devastated. I can honestly say that I have never experienced anything like it as a player. Rob and Brian were distraught. It was taking what had happened all in. We had never considered the possibility. We knew we were demonstrably better.

I turned to Geoff after a quarter of an hour and said: 'We've got huge problems here.' When Jerry ran in that try from half-way, I thought that might allow us to establish a pattern. You have to create some order, some continuity, especially against the Scots and Irish. It's the last thing they want. It's death to them. They want chaos, mayhem. The first inkling of trouble ahead was that slow march out. It made the hair on the back of my neck rise. It was Sole's greatest moment – brilliant. We could say that Stanger's try was fortuitous because of the bounce, or moan that the southern hemisphere referee awarded scrums and penalties when it should have been penalty tries. But we had only ourselves to blame. The defeat was physically painful. We had a hard time up there. It was as if Edinburgh had taken over from Cardiff as the seat of English loathing. We caught the flak for all the Thatcher years, for the English control of Scotland. The patriots redressed some of the balance that night.

Carling has always put on a brave public face in time of adversity. His mum, Pam, was in tears though. It was not his parents' day, either. Their south London home was burgled. On the bright side, when the crooks walked off with the video they also took the tape that had pre-recorded England's humiliation that afternoon.

Carling's captaincy honeymoon period was well and truly over. The Grand Slam defeat was not an isolated incident. It began a crisis of leadership that was nearly his last. England's captain had such a traumatic time over the next year that he nearly filed for divorce from the job. The stigma of the Murrayfield defeat proved difficult to shake off. The golden boy who could do no wrong was now trapped on the downward spiral. The rugby press and officialdom, who had had nothing but praise for him during his rise to the top, now appeared to concentrate their efforts on his destruction. They certainly got more than a little assistance from Carling himself. With his confidence dented and his judgement awry, the England skipper entered a period of doubt, suspicion and frustration. Eventually, he questioned whether leading the national rugby side was worth all the hassle. Murrayfield was the start of that thought process.

Carling had a busy end to the season, travelling to the Hong Kong Sevens with the Barbarians, then playing under David Sole when the four Home Unions beat the Rest of Europe at Twickenham to raise funds for Romanian rugby. England announced its preliminary squad for the 1991 World Cup. The surprise omissions were Mark Bailey, Nigel Redman and – though he actually played in the final – Simon Halliday. As Carling and England flew off to Italy for an international at the end of April, the *Sunday Times* reflected on the price of that Grand Slam failure. 'A forlorn group of wives and girlfriends will see the England party off at Heathrow tonight. Had things turned out differently at Murrayfield, they would have been joining the players on the two-day trip to Italy. It was planned to thank the group for their support of the men who won the Grand Slam. Evidently, supporting the men who came second wasn't quite enough.'

Brian Moore did not come second. The Nottingham hooker was named *Rugby World* 'Player of the Year'. The body of opinion which thought of England's hooker as a lightweight, a show-off, was dwindling. Moore was the proof of positive thinking. Everyone expected Ireland's Steve Smith to make the Lions Test team in 1989, but Moore soon showed that he was not going to accept second best. He had just announced that he would be joining Carling at Quins, although his coach at Nottingham, Alan Davies, was less than pleased: 'He's achieved everything in the game with us, from a teenager to mature player. It is sad when someone like him falls prey to those who have a job to offer. The whole things smacks of clubs like Harlequins and Northampton, with a lot of money and connections, organising themselves to get the players they want.' That view was repeated later in 1990 when Jason Leonard moved from Saracens to Quins.

England had been due to have a summer off. With the World Cup looming, those involved with the squad would have preferred it. But it was not to be. The decision was taken higher up, so Cooke's careful build-up was disrupted by a tour he knew nothing about. His charges would now have 18 months' continuous rugby through to the World Cup. Cooke had no choice, but his players did and several senior players made themselves unavailable. Carling led a squad to Argentina without Jon Webb, Rory Underwood, Jerry Guscott, Rob Andrew, Paul Rendall, Paul Ackford, Dean Richards and Mike Teague. Before leaving, the players spent time with Len Heppell, the movement consultant who had worked with Frank Bruno and the England soccer team and whose aim is to 'improve the reflexes, movement and balance of sportsmen'.

Carling appreciated that this trip would be a valuable learning ground for those outside the first-choice England XV. 'I don't see the main objective as to remain unbeaten. My main priorities are that we adapt the lessons we have learnt into our patterns of play, and that the youngsters learn about what is involved in the whole England set-up. It would be bad for us to be so negative and conservative that, at the end of the tour, we came away with played seven, won seven, but the youngsters had not been introduced into the hard games and not given a fair go.'

Only a missed penalty by Simon Hodgkinson cost England the Test series 2–0. Yet it was a disappointing trip, with the emergence of Jason Leonard the one saving grace. The lessons Cooke and Uttley learnt were negative ones. Several of the less experienced players were shown to be wanting when it came to that final step to the big time. England lost their first two Saturday matches. Afterwards Cooke showed his dismay: 'I can't believe what I'm seeing. We seem to have left our rugby brains back in England. We made a series of school-boy howlers and put ourselves under pressure.'

England's first Test team contained four new caps in Leonard, Nigel Heslop, David Pears and Dean Ryan. Carling read the riot act beforehand. 'It's a bit sad that we gave away 26 points in the Five Nations, yet it's nearly 100 already on this trip. I don't think we have sufficient pride in our defence. There has not been sufficient pride and dedication for an England tour.' The players respond-ed by giving their best display so far, winning 25–12. The tourists kept their nerve and tempers under severe provocation. The Australian referee Brian Kinsey offered England little protection.

The final week of the tour brought more problems. Stand-in skipper John Olver nearly took the team off the field during the 15–12 victory over Cordoba because of the local refereeing. Cooke again backed his players with some public pronouncements that did not find favour with the authorities at Twickenham. 'The referee was just incompetent. I don't normally comment on referees, but I feel I can because we got the right result. He had no concept of offside, how to set a scrum or throwing in at the lineout. He would not be allowed to referee a third-team game at home.'

England's attempt to be the first team to win both Tests in Argentina since France in 1974 ended in failure when Herman Vidou kicked a late penalty for the home side shortly after Hodgkinson had missed a simple kick to make the game safe. The disappointment of the 15–13 defeat accentuated the sense of failure hanging over the tour.

Behind the scenes, too, England had problems. Roger Uttley was beginning to feel squeezed out.

ROGER UTTLEY
There had been a lot of indications that Will wasn't happy with me. It came to a head after the third tour game. We had played in a football stadium with a moat and a tunnel underneath to allow the players access to the dressing-room. I waited there at the end of the game. Will was nearby, obvi-ously charged up. I asked what the problem was. He just told me to '****  off.' That was the end of it for me. I began to feel like an outsider and that lasted right through until I quit at the end of the World Cup.

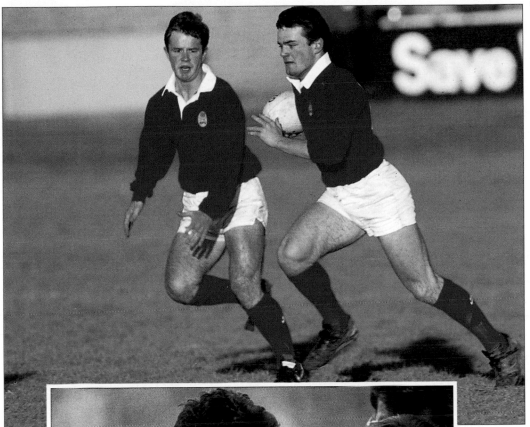

The 1986 Divisional Championship took Carling from nowhere to the fringe of the England team. This match clinched the title for the North as they trounced London at Wasps. *(Colorsport)*

Carling down, but certainly not out. Concussion forces Carling to make a premature exit from his first game as England captain in 1988, but not before the young centre had made the game safe. *(Colorsport)*

Carling powers through the Welsh defence on the way to scoring his third international try, which remains one of his very best. However, that 1990 season was to end in disappointment at Murrayfield. *(Colorsport)*

England's 16–7 victory over Ireland in 1991 set up a second successive Grand Slam opportunity. Unlike the previous year, this time they succeeded. *(Colorsport)*

ABOVE: The game was scrappy, but the result was emphatic. England beat Italy 36–6 and were on their way in the 1991 World Cup. *(Colorsport)*

INSET: Carling and manager Geoff Cooke in light-hearted mood before the 1991 World Cup campaign got underway. *(Colorsport)*

BELOW: Carling is consoled by the Queen after England's 12–6 defeat against Australia in the World Cup final. *(Colorsport)*

ABOVE: England celebrate Grand Slam No. 2 under Carling's leadership, 1992. *(Colorsport)*

BELOW: Carling in action for his club, Harlequins, as he goes past Bath's Stuart Barnes in the 1992 Courage League match. *(Colorsport)*

ABOVE: One of the few glimpses of the real Carling on the 1993 British Lions tour of New Zealand as he bursts through against Otago. (Colorsport)

LEFT: Carling gained compensation for his disappointing Lions tour of New Zealand when he led England to victory over the All Blacks at Twickenham a few months later. (Colorsport)

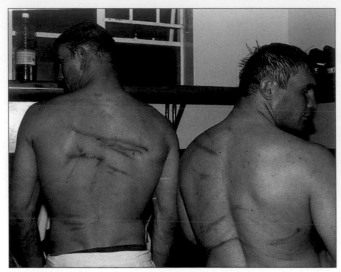

England forwards Lawrence Delaglio and John Mallett after the 1994 tour match against Eastern Province, which left Jonathan Callard needing 26 stitches and Tim Rodber facing a disciplinary hearing after becoming only the second player to be sent off in an England jersey. *(Colorsport)*

Carling and South African President Nelson Mandela at the end of England's 1994 tour. Contrary to expectations, it was Mandela, not Carling, who was one of the stars of the 1995 World Cup final. *(Colorsport)*

Carling celebrates at Twickenham in 1995 after becoming the first captain ever to lead his country to a hat-trick of Grand Slams. *(Colorsport)*

ABOVE: Carling on the attack in the gruelling World Cup quarter-final against Australia at Newlands in Cape Town. (Colorsport)

LEFT: Despite the most exhausting rugby game of his life, Carling still has enough energy to celebrate England's quarter-final victory over Australia with Tony Underwood and Mike Catt. (Colorsport)

Carling scores in England's second-half fightback against the All Blacks in the World Cup semi-final and, for once, Jonah Lomu is only an interested spectator.
(Colorsport)

Carling suffered his first defeat as England captain in nine meetings with France in the World Cup third-place play-off in Pretoria. Carling takes on Lacroix in a rare England attack.
(Colorsport)

The 1990 tour of Argentina was not an easy time for Carling. Relations with Roger Uttley were strained and England lost the second Test. *(Colorsport)*

It took us some time to find our feet with such an inexperienced squad. After about 10 days I was approached by Will and Geoff and told that they wanted to use Bestie [Dick Best] for a couple of sessions. The impetus for that had come from Will. He was obviously unhappy and worried with the way things were going. Bestie, who was coach of the London divisional side, was out there as part of his duties as a travel agent. I felt it was out of order. I think Will genuinely felt that he was not getting enough support, probably because his role as captain was being questioned after Murrayfield. He was finding it difficult to come up with the answers at the time. I don't know why he didn't turn to me. I remember being in a lift with him in Buenos Aires and at the breakfast table, but there was barely a word between us. I was finding it increasingly difficult to deal with him.

Carling definitely felt the need to assert himself in Argentina. The biggest criticism of his leadership at Murrayfield was that he failed to take control, that he depended too much on government by consensus. His first attempt to stamp his authority went badly wrong in the tour opener against Banco Nacion.

WILL CARLING

I lost it badly at the end of the match. I was disgusted with the attitude of the players. It didn't seem to bother them as much as it did me that they were losing while wearing the England jersey. I called them together at the end of the match and really ripped into them. 'You've got to have more pride. Otherwise we'll find someone else to wear your jerseys.' I was fuming.

Hillie [Richard Hill] came up to me and said: 'Calm down.' I quickly realised that what I did was wrong. It was far too much of an emotional outburst. I made a conscious decision that it would never happen again.

The trip came too soon for a few of the younger players. Some of the senior players performed below par. I know that Brian Moore and Wade Dooley were disappointed with their form. I believe that we lacked the necessary desire to win the second Test. We'd won the first Test. Maybe we were relieved that the tour was coming to a close. The Argentinians saw it as their final chance and came out with all guns blazing.

The tour finished with the traditional dinner. Beforehand Carling had been dragged before the players' court and his punishment was to attend the function with his face painted as a clown. His appearance was reported back in a UK paper with a critical piece that England's captain did not know how to behave and that he had insulted his Argentinian hosts. That was never the intention, and nobody was upset or complained. Carling was furious. He saw it as the latest attempt in an increasing trend to put the boot into the England rugby captain whenever possible.

# CHAPTER 6

# WINNERS AT LAST – GRAND SLAM 1991

The Uttley bust-up apart, Carling had done a good job in Argentina. This was his first overseas expedition as captain. No side can travel without eight key players and expect to function efficiently. Yet Carling was disappointed that some of those expected to stake a claim on this tour did not respond to his leadership. In this, the captain was being overly self-critical. The newcomers did not come through because they were not good enough. That was the fault of the selectors. Their choices had been exposed.

Carling had been examining his leadership style in much more depth since the defeat in Scotland. Never one to enjoy the prominent profile, he resented more and more being public property. Life had become much more painful since the back-slapping had become back-stabbing. Carling needed help. Unfortunately, the very body that should have protected him, the Rugby Football Union, had decided that it was time he was cut down to size. The more Carling asserted himself, the less Twickenham liked it.

Carling could have ended these problems at a stroke – the stroke of the pen which would have taken him to Warrington, and rugby league, for £400,000. That was not the last offer he received.

WILL CARLING
I have never been interested in playing rugby league. And I never will. The amount of money makes no difference. None of the England internationals is in the game for money. I remember the phone going. The voice at the other end offered me £1 million to play for Leeds. I said: 'Oh yeah.' But the offer was serious. That money was guaranteed over five years. I didn't say 'no' immediately. An offer like that has to make you think. But deep down I knew I couldn't go. It was no saintly act that I turned the offer down. I wanted to build up my business. It really annoys me when I'm accused of being in rugby for money. They haven't got a clue why I'm in this game. I talked it through long and hard with Jon [Holmes, Carling's agent]. I enjoy watching rugby league. I have great admiration for their players. I have no idea how I would have done. I played with Martin Offiah with the Barbarians. He's been a phenomenal success in league. Maybe he was a great loss to union, but those extra two defenders might have made all the difference. I have never had a minute's regret about not signing, even in the

worst moments. One thing is certain – I'm sure I would have regretted going. Rugby league is not my game. I've been in love with union since I was six. I would have been going for the money, nothing else. That would have been wrong. The ultimate price would have been too big to pay. I would have missed out on the World Cup.

Another rugby body was interested in Carling and money: the RFU. The whispering campaign against him was becoming deafening. Surely England's photogenic skipper could not be appearing in all those newspapers and magazines for nothing. His face was peering out from front covers normally the preserve of Princess Di, George Michael and Kevin Costner. How the RFU hated Mr Macho Rugby Player, good-looking, successful, pretty girlfriends, talking money, success and winning. If this was the rugby player of the future, then they were going to retreat back into the dark ages. So they got to work and, like the policeman who is determined to find something wrong with your car, they kept probing until they found something.

Carling was finding the resentment hard to take. His life revolved around rugby. If he was not playing, he was training or travelling to train or play, or thinking about playing or about how he could be a better captain or help give England that little edge. On top of that, Carling was trying to establish a new business. His first skirmish concerned a modelling feature for *You* magazine. Ignoring the normal principle of innocent until proven guilty, the RFU asked Carling to prove that he had not been paid, then dropped the matter when the magazine wrote to confirm Carling's story that money had never been discussed. The following month the rugby authorities were on his trail again, this time suspecting that Carling had received payment for opening a sports complex in London. This time Carling had to appear at Twickenham to answer the charges. Again, England's captain was exonerated, but this time his public ordeal led some to believe there could be no smoke without fire.

WILL CARLING

I had opened a leisure facility near Croydon and somebody thought it was their responsibility to send a letter to Dudley Wood [the RFU secretary]. Just for good measure, a copy made its way to the *Daily Telegraph*. I was hauled in front of the RFU to explain what had happened to the money. I told them the money had gone to charity. They said that I had to bring documentation to that effect and a letter from the charity. Then I had to sign a letter explaining where the money had gone – a solemn oath. The whole episode really annoyed me. In their eyes I was definitely guilty until I could prove my innocence, contrary to the law of the land. There was certainly no right of silence. I found it a very strange way to treat your national captain, or any of your players.

I have a regular charity to which I give money. It is a cancer hospital. But I have never felt that it is anyone else's business about how much money I give. I was accused without any proof. The payment, about £250, went to a third party. A lot of people actually resent that there is a fee in the first place and believe that the England rugby captain should turn up for nothing. My time is limited and valuable. Money was deducted for my travelling expenses and the rest went to the charity. Dudley Wood generously pointed out that if the cheque had been paid directly to the charity and not the individual, then tax would not have been due on it. By this stage, I really felt my personal world was being invaded. There seemed not to be a single part that was private.

After Carling was given the second all-clear, he assumed his problems were behind him. That was another error. His criticism of Paul Gascoigne at a Central Council for Physical Recreation forum in Bournemouth, where he was speaking alongside Prince Philip, made the sporting headlines. It was a storm in a teacup and the pair made it up a few weeks later, but it showed that Carling had lost his magic touch for the moment.

December 1990 turned out to be a terrible month for the England captain. The year ended with much speculation that Carling was about to quit as skipper. Stephen Jones of the *Sunday Times* was one sympathetic voice. 'What do you get the man who has everything at Christmas? I tell you. Carling needs help. He need parcels of understanding. He is feeling increasingly frayed, and the past few weeks have accelerated the process. There is another side to the coin of success, and Carling has seen it all too clearly. Carling is perceived as the kind of man to whom things come effortlessly. Too true. He is currently drawing heavy criticism without moving a muscle. As England captain he has controversially banded the squad together under an agency. The die-hards on the RFU committee blame Carling for the whole business.'

The rot continued with a bad car crash. Carling was finding the rugby field his only place of refuge. Playing had never ceased to be a pleasure. Soon even this was to be denied him. Once again, he felt betrayed by those he expected to offer some understanding and protection. Carling was about to suffer the ultimate humiliation. England's captain was dropped by the London divisional side after missing training. An ankle injury had kept him out of London's opening game in the championship. A delay in Glasgow while on business meant he could not make training the following week. Rather than be lectured on his responsibilities, Carling rang Rob Andrew to pass on his apologies.

WILL CARLING
I heard very quickly that informing Rob was not the correct procedure. Everyone involved in the London set-up was aware that I was going through a bad time. The London chairman, Graham Smith, rang: 'We can't make exceptions.' He added that he understood my position, although it was going to be difficult to pick me now. That wasn't true. I had already

been dropped. Victory for the team over the individual. Graham didn't have the guts to tell me. I was out in disgrace and I'm sure there were a lot of smiling faces around the rugby establishment when the news was announced. I went down to Gloucester to watch the London match. Graham's wife Anna came over to me: 'Please come and speak to Graham. He feels awful about it.' I was trying to do the right thing. No excuses. It seems that when you are England captain, you can't make mistakes. I was certainly making too many mistakes at the time.

I had written my car off the week before, coming back from divisional training at about ten o'clock. I just lost it. I wasn't used to the power of the car and shot down the road backwards. It was terrifying. I wrote off two other cars as well. It wasn't so much what could have happened to me, but someone else might have been killed. One of the other cars had the passenger door caved in. I didn't know if anyone had been sitting in that seat. It frightened me to think I could have killed someone through no fault of their own. It was the first time I'd been in an accident. I hope it's the last. The police arrived. Just my luck. A Welshman. 'Who's going to win at the Arms Park, then?' I couldn't believe it. 'Just at the moment, I don't give a damn.' I received nine penalty points and a maximum £400 fine. Maybe I should have offered him two tickets for the game.

Carling often found refuge at his parents' home in Clapham during this time. Whenever he needs to get a grip on life, his family comes to the rescue. That was evident from his earliest days. He was a toddler who was oblivious to danger. Carling was four when he toppled off the garage roof. A pile of leaves broke his fall. Many contend that luck has stayed with him. The Carlings are openly affectionate towards each other. The England captain will kiss his Dad in public without embarrassment. Yet, while his parents are at ease outside the close bounds of family and friends, Carling is not.

TONY ROCHE, *TODAY*
His Mum is very outgoing. Bill is more sombre. Will has Pam's character, but he doesn't feel it goes with the job of captain. Even when I first met him, I thought him too guarded for such a young man. Will was too serious too young. Strong character, talented bloke, too sensitive. His folks have always been supportive. That's been important. Bill is the strong, silent type. Pam is a bubbling person. She throws her head back and really laughs. I get the impression that Will would like to, but can't. Pam is warm and witty. Will looks like her, but doesn't reveal her traits. She talks. Bill gets on with things. It's a very close family. If there's anyone that Will listens to, it's his Dad. I think he has offered sensible advice at crucial times.

Bill Carling had retired from the Army in 1985, since when his base has been

the Brewers' Guild in the heart of London. Pam has returned to work as an interior designer. She had a second problem with breast cancer five years ago, and the England captain had lunch with her every day while she was in hospital. The Carlings had by now become familiar faces on the rugby circuit. Pam is careful to offer support without overstaying her welcome. While Bill has always had rugby ambitions for his son, Pam was annoyed that Will did not do himself justice academically.

LEFT: A satisfied Bill Carling and, as ever, a smiling Pam Carling with their younger offspring at the Parc des Princes. (Colorsport)

## PAM CARLING
I was very disappointed with his Durham results. William has got a good brain. I felt he owed it to himself to have done better. He was wasting a place for someone else. You must try to achieve your potential. He does on the rugby field. Why not in the classroom? Basically, William has a lazy streak. He had only three lectures a week. If he had been sensible, he could have achieved so much more. Mind you, he was like a ghost in the last two years, travelling back and forward from Durham to London.

RIGHT: Marcus takes the higher ground to emphasise Will's failure to reach six foot.

It was to his Dad Carling turned in the second half of 1990. Will is basically a private person, yet he was having to cope with his problems being played out in the media and in public. This increased the ordeal to unacceptable levels. His family and friends are always there to rally round, but wait for the call. In times of real stress, Will Carling goes to his Dad. If he has a real hero, it's Bill. That's not difficult to understand. Most parents visit school by car; his father came out of the sky and landed a helicopter on the lawns. Such schoolboy ideas of glamour soon faded, but his father's steadying influence has continued to make him a trusted adviser.

BILL CARLING

I always had a deep-seated ambition for him. I hoped he would play for his country and be captain. I wouldn't have regarded it as any sort of failure if he hadn't. I've always called him a lucky boy. The ball has bounced his way. He was born with some talents. Will made his England debut because the two first-choice centres were injured. Those are the breaks you need.

It would have been impossible for him to combine the Army with being captain of England. I thought the Army would have been more flexible. I didn't influence Willie one way or the other. He had to make his own decision. I didn't want him to lose his England place because of it. I think he would have been successful in the Army, but I always knew rugby would win if he had to choose. He was disappointed. He still regrets it. It was part of his life that he wanted to do. He hasn't. I've done it. So has Marcus. We talk about it and give him a hard time. Along with his other 'failure' – he's the only Carling male not to reach six foot. We keep telling him there's still time.

Willie certainly reached a crisis point with the England captaincy after the Grand Slam defeat. All along I believed he was prepared to weather the storm but the problems showed no signs of abating. He never said to me that he was going to give up the captaincy. Willie was finding himself. After losing that big game at Murrayfield, he found out how cruel the media could be. Every move he made in the months after was a bad one. He got depressed about it and his game suffered. He cuts himself off – that's his way of protecting himself. When that happens, he's accused of being arrogant. He certainly learnt a lot in this period. Will's not the type who asks for advice. He takes what he wants. He knows that our home is somewhere he can come back to and relax. And he will only relax if we don't keep asking him questions.

Personal scrutiny was not the only item on the media agenda. Carling's England were running out of time for coming up with the goods. The World Cup was only a season away and Cooke's side had won nothing. Another championship failure and the team manager would be forced to conclude that some of his senior players had reached their sell-by date. Cooke believed his charges were not over the hill, but he and they needed some silverware, imaginary or not, to prevent a wholesale clear-out before the summer tour to Australia. Cooke had no desire to experiment a few months before the World Cup. Even without pre-Christmas

Simon Hodgkinson's goal-kicking was a key part of England's first Grand Slam success for 11 years. *(Colorsport)*

victories against Italy and Argentina, England would have been installed as firm favourites for the Five Nations. But Cooke and Carling wanted more, believing that only a Grand Slam would satisfy the critics.

Carling headed for Cardiff in January 1991, well aware that England had not won in Wales since Harold Macmillan was Prime Minister. Cooke decided that his team must prepare themselves for the Welsh *hwyl*. Instead of the relaxed atmosphere of the St Pierre Golf and Country Club at Chepstow, England based themselves in the centre of Cardiff where there was no escape. It worked. After 28 years of frustration, England laid the Cardiff bogey. Mike Teague scored the try and Simon Hodgkinson kicked seven penalties in a no-nonsense, no-frills performance. It was a day and night for dancing in the streets of Cardiff. The England fans made up for over a quarter of a century of suffering. Unfortunately, Cooke and Carling were about to pull the biggest publicity blunder of their careers, a crazy stunt that would have cost them their jobs had the World Cup not been around the corner.

How an England management well versed in the business of communication and dealing with the media could transform a day of triumph into an unmitigated public relations disaster remains bewildering to this day. The management's crime? They refused to turn up for the traditional after-match press conference. Carling had some excuse: recent events suggested that he was not thinking all that clearly. Cooke should have known better. Getting the best out of the press was one of his strengths. Not in Cardiff. Upsetting the media can make life uncomfortable. The situation was worse for Cooke.

GEOFF COOKE
The players decided not to give interviews to the BBC. That was their choice. I can assure you that had nothing to do with our decision not to go to the after-match press conference. It was not a dramatic gesture. If I had thought about it rationally, it wouldn't have happened. But I wasn't thinking rationally. It was a very emotional time. England had just won in Cardiff for the first time in 28 years. We were told the press were ready. I replied: 'Give us a little more time.' The feeling was that we were being rushed. The players felt the increasing demands from the press had become unreasonable and unbearable. Then it just happened. We decided not to go.

It was an obvious blunder. I could understand the press being upset. But it was the RFU's attitude which really discouraged me. Whatever the press thought, it was a storm in a teacup. Some of those at Twickenham took it into their heads that it was a slight against amateurism. I was under no illusion. My position was under threat. The hotheads saw it as a chance to do a hatchet job. Fortunately, there are also a lot of good people at the RFU. The moderate thinkers won the day.

Much of the blame was put on the players' search for more substantial rewards. The squad had formed a company, Player Vision, to negotiate with commercial companies to look after their interests. They signed up with Bob Willis, the former England cricket captain, and his brother David. The players involved the RFU's marketing man, Michael Coley, to sit in on the discussions. The big problem was that nobody knew how far the players could go in pursuit of rewards. The Willis arrangement did not last long. It was difficult to escape from the feeling that money was behind the players' boycott in Cardiff.

## ROGER UTTLEY

I remember ringing home before the match and telling my wife Christine I was unhappy with what was going on. In simple language, it was player power. It was Will-led. I know the players were unhappy and I had sympathy for them. But it really brassed me off. All the extracurricular activities distracted us from what we should be doing. I have to admit feeling slightly blinkered. I was still suffering the after-effects of my experiences with Will in Argentina. I wasn't brave enough in Cardiff. Not turning up at the press conference in Cardiff seemed like a good idea at the time. I'd been around long enough to have known better. When we left the hotel by the back door to get to the dinner, I thought we were just taking a short cut. I didn't realise the press were trying to hunt us down.

To be fair to Will, he'd been through a lot since Murrayfield. He needed help. It was obvious he didn't want it from me. It was also obvious that he wasn't going to get it from sources within rugby. I found that sad. Our efforts towards the World Cup were being undermined by Twickenham's suspicions about the captain and players. The squad was being asked to commit themselves to England's cause in a way no others had been. But all Twickenham could see was pound signs and the players destroying rugby union. Unfortunately, Cardiff was grist to their mill. The management and the players got it wrong. Twickenham was going to make us pay.

*Today*'s Tony Roche had been Carling's first regular contact in the media. Carling got in touch during the summer of 1990. *Today* was his Mum's favourite newspaper and in the aftermath of Murrayfield the England captain felt he needed a media platform without worrying about sensational headlines. It was a feather in Roche's cap and the pair worked together until the 1991 World Cup.

## TONY ROCHE, *TODAY*

We only had a gentleman's agreement. I found him very reliable, very straight. We did first-person pieces before internationals. I rang him when he first got picked for England. Will didn't really know how to talk about himself. Very little was known about Will and, to a large extent, I still think that's the case today. He's a bit like an iceberg – most is hidden below the surface. He realised that I was someone he could talk to in the press who didn't always have a pen and notebook out. He was usually trying to find out how the press viewed him.

I thought he handled the press brilliantly after that Grand Slam defeat. His folk were close to tears. The stiff upper lip stood him in good stead that day. Cardiff was a different matter altogether. It had been brewing for ages. You could feel the tension, and not just because England hadn't won there for 28 years. The England players got it desperately wrong and never got their message across. It was a stance against the press, the RFU, arguments about money. I still rate it the biggest blunder of his career.

Carling's relations with the media have never really recovered from the Cardiff debacle. It remains his biggest weakness as a captain. He is the first England captain not to be readily available outside press conferences. His exclusive contract with the *Mail on Sunday* is a convenient excuse for not talking. This has caused resentment, partly based on professional jealousy. Every player deals with the media in his own way. If Rob Andrew had held a grudge for every time he had been ridiculed or written off, the England fly half would be the most bitter and twisted man on this planet. Andrew appreciated that he could never convince a large section of the press that he was a better fly half than Stuart Barnes. Andrew has retained his dignity and remained above the squabble by not departing from his charming, co-operative and affable self.

Carling does not possess such tolerance. Not that his head is turned by the 'Darling Carling' rubbish. It's the bad notices that he reads. Carling feels the pain and wants to lash back, though less now than he did.

## WILL CARLING

I've never given the press what they want. I'm not sure I want to. It's my weakest area, without a doubt, although I've worked hard to improve. There are certain rules when dealing with the press that you must obey and find out for yourself – they are not written down. You have to find out the hard way. I believe I'm honest with them. I'm not a manipulator. David Campese plays games and fools around. I can't do that. I find press conferences hard work. I'm definitely not a natural. I don't want the press to get too close to me because implicit in that relationship would be trust. I can't trust them. At some point they will criticise me, probably quite rightly, and that will hurt. I would have to push them away again. While I accept criticism, it still hurts. I know when I've played badly. I'm quite sensitive. I don't mark people for the paper they write for. Some are very knowledgeable, others are good at giving the reader a visual image. Occasionally, I wonder if the journalist was at the same game. I do have more time for certain journalists. But, as with players, I've got to be careful about showing it. They are quite a sensitive lot, too.

I got it wrong in Cardiff. I still believe our cause was just. All we managed to do was alienate people. We just wanted to put that awful Cardiff record to the sword, but we feared the after-match circus. I accept that things did get on top of us. We certainly did not expect such a backlash. It had nothing to do with finance. All we wanted was for guide-lines to be established. It's taken nearly five years to get down that path.

Murrayfield to Cardiff was a hell of a tough time for me. I felt picked upon. I don't care how strong you are, everybody needs help. My family was very supportive. Others in rugby who should have been were not and I have never forgotten that. The outside pressure can wear you down. I really got fed up with the business concerning amateur regulations. Where was the next accusation coming from? I felt under pressure in 1993 for other reasons. Expectations were high. I set myself an impossible standard. The strain was from within. But late 1990, early 1991 was different. My every twitch was examined under the microscope. All the pressures were from the outside.

If I have a weakness, it's insecurity. At school, I was concerned about doing the right thing the right way. My friends know it. They see it. I love being captain of England, but when it goes wrong, you are on your own. You can't share your doubts with the team. I don't think I've ever seriously considered giving up the captaincy. It has meant a lot to me. But five years ago when all those pressures were building up, it wouldn't have taken much to push me over the edge.

England's deafening silence in Cardiff made a Grand Slam even more of a necessity. The historic win in Wales did not make the front pages. The Gulf War had just started. Few felt the time was right for rugby players to be making a stance about money, press harassment or whatever it was England were protesting about. Rory Underwood knew that better than most when a colleague he had trained with, Lieutenant John Peters, appeared in a video that shocked the whole country. Peters' cruel treatment at the hands of his Iraqi captors was all too obvious. Later, England's flying wing dedicated his Triple Crown try to Peters.

England had a month's break before entertaining the Scots. Carling thought it best not to hide from the Grand Slam anguish of 1990. He rounded up all the press cuttings from the previous March. 'It wasn't pleasant reading, but it reminded us how much it meant,' was Carling's reason. The England squad nearly earned themselves another dose of bad publicity. Initially, Cooke refused to allow his players to be photographed wearing the red noses of Comic Relief. 'We want to help charity, but we don't want to look a bunch of clowns before a big match. It will make us look like idiots if we lose.' The players persuaded Cooke to change his mind, but the strain from Cardiff was showing. There was no slip-up against the Scots this time, as England won 21–12. The measure of their determination was obvious – and it was all needed a fortnight later in Dublin as the wind, the rain and the Irish conspired to try to deny England the Triple Crown. England were a point behind with seven minutes remaining before late tries from Underwood and Teague saw them home, 16–7. It was the sort of close encounter in Dublin that England have often failed to come to terms with. Yet, once again, Carling's England were hearing discouraging voices from the press. Winning, it seems, was not enough.

WILL CARLING

The press began to adopt a negative attitude towards us that remains to this day. Once they got it into their heads that we weren't playing expansive rugby, that was it. It's impossible to discard those labels. People have the romantic notion that the Aussies run the ball all the time. Not true. The 1971 British Lions had one of the all-time great backlines – Edwards, John, Davies, Dawes, Gibson, Duckham, J. P. R. Williams. Watch the Test matches in New Zealand. The ball hardly got past Barry John. The myth with England is that we don't play 15-man rugby, but I think we have played as much as anyone. The Aussies kick for position, then run it. That's the reality. The Aussies play very disciplined rugby. And quite rightly. Yet the image has grown up that they are great entertainers.

France, the northern hemisphere's great rugby entertainers, lay between England and a first Grand Slam since 1980. The French, who had demolished Wales on the day England collected the Triple Crown in Dublin, were also on the Grand Slam trail. Another Grand Slam showdown. England had the home advantage, but France had only lost once at Twickenham since 1979. Cooke was able to select an unchanged side – the first time the same England team had gone through the championship for 31 years and only the second time ever.

England should have won by a mile, such was the forwards' control. Yet that domination counted for little as France outscored England by three tries to one, ensuring a heart-stopping finale for the home supporters. France's opening try was as good as any seen at Twickenham. Berbizier gathered Hodgkinson's missed penalty behind his own line. The French were loose as Lafond, Camberabero, Sella and Camberabero again raced to half-way with England retreating in haste. Camberabero chipped ahead, regained possession and cross-kicked to the middle of the park where Saint-André was steaming through and went under the posts. Words fail to do justice to the adventure and inventiveness of that try. England were scattered around the park in disbelief. The England team of a year earlier might have cracked, panicked or recklessly caught the French mood; but Murrayfield had prepared them well. England carried on their way relentlessly, although Rory Underwood's try did not suffer in comparison with any of the trio of French efforts. Serge Blanco's team refused to concede defeat and were always too close for comfort, eventually going down 21–19. Finally, though, Carling was carried shoulder-high from the field, a year to the day since the worst rugby experience of his life. Two fans slipped away with his boots, special souvenirs of a memorable day.

WILL CARLING

I remember going up to Durham to see a mate after the Grand Slam. It seemed no time since I was just a young student trying to make my way in the rugby world. I thought about what had happened over the past year.

TOP: Carling tells his team that they just have to keep their heads against France for another 40 minutes to become winners at last. *(Allsport/Dan Smith)*

BELOW: Rory Underwood's Grand Slam try for England v. France, 1991. *(Colorsport)*

INSET: Carling and Jerry Guscott offer Underwood their congratulations. *(Colorsport)*

Carling, minus boots, finally leaves the pitch celebrations after England's 1991 Grand Slam. *(Colorsport)*

All my problems, the good times and the bad. There just seemed too much pressure being captain of England. Wouldn't it be nice to go back to being an unknown and just playing rugby for the pure joy of it? It was this time that I started wondering whether I was still playing the game for the right reasons. Those questions went on for a couple of years. If I wanted to be just another player, then I would have to lose the captaincy. I wouldn't have been happy about that. You have to keep reminding yourself. You can't go back. You can't have it both ways. There was a lot about the job that I could have done without. But those things came with the territory. The bottom line is that I love the captaincy. I would be telling a lie if I said I didn't enjoy many of the trappings. I'm lucky to have the job.

The pressure was off. Winners at last. Immediately, it was back on. The Grand Slam winners were obviously the northern hemisphere's big challengers for the World Cup. Blanco did not think so. 'We will face England in the quarter-final and the home side will win again,' predicted the French captain, confident that the Paris advantage would reverse the fortunes. Amid the congratulations, the sniping continued. England scored five tries to four, while the 1990 team managed 12–3. There was one gigantic difference. The boys of 1991 got the job done and went into the rugby record books as the 25th national team to achieve a Five Nations Grand Slam.

Uttley had had enough. He entered the record books as the one Englishman to have played in and coached a Grand Slam side. Before the championship, Uttley decided that the World Cup would be the end of his coaching road. His deteriorating relationship with Carling was not the main reason. Uttley felt the time was right, although it was becoming increasingly difficult to disguise his isolation.

The season had taken its toll on Carling, too. 'I seriously wonder how long I will continue to play because of the pressures. I realise that, at the age of 25, it is an amazing thing to say, but it may be I have only another year left in me. Everything that is happening around the sport is burning people out. It hasn't been made easy for us, but the most satisfying aspect has been the way the people around me have risen to it. I have been part of an England team which has had the character to ignore distractions. People don't understand the strains it puts on you psychologically, the difficulty of relaxing and forgetting about the championship in between games. The sad thing is it has been made clear to me that certain members of the RFU committee want me ousted from the captaincy.'

## ROB ANDREW

After Murrayfield, the heat was really turned on Will. Everyone was analysing Will. He didn't like it. His play, his captaincy, his lifestyle – an enormous amount of press coverage, lots of it bad. No other British rugby player has had to cope with that. Will's the same bloke I met in 1986, but he's had to shape his behaviour around being England captain. As the seasons pass, those who knew him in those early days get fewer and fewer in the squad. He was always quiet, but he's definitely more suspicious and wary. That's inevitable. I spoke to him a lot during this period. It really got him down. That's when you need people close to you reminding you: 'Stuff the rest of the world.' That might sound trite, but when you feel the rest of the world is conspiring against you, that's what's required. After losing the Grand Slam, the wheel of fortune – which to be fair had been rolling his way for a long time – turned with a vengeance. For the first time the press had Will Carling's head on the block. You can't ignore it. I don't care how confident you are. It gets to you. And you take it personally. I should know. You can't hide, especially with Will's profile. I don't think Will got a lot of support during his bad time. Although we are the England team, we are not together much, except on tour. I also think Will had had enough of being the front man in the players' fight over the amateur regulations. He wasn't the one leading the charge. Neither was Brian Moore or I. It was an issue every player in the squad was committed to. But Will took the flak from the RFU and the press because he was the captain.

If England's captain sounded rather thoughtful in March, he was back to his best in April. Carling accepted an invitation from the Oxford Union debating society to join Sir Arthur Gold, chairman of the British Olympic Association, in proposing the motion: 'This house believes that there is too much money in sport.' Opposing were the soccer star Garth Crooks and Graham Kelly, the chief

England's rugby captain patiently points the way to the Twickenham dressing-room after the 1991 Grand Slam success over France. *(Allsport/Dan Smith)*

executive of the Football Association. The motion was carried by 147–95. Carling's tongue-in-cheek address showed he was over the worst. 'First, I wish it to be known that I am receiving no fee for this speech. None was sought – nor indeed offered. I have, however, received superb hospitality. Potato soup served in its own skin, and something that looked remarkably like Bill Beaumont's ear, served in gravy. I say this in case there are members of the press present and, more importantly, members of the Rugby Football Union. It might surprise you that I, as an amateur sportsman who lives under such constant financial monitoring, should support the belief that there is too much money in sport. Surely you must expect me to claim that, in fact, there is not enough. I know some of you saw me arrive in a brand new Mercedes sports car. I can honestly claim that it is not mine – it's my agent's. And some of you will point the finger and accuse me of motivating the England team into one of the most money-grabbing outfits in rugby history. That is not the case. They needed absolutely no motivating.'

Carling continued by describing the joys of being steam-rollered by '300 lb of French livestock' and of 'voluntary acupuncture delivered by aluminium studs'. After a nightmare year, Carling's sense of humour was back. Lesser men would have crumbled under the pressure. Fortunately, England's young captain – a better and wiser man – had come through smiling. Now for the World Cup.

# CHAPTER 7

# WORLD CUP WINNERS AND LOSERS – 1991

England's summer tour to Australia was crucial in the build-up for the World Cup. Cooke and Carling could not afford another Argentina experience. That was in any event unlikely, as this time England took a first-choice squad away. There was much dispute about whether the trip would be beneficial after a busy season. The England management, who would rather not have gone to Argentina, believed the tour was the lesser of two evils. Forwards can very quickly get ring-rusty when laid up for four months and Cooke wanted to get his pack ticking over. Others, particularly the media, felt the rest would have been preferable. They believed the fact the England players had not had a break for 18 months would weaken their chances in the World Cup.

Ultimately, the tour was a factor in England falling at the final hurdle: not because of tiredness, but because it affected their strategy and selection. The defeat in the Sydney Test swayed England's tactical thinking when they next came up against Australia. The tour also marked the end of Simon Hodgkinson's reign as first-choice full back, and England missed his quality goal-kicking in the final. Hodgkinson's kicking had been an integral part of England's successes over the previous two seasons. His tally in the Grand Slam campaign was a record 60 points. In Australia, the Nottingham full back lost confidence after a bang early on and struggled throughout, allowing Jon Webb to reclaim the No. 15 shirt. England's Gland Slam set-up was further disrupted when Wade Dooley missed his first international for four years. An injury was the reason, but Dooley could only blame himself. The Blackpool policeman had broken a bone in his hand when retaliating against Queensland's Sam Scott-Young. That was one of three defeats England suffered before the Fiji international. Chris Oti returned for the Test, which is remembered for the debut of Martin Bayfield. The Fijians drew level in the second half as England looked anything but potential world champions. The tourists pulled away in the final quarter to a victory that was notable only for the first England try from Rob Andrew in his 37th international.

England returned to face Australia, who five days earlier had given Wales a 63–6, 12-try roasting. That, however, marked an improvement by the Principality, who the previous week had been hammered 71–8 by New South Wales. England were also well beaten and the 40–15 scoreline was a triumph for the Australian coach Bob Dwyer, who had lost 13 of his best players to the chequebook over the previous year. Beating a dreadful Welsh side told him little, but this win over England was a performance of pace and potential. England had not played that badly. The tourists were beaten by a side who were quicker in deed, quicker in thought and converted every scoring opportunity.

Cooke and Carling rejected suggestions that England's World Cup aspirations could be consigned to the dustbin. Cooke insisted: 'I like to think we have made some progress. As a country, we have a long way to go. We have had to recognise differences of style in Australia which have forced us to adapt. I still don't think that we are as good as we need to be. We're getting there. The players are much more analytical and have a better understanding of what is going on than I recall from the first tour here in 1988, when I was still wet behind the ears and discovering what international rugby was all about.'

ROGER UTTLEY

It was a good tour for us. It showed that we were not at Australia's level. We were left with no false illusions about what we were up against. We were well shafted in the Test. The Aussies' back row was exceptional. It was a relief when we learnt that Tim Gavin was going to miss the World Cup because of injury.

Rugby World Cup 1991 had been coming to the UK for four years. The players knew it; so did the media. The general public had little inkling of its existence. That the tournament became the overwhelming success it did was down to one team. By reaching the final, Carling's England ensured that Rugby World Cup fever reached epidemic proportions that autumn.

Carling needed no outside help to remind him that the World Cup was coming. The date had been on his agenda from the minute Cooke gave him the captaincy three years earlier. There were other reminders. England had a new World Cup strip, after signing a deal with Cotton Traders, a company run by former captains Steve Smith, Tony Neary and Fran Cotton. Members of the RFU complained that they had not been consulted. England reverted to the all-white jersey for the 1992 Five Nations until the threat of court action saw the RFU give ground. The England players were still trying to find a compromise regarding their own position. After brief flirtations with Prisma and the Willises and even an attempt to work with the RFU's own marketing man, the players felt they were no further forward. A 'Timberland' advertisement featuring England players not wearing rugby gear was rejected from the England–Scotland programme. Dudley Wood, the RFU secretary, who stood toe to toe with Carling until his own retirement in the summer of 1995, explained: 'The whole point of the new amateur laws is that what the players do should not be rugby related. If you have them appearing in a rugby programme, this is clearly rugby-related.' The whole point was in fact that Wood was determined to frustrate the players at every step. The players' company,

Player Vision, now joined Parallel Media. Eventually the RFU sanctioned their 'Run with the Ball' campaign to promote the game in conjunction with Virgin, Hutchinson, Telecom, Wilkinson Sword, Sony and Capital Radio, with Courage and the *Daily Mail* holding 'Run with the Ball' clinics during the World Cup. However, the RFU was very wary of this player initiative and the money that it might generate. It was still not a satisfactory situation, but Carling was not going to allow himself or his side to be distracted from the job in hand.

England's reserve World Cup strip, worn by Carling, introductions being made by RFU Marketing Executive Michael Coley. *(Colorsport)*

Carling was clearly in a much better frame of mind than a year earlier. That was not due solely to the Grand Slam. He had matured into the job and no longer felt threatened by the responsibilities and pressures. Carling had learnt that the best way was his own way, right or wrong. Some team members felt he had become too isolated, too aloof, too self-centred. Even they failed to appreciate the strain he had been under. Perhaps, like the public, they were dazzled by the public image of English rugby's golden boy.

England's World Cup squad gave no place to Stuart Barnes, Martin Bayfield, Neil Back, Ian Hunter or John Hall. England's players safely negotiated three warm-up games in September, including a 53–0 win on Russia's first visit to Twickenham. Five days before the off, the teams were summoned to a sumptuous dinner in London, where the Home Secretary Kenneth Baker wished 'Wayne Dooley and the British team' the best of luck. The opening ceremony was little better.

Carling did not care. England were to open the tournament in the traditional Hosts v Holders match and this was to be his first encounter with New Zealand. The All Blacks are Carling's heroes as the ultimate national rugby side. Defeat would not be disastrous for England as both sides would qualify from Pool A, although the runners-up had to travel to Paris in the quarter-final. Rugby World Cup 1991 got off to a stuttering start, with Scottish referee Jim Fleming keeping a tight control. Both sides were apprehensive. England led 12–9 at the interval. Flanker Mike Jones, unable to play on Sundays because of his religious beliefs, scored the only try of this Thursday afternoon as the Kiwis won 18–12. There was no rousing finish. Both sides seemed content with the result. England would go to France, while New Zealand would face Australia in the semi-final.

## WILL CARLING

We always knew that we would have to play a lot better and faster than we did to win the Grand Slam. The mistakes would also need to be reduced. I don't think I have ever played in a game where a side has dramatically changed tactics. If you are winning, why change? If you're being beaten, often there's very little you can do about it. The sides that come from behind do so by sticking to the tactics they worked out as being the best way of winning. You can vary the lineout and scrum or play a looser game. Occasionally, I ask: 'Anyone got any ideas about how we get out of this mess?' But I do remember the All Blacks slipping up a gear in that World Cup opener early in the second half. It was a deliberate ploy. They wanted to show us what they could do and who was boss. It was difficult to cope with. It was also very impressive.

The attention switched away from England's pool when Wales were beaten by Western Samoa at the weekend. England's players kept an eye on the rest of the action from their Basingstoke hotel, although the squad travelled up to Otley to watch the other two countries in their pool. Italy beat the USA 30–9. The players felt the trip had been organised for other than rugby reasons, a view confirmed when a dinner, at which Carling spoke, was slipped in the night before. It was two days of travelling, being pestered and smiling for the cameras that England could have done without.

England beat Italy 36–6 at Twickenham. Webb's record 24 points was overshadowed by referee Brian Anderson's 37 penalties, most awarded because of the cynical behaviour of the Italians. The game degenerated into a farce, but Anderson and Carling kept their heads. Anderson explained afterwards: 'I did consider sending off an Italian player for persistent infringement. I have never awarded so many penalties against one team in my whole career. When I thought of the ramifications, I decided that it would not have helped what was becoming a farcical situation. It could have inflamed the match. I repeatedly spoke to the Italian captain, but it was water off a duck's back.' Carling also took a philosophical approach: 'We want to play a fluid game. It would really have done us no good to kick 20 penalties. At the end of the day, we practised scrums in certain positions.'

England made eight changes for the final pool match against the USA. Gary Pearce came in at prop for the first time since 1988. There was no place for the understudy half backs, Morris and Pears, who sat out the entire tournament. Carling overtook Bill Beaumont's record of 21 games in charge. There was little else to celebrate: 'It was hard to concentrate for any length of time. That was because of the mix of some players coming in for the first time and being desperate to impress. Others were playing their third game in nine days and may have been a bit lacklustre.'

The quarter-final pairings were settled that weekend. Scotland beat Ireland to earn a home tie against Western Samoa, while the Irish entertained Australia. New Zealand faced Canada in Lille. Predicting the outcome of those three ties was easy. The clash of the round was the quarter-final in Paris between France and England.

That Saturday, 19 October 1991, was the day Will Carling's England finally came of age. Sadly, it was also the afternoon when rugby union lost its last, lingering glimpse of innocence. The game's most sacred tradition was violated when French coach Daniel Dubroca attacked the referee. Rugby union was now just another part of the pile of international sport with unruly participants. The affair rumbled on for nearly a week as the Rugby World Cup organisers dithered and delayed, and ended only when Dubroca resigned. The French coach was not the only rugby person to let himself down that day: Blanco, as it turned out, was playing his final game for his country. His participation might have lasted only two minutes, as he lost his cool and, with a little help from Eric Champ, floored Nigel Heslop with a flurry of quick-fire punches. There is no doubt that referee David Bishop would have been justified in sending him off. That would have been a sad end, although not as sad as the final memory Blanco left for us in a French jersey: one of the great modern rugby entertainers reduced to common thuggery. Blanco's and Dubroca's behaviour reflected the pressure of the later stages of the tournament. The World Cup had become a do-or-die scrap.

England's preparations had begun with a weekend family break in Jersey. Cooke hoped that the presence of the team's families would give an emotional edge to England's performance. From there the squad moved to Montmorency, just north of Paris. The relaxed atmosphere of Jersey vanished when Moore and Richards had a momentary dust-up. The following day, Richards was dropped, though it had nothing to do with the incident. Teague moved across to No. 8

with Micky Skinner taking the blindside spot. Heslop replaced Oti on the wing. Stories did the rounds that Oti was seen wandering the hotel armed with a baseball bat looking for the England captain. Far more significant than England being three games away from World Cup glory was the realisation that they were one game away from inglorious failure.

## WILL CARLING

I try to make my team talks fresh. That's not always easy when you're emphasising the same old things. It's impossible to come up with something new every time. Whatever I say, I always try to be positive. I don't highlight mistakes or things that have gone wrong in the past. It's about dos – not don'ts. There's some emotive stuff, but emotion is not going to carry you all the way through. It's not the English way. If I gave them the history bit, as the Irish, Scots and Welsh do, the boys would crack up. It's valid for the other countries, but not for us. There is certainly a lot more national pride in the English side now. My thrust is about England achieving their potential. The England rugby team has always had great potential.

I don't call for quiet. I wait for silence. I don't shout or pick on anyone. The players are fired up anyway. I like eye contact with all the players. You can tell immediately if you've hit the right chord. It was never more obvious that we were spot on than in the World Cup quarter-final against France. We always seem to be in a good frame of mind against the French. This was perfect. We couldn't have been in better shape as we ran out for the game that would make or break us as a team.

There was no disguising England's commitment as they took the fight to the French straight from the kick-off. Andrew hoisted a high kick, Blanco gathered, was enveloped and then churned out of the ruck as he had been dozen of times before. Champ and Skinner squared up. Bishop was used to such preliminaries: 'Champ. All right. Come on. Get out of it,' could be heard in the commentary box from the referee's microphone. Heslop gathered a wayward kick and returned it to Blanco, who called for the mark. Heslop arrived and barged into the French captain and full back. He was late, and Bishop would probably have given France a penalty rather than a mark; but Blanco took matters into his own hands, or rather fists. A sweeping left hook exploded into Heslop's face. Then, almost quicker than the eye could see, Blanco transferred the ball to prove that his right-hand punching was just as effective. Only the TV replay cameras showed that Champ had landed a combination of his own, the second right hand hitting Heslop round the back of the neck. Not surprisingly, the England wing slumped to the deck, involuntarily pulling out his gumshield as he hit the ground. The TV cameras also showed that Blanco and Champ were waiting for Heslop. It was no instinctive reaction. This was a premeditated assault that now turned the spotlight on referee Bishop. How could he let Blanco stay on? But

England's captain celebrates his quarter-final try and looks forward to a revenge match against the Scots at Murrayfield in the semi-final. *(Colorsport)*

how could he end a glorious career by sending Blanco off at the start of a World Cup quarter-final? Bishop consulted with the touch-judge, Keith Lawrence. Bishop took a long-term view. Of the next 77 minutes, in fact. He decided that this game could turn into a nightmare if Blanco were dismissed.

WILL CARLING
The quarter-final is the hardest game I've ever been involved in, mentally and physically. It was no different in 1995. Blanco's outburst showed how wound up they were. France were on edge. When he floored Heslop, my anger soon gave way to 'I'm glad I'm not the ref.' What Blanco did was so blatant. Bishop was in a no-win situation. By not sending him off, Bishop could have been giving the green light to an afternoon of mayhem. Similarly, the crowd might have erupted if their favourite had been given his marching orders. I wasn't unhappy that Blanco stayed. I was desperate to win, but I didn't want to see a rugby talent retire in disgrace. Anyway, I felt the incident had given us the upper hand. France were on the back foot. We had kept our cool. It was a black mark against the home side. They had to behave themselves now. If Blanco was that uptight, what state were the rest of the French side in?

England gained not only the upper hand, but also the lead as Webb punished Blanco's indiscretion. England turned round 10–6 ahead after Guscott had put Rory Underwood in the clear. It was a legitimate confrontation that decided this quarter-final early in the second half with Skinner's crunching tackle of Cecillon. The Frenchman was propelled back yards. France got back on level terms with Lafond's sixth try of the World Cup. More French indiscipline, this time by prop Pascal Ondarts, allowed Webb to regain the lead. The final action saw a try for Carling. England, 19–10 winners, were in the semi-final.

Bishop's problems did not end with the final whistle. He was grabbed by Dubroca, abused and spat at in the tunnel. Ondarts was also involved. A punch was swung at the referee. News of the confrontation spread like wildfire. The presence of an expert witness, in this case former Swansea hooker Jeff Herman, now working for the BBC, meant the Rugby World Cup organisers had to take decisive action. Even by rugby standards, statements like 'No further action against Dubroca' and 'There has been no official complaint from the referee' were hogwash. Fortunately, Dubroca resigned six days after the match, blaming the British media for a concerted campaign to get him out. Dubroca stole some of England's thunder. That was a great shame. It was a display of character, of resolution, of maturity, probably the finest by an England team abroad since that of the squad who beat New Zealand at Eden Park in 1973.

WILL CARLING
I knew we were through the second I touched down for that try. This win meant we were not World Cup failures. That was my first emotion. I remember the stigma the team carried round after losing to Wales at the quarter final stage in the 1987 tournament. I don't think many people expected us to win in Paris. But we did, and in style. We showed a lot of discipline, determination and character. I was proud that night. Not just for myself, but for the whole team and for all the supporters who had made such a noise that afternoon.

After that Paris victory Carling and England had to cope with a war of words that was to last through until the morning of the final. That propaganda certainly had an influence on England's thinking. Australia were very lucky to have joined England in the final four. Gordon Hamilton's late try in Dublin was the moment of the tournament, but Australia saved face with an injury-time try from Michael Lynagh. Australia stayed in Dublin to face holders New Zealand, leaving England and Carling to prepare for another Murrayfield showdown with Scotland. The semi-final never recaptured the passion of the Grand Slam encounter, although the prize was greater. The Scots led 6–0 after half an hour. Webb succeeded with only two penalties out of six attempts. England could easily have paid the ultimate price for discarding Hodgkinson and entering the knock-out stages without a world-class goal-kicker. England escaped when

Gavin Hastings missed a simple penalty with the scores tied at 6–6 in the final quarter. The tie was decided by a late dropped goal from Andrew.

England were in the final. The next day Australia, inspired by David Campese, joined them. Cooke and Carling's quest for the world prize had brought them back to where they had started out together three years earlier – with Australia at Twickenham.

The country was behind England, but some of rugby's major thinkers were publicly critical of England's approach. After the quarter-final Australian coach Bob Dwyer expressed his view: 'I am just a little disappointed with England's philosophy. They just restrict their game. But it's up to them. They have more capability than they show. It seems a shame not to utilise that potential.' A week later, Dwyer sounded this warning: 'I feel a bit sorry for England. I didn't think any team, apart from New Zealand, was capable of winning in Paris and Edinburgh. They would be stupid to depart from the game that has won matches for them. If I find it boring, then I find it boring. If England win the World Cup, it would have a terrific positive effect on the game here, which would outweigh any tactical approach they might have. We have considered the possibility that England might change. But I expect them to play a similar game in the final. It would be quite difficult to play a game that was remarkably different from your standard one.' New Zealand's John Hart was more succinct: 'If England win the World Cup, God help rugby.'

Cooke was getting fed up: 'It's all right for the armchair critics to sit there and pontificate, but I would say that for any side to beat France and Scotland in consecutive weeks is a major achievement.' Carling headed south to find that England had gone World Cup mad. Two matches were preying on his mind. Both against Australia. One win. One defeat. The victory was his first game as England captain, when England picked up the torch carried by the divisional sides. The defeat was that summer's, when the tourists tried to keep it tight and the Aussies took all their chances. How England were going to play the final was the question consuming Carling, although he publicly declared: 'The pressure has gone. In certain games you might need to run the ball to win the match. We have every intention of playing to the style that suits us.'

Carling's *Captain's Diary* revealed the internal conflict during that final week of the World Cup. 'I don't feel as emotional or as patriotic as at Murrayfield 18 months previously. The whole affair is low-key, amazing when you consider what was at stake. It is a much more relaxed team now that we have got to the final. All the dread of not getting there has vanished. We know that we are going to change tactics for the final. Not because of media pressure. We can't afford to take notice of what the press say. We will change tactics because we can't dominate them up front the way we've dominated France and Scotland. If we play solely a kicking game, we will not win, because the likes of Lynagh and Campese can kick the ball an awfully long way. If we get points up, we will win. But I worry that they're such a good defensive side. If we go points down, we will struggle. That's what happened in Sydney during the summer. We started playing catch-up rugby. They're lethal at exploiting any mistakes. It's got to be a tight game.'

Despite that semi-final victory, the Scots continued to get under Carling's skin, although Finlay Calder handed England the World Cup during the week. 'I think England will win because the Australian pack will not be mature enough to handle them. The England forwards will play as the Lions did in 1989. They will grind the Australians down and they will win.' That was not the Scots' stance on match day. They turned up wearing Australian scarves and rosettes, voicing support for anyone who was going to do down the English.

WILL CARLING

When I first met the Scots in 1988, they weren't like that at all. The change when we went up in 1990 was staggering. They were so nationalistic. We've been back several times since. I'm used to it now. David Sole certainly got tartan fever late in life. When I first came across him playing for Bath, that thick Scottish brogue of later years was missing. He was very English. When Sole moved to Edinburgh, he went the other way, maybe to prove himself. He very much became a Scot. I've nothing against fervent national-ism. It helped players like JJ [John Jeffrey] and Finlay [Calder] play out of their skins, especially against us. Their nationalism wasn't new. Nor was their hatred of the English. But it upset the England boys when we heard they'd turned up in Aussie gear for the final. Wade confronted Gavin at the post-final dinner. 'Why did you do that? We've been on a Lions tour together against the Aussies.' Gavin replied that the Scots thought it would be a laugh. I had a similar conversation with Craig Chalmers. It was obvi-ously the idea of a couple of senior players. The rest went along with it, not wishing to be seen siding with the English. It didn't go down well with the England fans. The final wasn't about England against Scotland. It was about the northern hemisphere against the southern hemisphere, which had traditionally ruled the rugby world. This was a chance to switch the balance. If Scotland had been in the final against Australia, we would have been supporting them wholeheartedly. England wanted the northern hemi-sphere to win the 1991 Rugby World Cup. If it couldn't be England, then we would follow whoever carried that flag.

The World Cup final was beamed live to 40 countries, almost treble the numbers of four years earlier. That finale had been disappointing. France had played their final in the classic 30–24 semi-final victory over Australia, and the All Blacks were never stretched, taking the trophy with a comfortable 29–9 win. This contest promised to be different. The Princess Royal and Prince Edward, who had officially opened the tournament, were in attendance. Politicians like to be associated with success, so Prime Minister John Major and the Labour leader Neil Kinnock lent support to England's challenge. The Queen was introduced to the teams beforehand. Her Majesty showed rather more restraint and impartiality than Nelson Mandela did four years later in Johannesburg when South Africa took on New Zealand and President Mandela took the field before the final wearing South African captain François Pienaar's No. 6 jersey and a Springbok cap!

This final was basically about Australia getting their noses in front and hanging on for dear life. Webb, with the wind at his back, missed penalty chances in the first half. England turned round nine points adrift. Lynagh kicked a penalty, then converted a try by Tony Daly from a lineout. That score came from a promising England position. Rather than kick, centre Tim Horan made a spectacular break out of defence. England could have been further adrift. Campese missed his chance after a kick and chase when the bounce, for once, was unkind to the Wallaby wing. It was not Australia's display which had the crowd aghast. It was England's. The host side were flinging the ball around with gay abandon. Even some of England's forwards were perplexed by the tactics. Prop Jeff Probyn: 'We'd win good ball, then look up expecting it to be drilled towards the Aussie line. Instead the backs were throwing the ball around, running from deep, getting caught and we would have to trundle back 30 metres for another scrum. The pack weren't happy. What had happened to our plan? Worse than that. It wasn't working.'

Webb eventually put England on the scoreboard, but Lynagh quickly regained Australia's advantage. England were getting desperate in attack. The Australian defence was able to plug any holes the England backs punched because the host side were attacking from so deep. But the Aussies were running on empty. The semi-final victory over the All Blacks had taken a lot out of them. The crowd sensed that if Australia lost that lead, England would win the World Cup. The decisive moment involved Campese, who had spent much of the World Cup criticising England's negative approach. It was not one of his more creative acts, but it saved the World Cup for his country. England had finally run the Aussie defence ragged. Carling passed to Winterbottom who had Rory Underwood outside him with Campese to beat. The nearest defenders, Lynagh and Horan, were alongside Carling. Underwood in the clear was a certainty for a try under the posts. The ball never reached him. Campese read the situation perfectly. There could be no pretence. He had to prevent the ball reaching Underwood however he could. This he did by knocking it forward deliberately. That act is often described as rugby's 'professional foul'. Carling took immediate revenge by stepping on Campese's privates as the Aussie was bowled over by Skinner. It was a futile gesture of retribution, but it gave England's skipper some momentary pleasure. The great David Campese was human after all. Like Blanco in Paris, one of rugby's most skilful performers had succumbed to the pressure. The World Cup was the overriding factor. Nobody blamed Campese, but England resented his action because Campese had been spouting all manner of

Carling sets up another attack in the World Cup final, but Australia's dogged defence stood firm to take the trophy. *(Colorsport)*

criticism about Carling and England. In the end Campese proved himself more calculating and less emotional about his rugby than the England players. It was England who lost the World Cup by getting carried away. Campese's knock-on was still a gamble. It paid off. England were still some way from Australia's line. Referee Derek Bevan felt justified only in awarding the penalty, not the penalty try. Webb made it 12–6, leaving England two penalties or a converted try from drawing level. It was a penalty kick too far. Australia held on to become the second World Cup champions.

Carling led England up to receive their runners-up medals from the Queen. He turned to the crowd, smiled and waved his right arm in salute, then lingered for a second and took a deep breath. England had been a fingertip – Campese's – away from the World Cup. Carling was choked. But, as at Murrayfield in 1990, the public face did not crack. He accepted the defeat with dignity and maturity. Adversity is a far tougher test of character than good fortune. Carling has enjoyed more success than any other England rugby captain. Yet he has been in charge on two of the most painful days in England's rugby history. At Murrayfield in 1990 and in the World Cup final 18 months later, nobody could accuse Carling of not being able to take a beating. In many ways, he copes better than with success.

Nick Farr-Jones was the man to raise the World Cup to the capacity Twickenham crowd. That act finished him off. A few minutes later, the

Australian captain and scrum half was soaking in one of the individual baths at HQ. It was over half an hour before he had the strength to get out.

This was Roger Uttley's final weekend with the national squad. It was not the send-off he had planned, either in its execution or in its result. Even now he wonders why England's game plan went so astray.

OPPOSITE PAGE: Carling shakes hands with World Cup official Russ Thomas after receiving his loser's medal from the Queen. (Colorsport)

## ROGER UTTLEY

We had enough possession to stuff the Aussies out of sight. The forwards did enough to win the game. There was a misapprehension that Geoff and I were not happy with England spreading it wide after losing at Murrayfield in 1990. That the potential of the side was stifled by us. That was and is not true. As we approached the World Cup final, we agreed to play the style that served us so well in Paris and Edinburgh. At some stage, the tactics changed. I couldn't believe it when the backs started running from so deep. There's no point running the ball from the middle of the park against a defence as good as the Aussies have. They have time to regroup. I've never felt so sorry for a group of forwards in my life. Mike Teague was in tears. I didn't blame him. The World Cup was there for the taking.

INSET: Carling salutes the Twickenham crowd as he comes to terms with the fact that England had failed at the final hurdle to take the 1991 World Cup. (Allsport/Russell Cheyne)

Carling and England, having been visited by John Major in the dressing-room, made their way into London to join Australia, New Zealand and Scotland at a special end-of-tournament dinner. The speeches rambled on. The England wives and girlfriends were excluded from the Royal Lancaster function. Unfortunately, many of the sponsors' tables were mixed, and pictures of some of the players with their arms round Virgin Atlantic air stewardesses took some explaining. Richard Branson, with his trained eye for publicity, had offered the players £30,000 worth of free flights if they won the World Cup. Branson is not a mean-spirited man, and the offer stood in defeat. Carling's girlfriend, Victoria, also made the papers. The *Sun* photographer recorded the fact that she was wearing stockings. That fact, coupled with her relationship with the England rugby captain who had just lost in the World Cup final, naturally made it front-page news. 'Scrum And Get Me, Will. Carling's Darling Dresses To Kill' was the headline. Rugby union had really hit the big time and would never be the same again.

## WILL CARLING

I believe that we played as well as we could. We lost to a great side. I don't have any sense of frustration about the result. The nine points the Aussies scored in the five-minute first-half spell was the turning point. We never came back from that. Still, I think it's probably the best game this side ever played. England had a great tournament. The reaction the players had from the public made it easier to come to terms with losing. We brought a lot of pride to English rugby. I know that it encouraged a lot of youngsters to start playing. That was the real measure of our success.

# CHAPTER 8

# NATIONAL ANTHEM FOR TWICKENHAM FAITHFUL – 1992

No sooner had England licked their World Cup wounds than Carling's team was packing its bags for trips to Paris and Edinburgh again, this time in the Five Nations Championship. The much-publicised mass retirement of his 'Dad's Army' did not materialise. Only Ackford called it a day, although Teague's neck injury kept him out for the rest of the season. Probyn returned to Wasps after one match for Askeans, while Andrew announced that his work as a chartered surveyor would be taking him to France and Toulouse. Tim Rodber, not Richards, took Teague's place, while Bayfield came in for Ackford. Morris and Hill swapped at scrum half, with the former returning to the side after three years of the understudy role.

The New Year's Honours list brought Carling an OBE. Uttley had been to the Palace to collect his during the World Cup. There was nothing for Cooke. It was suggested that RFU influence following the storm about the Cardiff press conference boycott had delayed his recognition. The World Cup had certainly changed the perception of rugby and the leading players in England. It was no more than a sign of the times when Jerry Guscott missed a Bath league game because of a modelling assignment in Miami.

Murrayfield was first on the championship schedule. Three of England's toughest adversaries in recent years were missing. Calder and Jeffrey had retired; Armstrong was injured. England struggled for the first hour. The all-powerful England scrum even suffered the ignominy of conceding a pushover try. It was only Webb's boot that kept them ahead. Rodber's debut ended midway through the second half when he was stretchered off with spinal concussion. Fortunately, the paralysis was temporary. His exit did, however, allow Richards to enter the fray and grab this Calcutta Cup by the scruff of its neck. England began firing on all cylinders as Rory Underwood raced away for his first-ever try at Murrayfield. Morris added a second before Guscott's lazy dropped goal ended the proceedings, England winning 25–7.

England made no such sluggish start against Ireland a fortnight later. The visitors never recovered from Webb's try after 23 seconds and England went on to win 38–9. Ireland's coach Ciaran Fitzgerald described it as the finest England

Will Carling, OBE, and trendy waist-coat-wearer, at Buckingham Palace after receiving his award.

performance he had witnessed. England pack leader Brian Moore did not agree: 'If we had played with more discipline in the second half, the score could have been 60 points. But we were tired and became greedy.'

England went to Paris and recorded their third successive win there in three years. Carling's side was showing no signs of any World Cup hangover. It was another big win, 31–13. Again England did well to control their tempers, especially in the closing stages when Irish referee Steve Hilditch sent off two Frenchmen. Stephen Jones of the *Sunday Times* commented: 'French rugby crashed in flames in Paris. It burnt itself to death. The team lost to an England side who were superior in rugby ability, but, far more significantly so, in heart and soul. France also lost their sense of shame.' The home side blamed the trouble on an Anglo-Saxon conspiracy. Blanco, now in retirement, singled out Moore as the *agent provocateur*. The most ridiculous point of the sendings-off was that they came long after the contest was over. England were playing out time when police inspector Gregoire Lascubé stamped on Bayfield's head.

Hooker and café owner Vincent Moscato followed for punching. Jean-François Tordo was lucky not to make it number three.

WILL CARLING

It's important to keep your discipline against France. It also helps if you can get them thinking about things other than the rugby. They can be distracted. Our guys are experienced enough to accept the physical intimidation. There's very little I can do out in the backs if someone gets punched and decides to take the law into his own hands. For the team's benefit, it's best to treat the macho stuff for what it is. The referee was brave, although he was left with no choice. Those incidents were more stupid than dangerous. I'm often asked what it's like to play in a game like that. It wasn't actually that bad until near the end when France had already lost the match. There are always flashpoints. England aren't blameless or angelic. We've done things wrong. The England side won't sit still and be kicked around. But I believe that we've shown we are mature enough to concentrate on the rugby. Our disciplinary record is good.

My *Captain's Diary* caused a furore when I wrote: 'I've come across a few players who you know will try and stamp on you if they catch you on the floor. Or gouge your eyes if you're stuck in a maul. A couple of Welsh forwards spring to mind. Some French forwards are tricky, too, but for them it's only an extension of their club rugby, which is the most brutal in the world. You don't feel that their violence is directed against you personally. But those Welsh forwards I mention go in to maim individuals, and everyone knows what they're up to. You look at those blokes as you leave the pitch and think: "Do I really have to drink with you tonight?" Which is a shame.' I still stand by those words. But they were a mistake. I'm not one who abides by rugby's unwritten rule of silence on all matters of violence or matters unpleasant. But I should have identified the culprits if I felt that strongly. Or kept quiet.

I'm a marked man. It's something else that comes with territory. There's no use complaining about it. If a player wants to make a name for himself, get Will Carling. The best thing for me to do is keep moving on the field – and keep quiet. I know Jerry [Guscott] has the same problem. The plus side of being a well-known name is that you have the best people to look after you. The incidents increased after the World Cup. I seemed to be getting stamped on a lot. Referees generally look after me. A few don't. 'You're a big star. Can't you look after yourself? Do you want special protection?' I've been lucky with serious injuries, much luckier than Melville, Halliday and Oti. Rugby has become much more competitive at international and club level, though that has been balanced with the greater involvement of touch-judges. I also believe that rugby is much cleaner than it used to be. I'm amazed when I talk to the older players about what used to go on. I hear officials laughing in the bar about the gratuitous violent behaviour of their day, then they moralise about the modern game and how it needs to be cleaned up. Referees could do with more help from touch-judges. There's so much to watch. The referee can't be everywhere. Good referees are hard to find. That's why I was amazed when Fred Howard was dumped from England's panel in 1992. Fred was one of the best, and recognised as such by the top players. Suddenly, he was out. The same thing happened to Clive Norling. There is too much sharing of top matches. If we had a couple of really good officials in the UK, then they should do most of the Five Nations Championship.

Another problem is interpretation. Not just between the northern and southern hemisphere referees. But among Irish, French and Welsh referees. That can cause problems in the Five Nations. You can play one way without a problem in one game and be whistled off the park for the same style next time out. I'm afraid who is refereeing a match is still a key factor. I try to keep as quiet as possible with refs. Smile politely and accept their decisions. Some officials don't like explaining their decisions, even to captains. Occasionally, I'm told to clear off in no uncertain manner. How can a captain sort out a problem if he doesn't know what it is? Often refs create a rod for their backs. They call the captains together, get us to issue a general warning that the next offender is destined for an early bath and then don't carry out the threat. Where do the players stand then? We have always preferred referees who mean what they say. Players like strict disciplinarians. I don't mean whistle-happy with regard to the laws – most of the good ones let the game flow. But when they issue a warning, that's it. The best officials are those who have a feel for the game. I like refs who talk a lot. Players find that useful. The Welsh panel worked well in my early days. All three – Norling, Bevan and Peard – were top referees in their own right. The best referees – like the best players – seem to be resented by the authorities when they enjoy too high a profile.

England were now one match away from the first back-to-back Grand Slams for nearly 70 years. England had been the last to achieve it, under Wavell Wakefield, another former pupil of Sedbergh, in 1924. Already this latest Sedbergh old boy to lead his country's rugby side was a firm favourite to lead the British Lions to New Zealand the following summer. Many had expected David Sole would do the job, but he shocked the rugby world by announcing his retirement at 29, an age when most front-row experts are still considered to be in their nappies. England's Jeff Probyn was not capped until he was 31. Sole's explanation was simple: 'It's not the year the model was made that matters these days. Look at the miles on the clock.' Sole had achieved rugby fame way beyond that predicted when the Bath prop first appeared in a Scotland trial. Under the influence of Jack Rowell at Bath and Scotland's Ian

McGeechan, Sole became an international player of distinction and a captain of considerable stature. Murrayfield 1990 was his finest hour. Few Scottish leaders have walked out so confidently – or so slowly – at the head of the Tartan Army. Less than two years later, Sole was ready to quit. He told Carling of his decision after the Calcutta Cup match.

WILL CARLING

I was surprised. I asked him why he wasn't staying on until 1993 to lead the Lions. David said that he had had enough. Jokingly he added that he was leaving the path clear for me. In all seriousness, he added that it would be very hard for a so-called pretty boy England three-quarter to captain the British Lions. It wasn't a judgement on me. More the image that was perceived among the other nationalities.

ROB ANDREW

I don't think Will's absence from the 1989 Lions tour did him any harm from a playing point of view. But it would have done him a power of good in a lot of other areas, especially having such close contact with players from other countries over two and a half months. Going away with the Lions is an amazing experience. The Home Countries hate each other for two or three years, then all come together for the Lions. Usually, up to that point, you have been on opposite sides in a pretty competitive environment. The press love feeding on that national fervour. Suddenly, you are rooming, drinking and playing together. You find out that most of these blokes are not as bad as you thought they were. Sharing a common cause breaks down all sorts of barriers. Not that it prevents you knocking lumps out of each other once the Five Nations Championship comes round again. Those friendships remain. Often for life. That's why the British Lions must survive.

Most of us know each other from those tours. Or from the days when we started playing international rugby. Will missed out on the 1989 Lions tour. And he missed out on those early days with the lads. He's there on a pedestal and has been since the second season of his England career. Being the captain stuck on the top table wouldn't matter if Will had made his friends on the way up. He didn't. Will was at Durham University when he was first capped in 1988. Nine months later he was England captain. Players from the other countries never got a chance to know him. The number of big games that England play doesn't help, either. There's a lot of tension around. Even after matches, others seem reluctant to approach Will. Basically all they know is what they read. And there's been an awful lot of rubbish written about Will. He is shy and not an extrovert. He won't push himself forward in a group he doesn't know, so he can appear aloof and arrogant. The only guys who really got to know him before the press got to him and the big time beckoned are some of the older England lads from the North.

A second Grand Slam would certainly give Carling pole position for the Lions job. As England prepared for the visit of Wales to Twickenham, the president of the RFU, Peter Yarranton, gave the rugby team this glowing testimony. 'I believe this is the most skilful and fittest team England have ever fielded. I take enormous pride in the way the side has conducted itself. This was epitomised by their tremendous discipline in Paris. But the truly great thing has been their total dedication to the things in hand.' Here was a president who believed that his year of office was in some way connected with the success of the national rugby side. At least Yarranton just basked in the glory. Three years later, another president saw his role as more of a participatory one with regard to the England team and the captaincy. Cooke was not quite as willing as Yarranton to pat England on the back. 'We are still a bit off being the best in the world. Until we can beat New Zealand, Australia and South Africa, we are still only a step down the road. The job is only half-finished. We had one chance to beat New Zealand and we didn't. And we have managed to beat Australia once in five attempts while I have been manager. The measure is sustaining a run of success over a period of time. I think we have closed the gap. But they are still running ahead of us. We are running like hell to keep up with them.' Despite England's recent success, Cooke was still waiting to hear if the RFU were going to extend his appointment beyond April.

Rory Underwood confirmed his decision to retire after the Welsh game, while Jon Webb announced he was reconsidering calling it a day. That Saturday was a big day for farewells. The Twickenham East Stand was making its last appearance. Carling allowed Dooley to lead the side out to celebrate his 50th cap. The captain had the ball back within a minute after chasing up a kick ahead for England's opening try. Dooley, not to be outdone, scored the third and final try in England's 24–0 victory. The Twickenham faithful had another Grand Slam to celebrate. A day for farewells was also a day for records. England's 118 points set a new Five Nations tally, 16 more than Wales scored in 1976. Webb's score of 67 points was seven more than Hodgkinson notched up in the previous Grand Slam, and his career total was now 246, taking him past Dusty Hare's 240.

Records apart, it was a much more subdued affair than the 1991 victory over France. After Carling's quick try, there was an inevitability about the result. England did not score for 48 minutes in the middle of the match as Wales concentrated on defence. It appeared as if the visitors were happy to keep the defeat down to a respectable level. Carling came off five minutes before the end with a dead leg. Cooke was honest about England's display: 'Everyone was a bit disappointed with the quality of the performance. We just couldn't control it for long enough to produce the quick ball we wanted.'

Carling beats Tony Clement to the ball to score after only 61 seconds at Twickenham to set up England's first back-to-back Grand Slam since 1924, when Sedbergh old boy Wavell Wakefield was captain. England's 118 points in the championship surpassed the previous record of 102, set by Wales in 1976. *(Colorsport)*

Cooke was confirmed the following day as England's team manager through to the 1995 World Cup in South Africa. It seemed ridiculous to the outside world that someone who had helped England's national rugby side to such success should have been kept waiting. Cooke did have the support of the majority of the RFU committee. The dissenting voices, though, were some of the loudest and most influential. One man, one vote has never been the way of the RFU. Most of the opposition came from Cooke's home ground, the North. Cooke had succeeded where many of them had failed. That was resented, along with his high and public profile. If anyone on the committee started recounting Cooke's many achievements with England, the diehards would simply recall the problems in Cardiff and Cooke's failure that day. Meanwhile, Cooke announced he was stepping back from his 'hands-on' approach. 'The time has come for me to step aside a bit.' Dick Best, as expected, had taken over from Roger Uttley.

England had confirmed their status as the top team in Europe by taking another Grand Slam. The predictability of the achievement removed some of the gloss. Rob Andrew recalls: 'We were still living the World Cup. The championship was on us before we realised it. I really enjoyed it, though. There was less pressure than I can ever remember in the Five Nations!'

Carling had one big game left: the Pilkington Cup final against Bath. Harlequins' chances were not boosted when Micky Skinner and Richard Langhorn, who tragically died a couple of years later, were sent off the week before the final and so became ineligible. Paul Ackford was persuaded to come out of retirement to fill the breach. 'It's a one-off game. I'm doing it out of loyalty to the club and to Dick Best, who was instrumental in my rise to international rugby.' There was plenty of life left in the old dog: Ackford played a blinder. The final went into extra time and the cup went Bath's way with the final kick of the game as Stuart Barnes put over a 30-metre dropped goal. Carling was magnificent in defeat. Defending, attacking, Carling was in tip-top form. His tactical kicking had often let him down, but he showed he had

England celebrate another Grand Slam. When the picture was used in the 1992/93 RFU Handbook, Micky Skinner's shirt was painted on. *(Colorsport)*

mastered the art that afternoon. Carling looked the complete article. Stephen Jones of the *Sunday Times* remembers: 'I rate his finest performances as England captain those two games against France, the World Cup quarter-final and the 1992 match. England are no angels, but, under his influence, they conducted themselves well. As a player, Will was immense in that Pilkington final against Bath, when he was under a lot of pressure. He has always been a guy with talent. I think he's probably been a bit conservative. A man with his talent should be more extravagant. He has continued to develop. Will is very much the strong man in the middle. He's always been assured. I rate him highly as a player. Sella has great ability, but he has not contributed as consistently as Carling. As for Charvet, how many games did Charvet's genius turn? The great players do it all the time.'

## WILL CARLING

I don't worry about opposition centres that much. I accept their strengths and weaknesses. Most of my build-up is visualised. How I am going to play. I've never been deeply into other players. It's about me, not him. Scott Hastings is a tremendous defensive player, very committed, but he doesn't possess the subtlety of a Charvet. Sella is strong and skilful, and has vision. I didn't think he was as effective when he lost the edge on his speed. Tim Horan is a good finisher, very strong with pace. Like Jerry Guscott, he has the knack of being in the right place at the right time – and doing the right thing. Horan works well with Jason Little. Jerry and I have to be on our toes when up against them – or the All Blacks Frank Bunce and Walter Little. Both pairings have a good understanding. I can predict fairly well what Jerry is going to do, his angles. I know what he prefers to do. Occasionally, I just have to admire breaks he's made or even his passes – the miss-pass that put Ian Hunter away against Canada, or the break for Rory's try against Scotland in 1993. We don't do a lot of talking during matches. It's mainly calls.

Carling's status was confirmed when he was named *Rugby World* Player of the Year. He was photographed alongside his old adversary David Campese, who won the International award. Now Carling really did have the rugby world at his feet. He was the outstanding captain of the outstanding rugby side in the northern hemisphere. On his horizon, after a rare summer off, was a hat-trick of Grand Slams and the leadership of the British Lions on the tour of New Zealand.

Will Carling, the 1992 *Rugby World* Player of the Year, with his old adversary, David Campese, the International Player of the Year. *(Colorsport)*

## ROB ANDREW

Will's game has improved every year. He knows what has been required and he has done it fantastically well. He's always been a quality player. He quickly became world-class. There have been times when his game has been picked to pieces. That's been unfair. When he's playing well, his captaincy has been attacked. When his leadership is no longer an issue, Will's game is put under the microscope. The only ones who really appreciate his performance are those on the field. Coaches and team managers have a fair idea, but deep down, it's only the players who see everything. He's been the first name on the team sheet for the past seven years. That's a tremendous achievement. Will's got phenomenal pace and strength. He works hard at his game, both his skills and his physical attributes. Will is naturally strong, but works hard to improve his body strength and mauling ability. He also has great determination. Aside from the captaincy, which he holds in great store, Will is very proud of his own playing performance. Once you get to a certain level, people are looking for you – and at you. Will knows that. His pride refuses to allow his standards to drop.

Canada and South Africa provided a busy end to 1992 for Carling. England's captain was at Twickenham in early September to launch the Young England Club, a grassroots scheme for kids aged 6 to 16. Carling appreciated that the impetus given to rugby in England by the World Cup had to be sustained. 'There is a tremendous opportunity to get children involved and interested in rugby. It's vital for the future. Children have so many sports to choose from. I would like to help ensure that they choose rugby football. Both cricket and rugby are not played as much in state schools. We need as many as possible playing rugby. That's why current players, at whatever level, have a part to play.' The making of rugby safe for schoolkids to play was another concern of Carling's.

England were to have real problems with changes to the ruck and maul law that season. Possession used to be everything. Not now. If the ball was not produced quickly by the attacking side, the scrum went to the defenders. Bob Dwyer, Alex Wyllie, Ian McGeechan and Geoff Cooke all condemned the changes. It took England longer to adapt than most.

WILL CARLING
I think it's just common sense to involve all the top participants in major changes to the game, laws or otherwise. They are the ones with hands on, who can offer interesting observations and thoughts about the effects of the new laws. Often, it appears that the full ramifications of changes have not been considered. I've often wondered why they have to change the laws for all levels of the game. Often new laws are tried at schoolboy level first. Because they work there, the authorities introduce them in all rugby. By and large, though, you don't get cunning players at schoolboy level. The first reaction at the top level when a new law appears is 'How best can we use this to our own advantage or to disadvantage the opposition?' They are a bit like tax laws. You either look to avoid them, which is legal, or evade them, which is not.

The international game is the shop window. The authorities have to reflect on how the changes will affect the top level, not the grass roots. People judge the game on internationals. They are what attracts the sponsorship money and other revenue that keeps the game ticking over and making a healthy profit. I am only too well aware that safety is an important factor, especially when dealing with schoolboys. There is nothing to stop rugby having different laws for junior and schoolboy players to make their game as safe as possible, more attractive and fun to play.

England's season received a bonus with the news that Rory Underwood would be carrying on, despite his newly released autobiography explaining his decision for 'quitting'. Andrew, too, returned from France, but under the ludicrous Senior Clubs registration regulations England's fly half was prevented

'At least the model might pass to me' was Jerry Guscott's remark when Carling's Madame Tussaud's waxwork made an appearance before the game against Canada at Wembley in October 1992. *(Madame Tussaud's)*

from playing league rugby until February. Andrew could not believe that his genuine work commitments could lead to such a ban. 'So much for the amateur game. It is the reasons I have been given which so confuse me in this matter. I have been informed that the decision was taken on the grounds that I have played for another English club prior to joining Wasps. That club was Nottingham, but I left them in 1985. I found it strange that the committee has to go back seven years to find something on which to prevent me playing. That was pre-registration and pre-Leagues.' The authorities who were always banging on about this 'great amateur game' were making the simple business of playing rugby union as complicated as anything in sport.

Carling was looking forward to playing at Wembley for the first time. The new East Stand would not be ready until South Africa's visit a month later. Dean Richards was photographed sparring with Frank Bruno, who was fighting Pierre Coetzer at the Wembley Arena after the match. Most of the England boys reckoned Richards would have been a better match for Bruno than many opponents the boxing promoters saw fit to put in the ring with him. Wembley was treated to two Carlings – his Madame Tussaud's waxwork was unveiled. Jerry Guscott looked it up and down, then reflected: 'At least the model might pass to me.' When the media met Carling for the usual pre-match captain's press conference, the Guscott joke was passed on to the captain. It hit a raw nerve.

TONY ROCHE, *TODAY*
Instead of laughing, Will took it to heart. 'Everything seems to be at my

expense,' he moaned. He saw it as another personal attack. A month later we saw him at the Lensbury Club before the Barbarians game against Australia. It was a cold, wet, windy Thursday. As we passed the time with him, he tried to trip Coops – Terry Cooper of the Press Association who had mentioned the Guscott joke. His body language was so different. He had his hands in his pockets. His shoulders were relaxed. That day he wasn't wearing his usual hat. Will Carling wasn't captain of England.

Canada gave England a good work-out at Wembley. Carling enjoyed the atmosphere of the venue that had witnessed England's and Bobby Moore's soccer World Cup triumph in 1966. 'It was always going to be hard this early in the season against a very committed side. It was a one-off blast for them and they played well. It was the biggest match of the year for them.' That same afternoon South Africa enjoyed their first win, 20–15 over France, since returning to the international fold. They lost the second Test a week later. For a time it appeared as if England might lose their leg of the tour. The National Olympic Sports Congress announced from the Republic: 'We don't feel obliged to protect rugby any longer.' They objected to references to the South African rugby side as the Springboks, a reminder of the old white supremacy and of apartheid. Less than three years later, President Mandela was cheering on the 'Springboks' to World Cup glory at Ellis Park. At first the ANC backed the NOSC, then decided that the tour of England should go ahead. There was a casualty – 'God Save the Queen'. The British national anthem was dropped to prevent the South Africans singing the old Afrikaner favourite 'Die Stem' – the call of the old South Africa. Its passionate singing by the South African team in a French hotel suggested yet again that the old apartheid ways had not died completely. The RFU decided that the safest course was to have no anthems at all, especially as the South Africa state president, F. W. de Klerk, was scheduled to attend.

## WILL CARLING

The anthem has come to mean something very special to the England team. We were very angry that we were going to be denied part of our normal build-up through no fault of our own. It's a tense time in those few minutes before the kick-off. You are ready for the off, desperate just to get started. I'm not keen on presentations to officials. It was a great honour and privilege to meet the Queen before the World Cup final, but I would have preferred different circumstances. You are so keyed up for the game of your life, but expected to make small talk.

I really do feel it's time England had its own song, its own anthem. Everyone else does in the rugby world. I'm not unpatriotic or disloyal, but 'God Save the Queen' is Britain's national anthem, not just England's. I've actually talked to Prince Edward and the Princess Royal about it. They both hinted that it's not a bad idea. I would like something like 'Jerusalem' or

'Land of Hope and Glory'. Something that is English, not British. That would give the team an incredible lift. Look at the impact of 'Swing Low, Sweet Chariot'. That has become our anthem, although it seems to have been adopted by supporters of other England teams. It's a tremendous feeling to hear it being sung and remember how it all started back in 1988.

Carling's complaints paid off. The anthem was restored the day before the game.

South Africa showed for half an hour that they were going to be a real threat on home ground in the 1995 World Cup. England were in some disarray as the visitors took a 13–8 lead towards the end of the first half. The game turned England's way when Andrew chipped ahead for Guscott to jump and score. England's 33–16 success was completed when Carling once again chased and jumped – this time with a hint of a knock-on – to notch up his seventh try for his country.

Next stop was the Barbarians. They would provide the traditional finale of Australia's tour to Ireland and Wales. Carling was chosen in the centre, but not named as captain. It is a way they have in the Barbarians not to announce the leader beforehand. Carling had a long-standing business appointment in Southampton on the Friday. He offered to move the time and catch a helicopter back. Carling was discovering what Campese had discovered the previous year: the Barbarians believe the biggest stars will drop everything for the honour of playing for them. The Barbarians' training requirements have increased because these days even the best rugby players in the world cannot just turn up and turn it on against well-organised and super-fit national sides.

The match brought Carling and Campese into opposition again. Campese had claimed that Carling had refused to shake hands with him after the World Cup final. About England's latest Grand Slam he said: 'England have beaten no one. Scotland have lost a lot of players, Wales are rebuilding from the bottom up, France have all sorts of political in-fighting, and Ireland are still celebrating the World Cup. England should be more realistic. The claim they are a "Run with the Ball" team. That is a joke. I am fed up reading about Captain Marvel this and wonderful Will that. I saw him in action and if he gave me a team talk, I'd fall asleep.' No one can doubt that Campese has been one of the great players of the modern, or any other, time. The Australian had a marvellous World Cup, especially in the semi-final. He has the rare ability to think and react immediately in the heat of battle. Former Wallaby coach Alan Jones called him the 'Don Bradman of rugby'. But his mouth has been known to run away even more quickly, and more often, than his legs. He had already upset the Irish on this tour with a typical pre-match barrage. Fortunately, Campese's rugby usually has the last word. That rarely leaves a bitter taste. Carling refused to get involved in a war of words, and the pair shook hands in front of the TV cameras after the Barbarians had lost.

# CHAPTER 9

# CAPTAIN CARLING IN DOUBT – 1993

Carling's New Year did not begin promisingly: England's captain was laid out by a crunching tackle by Phil de Glanville during England's training trip to Lanzarote, which put an end to his active participation. The injury problems continued the following week when he limped off after 14 minutes against Orrell. Carling was a spectator at the squad session the next day. Those 14 minutes were all the competitive rugby Carling had under his belt in the seven weeks leading up to the visit of France. Dooley had withdrawn the day before to give Martin Johnson his first cap. Carling had great respect for the policeman's honest endeavour and continuing enthusiasm. Before the 1991 Grand Slam decider Carling had slipped him a note under his door: 'Wade, with over 40 caps, there's bugger all I can say, but you know how important you are to us tomorrow. You've carried us through three games. Let's kill these buggers off in the fourth. Make sure you get to run with the ball, too. Hurt those idiots in the tackle. This is our biggest game, so let's show everyone how powerful we are. Good luck, mate. Will.'

Carling felt it necessary to reassert his claims to the captaincy before the French game: 'I'll never give up the captaincy. I don't see myself being just a player. I'll never relinquish the captaincy voluntarily. I'd find it very difficult to play for the side if I wasn't the skipper. I love the job and I'm getting better at it. I want to go on leading England until 1995 – and maybe even beyond that. I'm very aware of the dangers of getting stale and players not responding to what I say to them. I would still want to play for England if the captaincy was taken away from me. But it's not what I want.'

New cap Johnson played well. England did not. Only the woodwork enabled the home side to scrape home 16–15. The post provided the opportunity for Ian Hunter to score from Webb's penalty attempt before the interval, and the bar denied the French a late dropped goal by Lafond. The French full back had given an outstanding display in wretched conditions. Cooke was more than a little disappointed. 'We made more errors than we would expect to do in the whole of a season. It was the most disciplined and well-organised French performance against us for a while. Given that sort of start, they are likely to win their next three games.' Cooke got that right.

David Miller, the respected sports columnist of *The Times*, is well used to the post-mortem press conferences. He observed: 'When Geoff Cooke and Will

Carling came to the interview room, it was hardly with the smile of victors. They revealed the slightly gaunt expression that people used to have when emerging from air-raid shelters after the all-clear. In 1991 France lost at Twickenham by only two points when victory would have given them the Grand Slam instead of England. Carling said afterwards that being captain of England had become easier over three years. That would be enough to infuriate the French even further. What had become grindingly evident was England's refusal, no matter how close the call, to become frayed, to lose their presence of mind whatever the pressure. That is part coaching and organisation, part captaincy. You can picture Carling still pouring the wine in a restaurant that was on fire. No panic.'

Carling may have appeared calm on the outside. The truth was somewhat different. The captaincy was getting to him again. This was not the same problem as 1990 and the aftermath of Murrayfield. Carling had done his best to make himself a sitting target three years earlier; not the most sensible ploy when you are being attacked from all sides. This time the pressures were coming from within. Carling had set himself such high standards and expectations that they were becoming impossible to live with. Winning and winning well was the norm. Anything else was failure. Carling knew only too well the price of failure. As he predicted before the start of the championship: 'If we lose a game in the championship this year, I'll get absolutely murdered again. I've been up there and I'm a target. Gary Lineker didn't get that when he was captain of England. The soccer skipper doesn't get slagged off for the national side losing. I have always seen the England rugby captain as midway between the cricket and soccer jobs. I am not as involved as the cricket captain, but much more than the football. I'm much more actively involved in selection and tactics than Gary ever was. But the cricket captain does the job all day. He has much more time to make his decisions, and even longer to live with them.'

The strain had showed earlier in the season when Carling clashed with former Wales captain Eddie Butler. Butler had suggested on BBC TV's *Rugby Special* that the only breaks Carling was making were in the commercial world. It was a cheap shot, one which Carling would have normally ignored. Instead, he gave Butler a piece of his mind at the post-match Barbarians dinner.

COLIN HERRIDGE, HARLEQUINS
Will has always tried to keep his emotions and thoughts in check. He doesn't get out of control. But when the adrenalin flows and he lets his hair down after a match, he'll tell you what he thinks. As he showed with Butler, there is a lot pent up there. Will felt a top-class player should have shown a better understanding of his situation, not make fun of it. Butler has been through the mill himself.

The England captaincy was not the only problem. The almost daily analysis of his suitability to lead the Lions quickly became more than just an irritant. Carling was such a certainty that the media had to examine each and every reason why Will Carling should not do the job. England's captain was already thinking along the same lines. Cardiff offered no relief. It only made matters worse. The 'upset' has always been an integral part and major attraction of the Five Nations Championship. Because England have been so strong during Carling's reign, the only time England's captain has been involved in such afternoons has been on the receiving end. It is not a pleasant experience. The other countries salvage something out of their season if they beat England. It is doubtful whether the National Stadium, even in the glorious seventies, has ever made as much noise as it did when Wales overcame England in 1993. Destroying England's dreams of a hat-trick of Grand Slams was reason enough; yet the cheering was as much in relief that Welsh rugby was competing with the rest again as in celebration. The contest turned on a few seconds' aberration by Rory Underwood. It was not the first time England's flying wing had lapsed under the influence of Welsh *hwyl*. Flanker Emyr Lewis kicked ahead down the right wing. Welsh captain Ieuan Evans set off in pursuit, more in hope than intention. Underwood's 58-cap experience went out of the window. The only person on the Welsh side of the Severn Bridge who did not see the danger was Underwood himself as he covered across in something less than haste. He admitted afterwards: 'I didn't think there was any urgency.' Underwood cottoned on a split second too late. Evans steamed past him, hacked on and won the race for the touchdown. Cardiff went wild.

England had half the match to recover the situation. But the tide had turned. Morris had already been denied a try by French referee Joel Dumé. Bayfield had lost the ball over the line. Carling was as guilty as anyone of fumbling chances. Webb hit the post. England did not take a last-minute 50 metre penalty shot when only 10–9 down. It was just not their day. It was a day of mistakes, below-par performances. Cooke reflected: 'Simply getting to the other end doesn't necessarily bring you points. When there's a mistake, it's a collective mistake, and everyone shares Rory's disappointment. It is a major setback. But we simply have to pick ourselves up and go on, even though it hurts. It was a combination of skill and judgement failure.'

WILL CARLING
It had dawned on me suddenly. Why was I playing? Was I captaining England for the right reason? Was it just ego? I began to question my motives. Was I interested in me, or the team, or in just being heralded? Did I want to be the greatest captain there ever was? If the answer to that question was 'yes' – then I had got it all wrong. I always felt I'd been for the team. Now I wasn't so sure. Cardiff gave me the answer. It was sad to lose. I knew afterwards that I was still doing the job for the right reasons. I don't like being in the dressing-room with my team-mates when we've lost.

At least there was no more talk of the third Grand Slam. But the debate about Carling's suitability to lead the Lions intensified. In the *Sunday Times* Stephen Jones gave this view of the current state of thinking: 'What of Carling and the Lions? How did Cardiff change his life? He did make one or two electrifying bursts, but they were delicious single notes of a symphony which remained unheard. Carling is a brilliant player, but for an inside centre who is also captain, he was disturbingly peripheral. He was peripheral because England do not have the capability to launch him to strike for victory, and because he showed again that, in tight games, he can allow the England tactics to meander. England captains of the past would have killed for results half as good as those of the Carling men. Yet, in Carling's era, had England been tactically harder of head and more inclined to chase the close games, they could have been unbeaten in the northern hemisphere since 1988 – a run which would have included victory in the World Cup final and against Wales last weekend. All this is Carling's triumph and failure.'

England and Carling struggle to get into the action in Cardiff in 1993. There is no way through as Stuart Davies, Emyr Lewis (with ball) and Richard Webster keep Carling at bay. *(Colorsport)*

The heat was on, off and on the field. Carling was only too well aware that his performance out of a rugby jersey was being analysed just as closely. Carling's leadership style demands loyalty and respect, not popularity. Seven years into the job, his captaincy style is well established. He sees no reason to trust the media or the rugby authorities. His players expect certain standards, so he keeps himself apart. Carling has worked closely with Geoff Cooke, Dick Best and Jack Rowell in varying degrees. He devotes a lot of time to his role as captain. Those responsibilities, coupled with running a successful business and married life, leave little time for being social. Will Carling is the first England rugby captain who does not hang around bars and clubhouse chatting. He does not have the time. He does not have the inclination.

WILL CARLING

I don't enjoy the spotlight that much. Many make the mistake of thinking I do. But I hate going to functions and dinners if I'm not working. I don't like people pointing and staring at me. I much prefer being with a few close friends. That's where the press have never worked it out. I don't crave TV and newspaper coverage. I admit I'm no shrinking violet, but I choose carefully. I've become the symbol of England's recent rugby success. That's lovely. But it's not the truth. I place far too much importance on the rest of the squad who've been there all the way through to believe it. It's been a hell of a team and I think there are four or five people who would have made good captains. Rob Andrew, Peter Winterbottom and Simon Halliday are the most obvious, but there were other potential leaders around. I don't think I've done anything startling. It's not a big deal. It's not fair to attribute England's success to one person. I've done my bit. So has everyone else.

The perception of me as arrogant and aloof is strongest in the media. That is not how other players view me. I know Geoff Cooke talked to Ian McGeechan and others from the Home Countries about it before the Lions tour in 1993. I certainly got on with everyone when I captained the Barbarians. One reason that Nick Farr-Jones was so successful as a captain was that he was always slightly detached from the other players. As skipper, you room alone. The players know you sit in on selection. You have to set standards. It's doesn't work if you try to impose standards that you don't adhere to yourself. By definition the job is a lonely one. I keep my emotions in check, most of the time. The Scots are fairly canny like that. My grandmother is Scottish – I was eligible for Scotland. I was sent away to school. I don't know if that had anything to do with it. I was a year ahead of myself in sporting teams at Sedbergh. That singled me out. I couldn't come back to my own year gloating. My team-mates didn't want to know me. I was from the year below. A lifetime at school. So I kept things to myself. I concealed the fact that playing well at sport meant a lot to me. I didn't want to appear arrogant and different from boys in my year.

Arrogance is not my style. It's not England's. Players like Blanco and Campese have a lot to say for themselves, but that doesn't make them superior in my book. If I'm facing those sort of blokes, I don't give a damn about them. I know I can beat them. England players have arrogance. But it's inside. Not to be shown. I'm arrogant on the field, but I've got to be if I want to win. I have to believe in myself. That I'm the better man. I would like to believe that the best thing about this England side is that they can turn off. If you meet them off the field, they are not arrogant. They prove that you don't have to live the part all the time. Jerry is arrogant. He has a swagger. That's his style. It's not put on. We don't attack people off the field. I have never been a great believer in that. We get our satisfaction on the field.

There was not much satisfaction after Cardiff. Rob Andrew was the main casualty of that first championship defeat for three years. That cost Carling his main link with the players. Andrew often relayed the team's mood and Carling used the fly half to gauge the general reaction to his performance as captain. The long debate about the England No. 10 shirt continued when Stuart Barnes was brought in to replace him. Cooke announced the side to play Scotland five days after Cardiff, despite England missing the next round of championship matches. 'Now the players brought in can prepare themselves mentally for the game and the two we have left out can reflect on their roles in the squad.' Ian Hunter was also dropped, making way for Tony Underwood. Andrew's demotion put a strain on his relationship with the skipper.

ROB ANDREW
Will and I have always been close. I wasn't expecting the chop. I obviously misread the situation. I didn't think that there would be any changes. I believe that if we had played that game for another three weeks, England would still have been destined to lose. You just have to look at the circumstances of their try. It was Geoff who rang me with the news. Then I talked to Will. These things happen. When a guy has picked you for 39 consecutive Tests, you can't argue. That's the way it goes. I know Will is involved in selection. Ultimately, it was Geoff's decision. What disappointed me was that mistakes led to the try. There were others, too. I wasn't involved in any of them.

In a way it was more awkward for Will than it was for me. We've discussed it since. We've been in the same side since 1988. We are close, on and off the field. I had been heavily involved. Suddenly, that changed. That made the dropping all the more difficult. Will finds that part of the captaincy difficult. England have had a settled side in recent times. That's probably made it even harder when senior men are dropped – when Deano was left out, Webb coming in for Hodgkinson, Hill for Morris, Morris for Hill, Probyn in and out. Defeat in Cardiff was difficult. The press were really gunning for the side. That had started right back in September. There was a lot of speculation about Stuart Barnes and myself. I had a good game against South Africa and didn't play badly against France. Luckily, the British Lions tour gave me the chance to compete with Stuart again.

WILL CARLING

I'm glad I have some say on selection, but it comes at a price. When players are dropped, they know I've had some input. It helps to know why players are picked and the thought process behind the selection. Cookie was clever. He knows he gets an input from the players through me. That has never happened before. Sometimes we argue. Cookie got his way, just as Jack Rowell does now. I remember Geoff wanted to bring in Simon Hodgkinson at full back against Romania, while I wanted to play an attacker, someone outrageous, like Simon Halliday. I suppose we had half a dozen such clashes over the years. Nothing serious. I've always felt disloyal leaving out Deano. He's such a tower of strength. Bringing in Jerry Guscott, who I didn't know at all, for Simon Halliday was another hard decision. Dropping Rob was the toughest of the lot. It's about the strength of mind to be honest. Provided the change has been done for the right reason, I can live with it. It would be terrible if personal reasons clouded the argument. I felt Rob's dropping did take the edge off our relationship for a while. I don't know what was said behind my back. I can't disassociate myself from the process. It's not my decision alone, but I am involved. I can't make excuses. 'Sorry you're out. Personally, I didn't agree with it.' You have to toe the party line. That's best for all concerned.

The Welsh revival came to an abrupt halt at Murrayfield. Scotland's victory highlighted Carling's emerging challenger for the Lions captaincy. If the main thrust of Carling's leadership is using the head, Hastings' motivating force was focused on the heart. Hastings is a much more extrovert character, more at ease with the public, the responsibilities and the authorities; and he was a leader more by instinct than design, who felt no great need to wrap himself up in the off-the-field planning. The Scottish full back had an obvious advantage in being an integral part of the Lions success in Australia four years earlier. The Calcutta Cup was billed as a duel between the pair for the Lions leadership. It was rather an unfair contest. Carling couldn't win. If England triumphed, the jury would stay out. The battle for the captaincy would only be decisive if Scotland took the Calcutta Cup home. By now Carling was beginning to feel the tide had already turned the Scot's way.

It was not all Hastings and Carling. The spotlight was firmly fixed on Stuart Barnes. The Bath fly half and captain was winning his ninth cap. It was a new beginning, his first game under Carling, his first at fly half in the championship, his first start at Twickenham since his debut against Australia nine years earlier. Four times Barnes had come on as a replacement. His four full games at fly half had been against Australia, the All Blacks (twice) and Fiji. Twice he had announced his unavailability for England, fed up with waiting for Andrew to falter in Cooke's eyes. His influence on Bath's rise to dominance at the top of English club rugby had been considerable. That success had kept him in the public eye, even during his periods of self-imposed exile.

Carling treated him no differently from any other player.

WILL CARLING

I'm very trusting of players. When they come into the squad, it doesn't matter what's gone on in the past. Everyone starts with a clean slate. You have to trust players in order for them to trust you.

The captain also appreciated that, for all Barnes's experience and confidence, much was expected of him. It is not always easy or possible to turn it on in the cauldron of the Five Nations Championship. Barnes started nervously. The visitors' rhythm was disrupted by an injury to fly half Craig Chalmers. Almost immediately Barnes started buzzing. England's backs were given the space and opportunity Guscott revels in at Bath. Barnes instigated one of the most famous tries of the Carling era. Barnes stretched high to take Morris's pass from a lineout deep inside England's half. Safety first would have been Andrew's order of the day. Instead, Barnes stepped inside Ian Smith's charge and was away. The burst caught Scotland off guard. Barnes reached half-way before throwing a long pass. Guscott did not even have to check his stride. Guscott then drew the two covering tacklers as his scoring pass found its way to Rory Underwood. Guscott had already scored. Rory's younger brother Tony added a third. That set off the proudest Mum in Twickenham, Mrs Anne Underwood. She was captured by TV cameras celebrating the Underwood double with a one-woman Mexican wave.

Scotland rallied in the final quarter, but England's 26–12 victory was conclusive. Nevertheless, the margin was almost certain to cost England the championship. Midway through the Five Nations, the powers that be introduced a trophy. There were to be no more ties or titles shared. The winner would be decided on points difference if countries were level. Nobody had argued about shared titles. Normally the winner of the match between the countries stuck together at the top claimed a moral victory. France's points advantage now made them firm favourites for the 1993 championship. Cooke reflected: 'It is unfortunate that we did not show the killer instinct after going 23–6 up. We should have gone to town. But our supply of ball dried up and we did not get our lineout working.'

Carling had little time to celebrate the success as he flew off to join his Harlequin team-mates in South Africa. He did make the Rose Room immediately after the Calcutta Cup, and that gathering marked one of his first public appearances with Julia Smith, whom he was to marry the following summer. Even there Carling had to evade the lens of one or two prying cameras. There was no escape in South Africa, either. By accident or by design, one of Julia's faxes to Will was delivered to another member of the side. Its contents were made public to the team at a later date, to much merriment.

Carling tries his luck at scrum half in the 1993 Calcutta Cup match. *(Colorsport)*

Generally, though, the Harlequins has offered Carling a great deal of consideration and relief from the fray. It has been the perfect club for him. The fact that it was a glamorous club with glamorous traditions and glamorous players was not important. What has mattered is that club officials, especially former secretary Colin Herridge, have been sympathetic to Carling and his situation as England captain. The club–country conflict has not really affected Carling. He is not required to play in every club match, or even every league match. The club scene, even in today's competitive world, is simply a means to an end. Carling would certainly not have enjoyed life as a big fish in a small pond.

The week before the final round of championship matches, Stephen Jones of the *Sunday Times* wrote an article that appeared under the banner: 'Why Carling Must Not Captain The Lions'. The unfortunate headline angered Carling. The content did not. The Jones verdict was more a plea for Gavin Hastings to be given the job, arguing that Carling would benefit from a period away from the responsibilities of leading an international rugby side.

Lions or no Lions, Carling and Cooke were worried about the Irish. 'They won in Cardiff. We didn't. Their crowd support will have picked up because of that win. Lansdowne Road can be a very daunting place. And Ireland will be more used to the referee, having had him in their last match.' The final statement was Cooke-speak for 'we don't think much of Aussie official Sandy McNeill.' The *laissez-faire* refereeing of the French and the Aussies cost England dear in 1993, as did the new laws.

Once the Irish realised the law-makers had given them a licence to hang off, fringe and generally run amok, the men in green found a new lease of life. It was no surprise when England, Grand Slam champions, World Cup finalists and the northern hemisphere's most successful side of the nineties were hustled, bustled and brow-beaten 17–3 by an Irish side full of passion, pride and personality. Slowly and surely England drowned in a sea of Irish green. England forwards continued to struggle. The visiting backs rarely received the ball without an accompanying tackler. That is how Carling's championship misery ended. England's captain was bulldozed backwards, the ball went loose for Mick Galwey to pick up and score. Carling, who had started the Five Nations campaign looking every inch a winner, was now down for the full count.

WILL CARLING
We were really struggling. I remember talking to Barnsey. 'What can we do to get into this game?' I had a terrible sense of frustration. You have to persevere. It's said that you should never look at the scoreboard or the clock. You should concentrate on the basics. And don't panic. Don't try to force the pace. That's probably right and makes a lot of sense. But common sense is in fairly short supply when the Irish are flying around at a hundred miles an hour, smashing into everything in a white jersey. I was really annoyed to give that try away at the end. I was trying to make something happen. But I should have held on to the ball. It summed up the whole miserable afternoon.

Seen against the outcome of the 1993 championship, the decisions of Rory Underwood, Webb and Dooley to reverse their retirement plans were a mistake. So was the notion that England's experienced pack would be the unit quickest to adapt to the law changes. Brian Moore's forwards were too set in their ways. Ben Clarke apart, they struggled to do the new things instinctively.

Ireland, jubilant, Martin Bayfield stunned, as Carling suffers his biggest Five Nations defeat as captain at Lansdowne Road in March 1993.
*(Colorsport)*

Nevertheless, Ireland always offers consolation for Carling, for Dublin is his favourite rugby weekend.

### WILL CARLING

The Irish play their rugby hard, then play hard. In Cardiff and Edinburgh, the result is everything. The Irish celebrate whatever. That philosophy is catching, especially when the Guinness flows. The most horrendous night I ever had was with Paul Dean and Michael Kiernan. To this day, I have no idea what happened. I must admit that I prefer waking up in London on international Sundays for two reasons. It's easier getting home. It usually means we've won. Sunday morning in Dublin is hard work. We fly back after lunch. That gives Wade Dooley plenty of time to organise compulsory Guinness for the whole team. However badly you've done, the result doesn't seem quite as life-shattering as it had the previous afternoon.

The difference between 1992 and 1993 is that we took our chances in 1992. The slightest chance and we took it. That's the key in the close matches. The 1992 Grand Slam had almost been too easy. We were still on a high from the

World Cup. We had so much support and the team was going well. It was incredible. Winning seemed to take so little effort. The atmosphere was so relaxed and so different to 1991. Every game had been hard in 1991. The final game against France was so tense and so close. There was so much relief that we had finally won something. We didn't have a close game in 1992. The second Grand Slam was more a matter of fact – we'd already done it. No game was on the line. The final game against Wales was won in the opening quarter of an hour. People were claiming that we were beating weak sides, but it was still a great year for us.

The level of expectancy did weigh on us in 1993 after two Grand Slams. Most people were putting good money on a third, but the edge had gone. No one from the outside could assess that. To be brutally honest, the Lions did have a distracting effect. It was hard for Cookie and Bestie in their dual roles. Certain players took their eyes off the ball. They were looking too far ahead to the Lions. Basically, England did not come up to standard. The new laws affected us much more than we thought. England were not able to establish a pattern of play early on, as we had done in the previous two championships. We had chances against Wales. But we did not put them away. We could not maintain pressure under the new laws. Nowadays, it's a case of getting down there and scoring because it can be 10 minutes before you might get another chance. The new laws changed the whole emphasis of the game. I have always believed that rugby is about going forwards by passing backwards. That's the way I was taught to play. You play that way until you are stopped. The new laws reward good cheats – get to the ball and tie it up. It's disheartening as a back to look up and see so many forwards hanging around on the inside. There's no space. It's man-for-man overlaps these days.

# CHAPTER 10

# RISING FROM THE LIONS MIRE – 1993

Carling flew home from Dublin with his Lions future assured. He had revealed to the press that he did not expect to be named captain the day after. Why should he? Carling had already told Cooke that he did not want the job, a view shared by the Lions selectors.

WILL CARLING
I was never obsessed by the Lions captaincy. I never sought it. So much can happen – injuries, loss of form. Shin splints had cost me my place on the 1989 Lions tour to Australia. That denied me a chance of playing with players from the other countries and working with coach Ian McGeechan. I took nothing for granted, although I desperately wanted to go on the tour. My main interest during the season was England. That Cardiff defeat was the crunch. It dawned on me that the England captaincy was tiring me out a lot more than it used to. My own performance disappointed me there. I felt I needed to concentrate on my own game. Had we won a third Grand Slam, I might have felt fresher. I might have been given the Lions job. I might have accepted. I might have done a good job. But it worked out differently and I'm happy with that.

The pressures were intense, even before Cardiff. I had been in the job since 1988, so I knew what the score was. Success brings its own pressures. I had also created a few of my own. In the summer with the Lions, I was relieved to take a back seat and let another management team do the work. I've always felt the England job was a big enough challenge. I didn't need to captain the British Lions from an ego point of view. I'm not belittling the Lions. The 1993 tour was a unique experience. At that stage of my career, it was beneficial not to be given that responsibility. Maybe I was selfish. I had long-term plans. I was looking to take England to the World Cup in 1995. The next two years were going to be tough. One summer out of the hot seat was as good as a rest.

There was no feeling of being slighted when the Lions squad was announced. I had already made my feelings clear to Geoff. I don't think he was surprised with what I said. Nor did it go against what the Lions selectors were thinking. The Lions were looking for an emphasis away from English bias. Two of the three management team were England – Cookie and Bestie. England players were obviously going to provide the majority of the squad. To be Lions captain would be a great honour. No one would ever turn it down. Gavin knew how I felt. We discussed it when we worked together for ITV at the World Sevens. When the squad was announced, Rob Andrew said to me: 'You've been captain for five years now. You've never been able to enjoy the company of the lads without being their captain.'

Carling knew that England's poor showing, especially in Dublin, had muddied the waters for the Lions selectors. When proven players of a certain age are not producing the goods, selectors are left in limbo. Several of England's most experienced forwards, especially Peter Winterbottom, who some thought should lead the tourists, and Wade Dooley had only shown glimpses of their best form. Coach Ian McGeechan had to decide whether the decline was temporary or permanent. McGeechan was only too well aware that New Zealand is not the place to take a forward on a downward slide, although he knew how valuable experience is against the All Blacks. Ireland's rousing finale had many pleading for a serious rethink. Cooke and McGeechan are not men to be easily swayed. They went for experience. The two major influences were the Lions success in Australia in 1989 and England's subsequent domination of the Five Nations. Hastings was put in charge of 16 Englishmen, although Jeff Probyn again missed out. The eight Scots included their entire front five. Dean Richards, who was not a current member of the England pack, was one of a dozen 1989 Lions chosen again. For the first time since 1959 there was no Welsh scrum half in the party. Robert Jones put that straight when Gary Armstrong dropped out through injury. McGeechan made his policy clear: 'Those who were with the 1989 Lions have a head start. They know what the pressures are. That experience must be used, while the challenge to the England players will be crucial to the development of the squad. I hope to set challenges to some very experienced players who can achieve great mobility and pace. All I am asking of them is seven games of top rugby.'

GEOFF COOKE

I always thought there were other players than Will who could captain the Lions. We kept an eye on them all the way through. For the Lions job we perceived that a different approach was necessary. One point of view was that Will needed a break from the whole business of being captain. The job and the make-up of the party then pushed us towards Gavin Hastings. The fact that the management was mainly English was part of the process. If the Lions captain, who is an integral part of the set-up, had been Will, then three out of the four would have been English. There weren't any votes during the selection discussions, not even on the captaincy. It was done by consensus. Will sets high standards. He puts pressure on himself. It's all about finding a balance. Sometimes you get it wrong and that causes

Carling and Julia Smith at Chelsea Harbour at the time their engagement was announced just before he left for the 1993 Lions tour to New Zealand. That separation proved costly. 'My phone bill was horrendous,' explained Will. *(Mail on Sunday/Solo)*

problems. I believe the break from the captaincy was of benefit. The only doubt about his future as captain was a loss of form. That's been the proviso from the day he got the job.

There was general agreement that not giving the captaincy to Carling was a good thing. If Carling felt a sense of failure, he did not show it. There were compensations. Three days later England's captain was pictured with top pop PR Julia Smith. Carling's team-mates were surprised that he agreed for the pair to be photographed together, for Carling guarded his private life fiercely. In fact he felt he had little choice. Julia rang him from her Kensington office and told him the photographers outside had promised to follow her day and night until they got a picture of her with the England rugby captain. But even when they had it, the matter was not closed. The following day his previous girlfriend Victoria, who had split from Carling before the Five Nations, went into print under the heading 'Life Without Will'. Carling, single and good-looking, may have been one of England's sporting sex symbols, but he was always embarrassed and uneasy with female adulation. He also disliked the intrusion into his private life. He had done his best to keep his sex life under wraps, but most top sports stars have noticed a growing interest in their off-the-field activities and habits, and Carling is no exception. His elevation to the captaincy had young girls swooning and mothers plotting. Carling's name was even put forward as a suitable replacement when Charles and Di separated. That royal connection was to cause problems in 1995.

Carling has never denied the existence of girlfriends. There would have been much more press interest if there had not been any. He has always insisted that they have had nothing to do with his public profile or rugby career. Generally, Carling has been accompanied by blondes, although dark-haired Sky Sports presenter Beverley Webb was a brief exception. That relationship did not last long. Business and pleasure do not mix. The other players knew about it. So did the press. That made Carling seem vulnerable. Discretion has always been the hallmark of his friendships, male and female. Carling was very upset when Victoria went public after he started seeing Julia. His relationship with Victoria had been on rocky ground for a while. They had met in March 1991 at a sports dinner at London University, where she was studying economics. Like most of Carling's ladies, she had little interest in rugby. When she saw his collection of Five Nations shirts, she asked if they were all the teams he had played for. They had split briefly the previous summer, but went on holiday together in August. Carling finally called a halt after their December break in the Far East. His explanation was that rugby was still the most important thing in his life, and that there was no room for a serious relationship in his current plans. The break-up was made public mid-way through the Five Nations. Carling insisted: 'There's no one else in my life. We are both sad it is all over. But I feel the relationship had run as far as it was going. It was an unpleasant day for both of us, but there seemed no kindness in prolonging it just for the sake of it. Neither of us has any intention of discussing our time together in public.'

That lasted a month. When Victoria saw the picture of Carling with Julia, she felt aggrieved that England's captain was now able to accommodate a serious relationship. Carling was horrified by her public pronouncements. Hitherto his battles with the press had all been rugby ones; now, for the first time, his private life was on view for general consumption. The article began: 'Victoria Jackson is fed up being cast as the spurned lover.' She was less dramatic. 'It's happened. Romances break up all the time. The thing that makes it so difficult is that it's so public. The private side of Will, the part that made him so attractive to me, is still very private. We used to have other girlfriends and boyfriends, separate friends, and Julia was one of Will's. That did not stop us having a close relationship, and neither of us was sexually involved with friends of the opposite sex. I don't really know if he was romantically involved with Julia before we split. I never thought our relationship was for life. He phoned to tell me about Julia. I was so surprised he posed for the newspapers with her. I think it's sad because that's what we agreed on. That was the golden rule. People change. Will is now definitely a past stage of my life.'

Carling had first met Julia when he was going out with Nikki Turner, another PR girl to whom he was attached for a year before she headed for Australia after they split in 1990. Julia's world was the pop world, not the rugby one. Her clients included INXS, Right Said Fred and Vanessa Paradis. She had had a six-year relationship with pop guitarist Jeff Beck and her name had been linked with Mick Jagger, Bob Geldof and Eric Clapton. The seriousness of her relationship with Carling was evident when they were pictured together and Julia emphasised it was 'very special. It is in its early stages and we both hope it will develop. We have known each other for four years. We met at a supper party. Over the years we kept in touch and, suddenly, two months ago, we found ourselves together again and realised that our long-valued friendship means much more to both of us.'

Just how special was revealed four days before the Lions left for New Zealand. The pair announced their engagement, with marriage planned for the following summer. 'It was fairly obvious to me that this was different to other relationships. I realised that Julia was the one. We share the same sense of humour and, for the first time, I feel comfortable with a woman and can talk about things that are important to me. I have some very, very close friends and Julia gets on well with them. Her being there hasn't made any difference. I'm very much a man's man, but Julia is a man's woman. Marriage is not going to change me a lot. I'm not a hell-raiser.' Carling and Julia had spent a lot of time together between the end of the championship and flying out to New Zealand early in May. Carling had injured his shoulder against Ireland, and his only subsequent outing was the Pilkington Cup final, which Quins lost for the second year running, this time to Leicester. A fortnight earlier, Carling and Hastings had worked together for ITV at the World Sevens. Carling offered the Scot his full support and help at any time. It wasn't called upon. The Hastings way was to let the coach run things. That was just as well. Carling would have a lot on his plate over the next ten weeks as he hit the lowest point of his playing career.

The Lions gathered together for a weekend in London at the end of April. After five years as captain and the privilege of a single room, Carling found himself sharing. Scotland's Andy Reed was the man chosen to acquaint Carling with a few facts of life. After half a day together, Reed felt the time was right for a talk. 'You carry on, Will. Don't mind me. Just use my bed as an office. That's not a problem.'

Carling did not make a good start to the trip. He had not even made the park before there was speculation that his Test place was under threat. Scott Hastings and Jerry Guscott, the centre pairing, impressed in the opening match. So did Scott Gibbs, alongside Carling, in the second. Carling and Hastings were the partnership when the Lions, 20–3 down as the match entered the final quarter, staged an amazing fightback to beat the New Zealand Maoris 24–20. The recovery should have been the perfect stage for Carling's power and pace, but something was missing. He limped off dejectedly in the final stages. The tour was already a strain. Training and playing apart, Carling had little to do. That was a new experience. So he was feeling homesick – or rather, lovesick.

The likely Test lineup was given a dress rehearsal against Otago, with Guscott and Carling together in the midfield. The Lions led 18–8 at the interval, but the second half was a catalogue of injuries and mistakes. Carling was first to go with a thigh strain. His replacement, Scott Hastings, had his tour ended

Carling breaks through the Otago defence for the Lions. He was forced to withdraw with a thigh strain as the tourists plunged to defeat. *(Colorsport)*

with a broken cheekbone. Then Martin Bayfield was stretchered off after being upended at a lineout and landing on the top of his spine. The visitors conceded five tries, going down 37–24. The Lions' problems mounted in the week when Wade Dooley had to return home because of the death of his father and Gibbs and Barnes were both injured in the final game before the first Test. Carling, after declaring himself fit, was paired with Guscott almost by default. His mood was buoyant. Julia, who had been working in Australia, had flown to Christchurch to join him. Morris and Andrew were the half backs, but Moore, Leonard and Teague failed to find places in the scrum. Few predicted a Lions victory. New Zealand did emerge victors, but the Lions were left shouting 'robbed'. A Grant Fox penalty two minutes from time gave the All Blacks a 20–18 win.

Australian referee Brian Kinsey gave New Zealand a try early on when Bunce and Evans crashed over together. Kinsey consulted the touch-judge first. Yet from where the touch-judge was standing he could not have seen whether Bunce had made the touchdown first. The All Blacks led 11–9 at the interval, signifying an impressive recovery by the Lions after that setback. Three more penalties by Hastings to two from Fox gave the Lions an 18–17 advantage. The almost inevitable penalty came when the Lions were being so careful. Kinsey blew up after Richards tackled Bunce and, supposedly, killed the ball. Fox, who had earlier passed 1,000 points for the All Blacks, made no mistake.

WILL CARLING

I felt on trial from the moment I arrived in New Zealand. 'Carling under pressure' – that gave the media a great story straight away. I'd heard about New Zealand rugby and how much it meant to the nation. But I wasn't prepared for the overwhelming interest. I felt on trial as a person as well as a player. And I made the mistake of worrying about the personal side. How was I getting on with the Welsh, Irish and Scottish lads? That was important, but not the most important thing. I didn't spend enough time thinking things through. That was strange because I had time on my hands. I was desperate to do well in New Zealand. I didn't prepare properly. I am normally very thorough. That showed there was something seriously wrong. I don't think I arrived in bad form, although I had played very little rugby in the previous two months. Once there, the harder I tried the worse it got. The thigh injury came at a bad time. I wanted a good game against Otago. I don't know what would have happened if Scott Gibbs had been fit because he had been playing so well. I was worried that I might be on my way home after the injury. My leg suddenly had no power in it. Nobody could find out why.

I think we psyched ourselves into thinking that we were under more pressure than we actually were in the first Test. I threw out one pass when I thought I was under pressure. I wasn't. We thought they were going to play

Carling kicks clear during what was to be his only Test on the Lions tour. *(Colorsport)*

at pace in the backs. As soon as the referee awarded that final penalty, I knew it was going over. It was an amazing decision, to say the least. We can't blame the referee, though. We should have been further ahead by then, so the penalty points would not have mattered. If you play the final 10 minutes and the opposition only need a penalty to win, you leave yourself wide open. The All Blacks did enough. We allowed them to win the game.

Fox appreciated how lucky the All Blacks had been. 'Unless we improve by 30 per cent, we will probably lose the next one and the one after that. We can't expect to play like that and get away with it.' Coach McGeechan's side had lost the first Test in 1989. He had a dozen survivors from that tour who could help him pull it back.

The biggest row between the Tests had little to do with the playing side. Dooley had decided to accept the New Zealand Rugby Union's kind offer to return after his father's funeral. It was the British officials who told New Zealand that his return as a player would be in breach of the tour agreement: Dooley could fly back, but not as a player. The Lions were incensed at such an insensitive attitude at such a sensitive time. Cooke spoke for the squad: 'It's an appalling way to treat a person who has done so much for the game. We are talking about the amateur ethos in our game. If there was ever a case for displaying the amateur ethos, this was it. On the grounds of sheer compassion, he should have been allowed to rejoin the party without conditions. For our people to raise objections is staggering. It started with the secretary, Bob Weighill, who was very negative in his approach to Wade, raising objections about insurance that were nonsensical. As for the grounds of precedent, that is even more illogical than it being outside the tour agreement, which is the rules and regulations bit.'

Carling's tour also effectively ended that week as well. Scott Gibbs was given his chance alongside Guscott in the Saturday match before the Test. The writing may have been on the wall, but it came as a big blow to Carling. He thought he would get one final opportunity against Auckland.

WILL CARLING

Auckland was a shock. For the first time in my life I had been dropped. I had no inkling about it. Nobody had spoken to me or warned me. The team was read out and my name was not there. I had this terrible sick feeling in my stomach. It wasn't that I really thought it was unfair. Scott deserved his chance. I wondered what I was doing out here. I had drifted along for four weeks and had just paid the penalty. Brian Moore had a beer with me after the Auckland game: 'I'm sorry you didn't play. I wanted to say something at the time, but I didn't know how.' I wasn't the only person dropped, but you would have thought so the way the press bombarded me. One even asked me how I reacted to those who said I hadn't been concentrating on my rugby because Julia had been out to see me.

I was very disappointed to be left out. Still, it was nothing to what Wade had been put through by the rugby authorities. The England lads were especially upset. We had all known his Dad. It had been the perfect chance for this great amateur game to show the rest of the world what a great amateur game it was. Here was a man who had played over 50 times for his country, whose father loved rugby, who had announced that he was quitting the big time after the tour and who had been invited back in a kind gesture by the home Union. How could the four Home Unions get it so wrong? We instigated a 50 dollar fine for any member of the squad caught talking to Weighill.

The Lions lost for the third Saturday in a row, after leading Auckland 18–11 at half-time. Gibbs maintained his form. It now needed a miracle if Carling was going to hang on to his Test place. England's captain came on to replace Gavin Hastings at the interval. His lack of familiarity with the full-back role was exposed a couple of times. Carling also damaged his shoulder again. Relegation to the midweek side – the dirt-trackers – brought Carling little relief, though he put over his first points of the trip, a dropped goal, when the Lions went down to Hawke's Bay. Skipper for the day, Barnes, was especially vocal: 'Not all the players showed 100 per cent commitment here. I simply cannot understand that. I'm bitterly frustrated. I'm not accusing all 15 players, but the boys working hard to get into the second Test team in Wellington on Saturday have been badly let down. Unless certain people react in the right way, this performance will cause internal divisions in the squad. This defeat hurts my pride. I just hope it hurts everyone else's pride as well.' Cooke arranged a clear-the-air meeting for the following day.

This was do-or-die time for the Lions. Three Englishmen – Leonard, Moore and Johnson – replaced three Scots – Burnell, Milne and Reed – in the pack. The only change in the backline was Gibbs for Carling. A record 11 Englishmen were picked, but there was no place for the national captain, even on the replacements' bench. Instead, Carling joined John Taylor in the ITV commentary box. The pair had a grandstand view of the best Lions display in New Zealand for 22 years as Gavin Hastings overcame not only his hamstring problems but a nightmare start. His elementary error gifted the All Blacks seven points after a quarter of an hour. But two penalties from him and an Andrew dropped goal gave the Lions a 9–7 half-time lead. Hastings made it 12–7 before Rory Underwood left the New Zealand defence for dead with a scintillating try. Even the All Blacks could not come back this time. Nor would Carling. This emphatic and dramatic turnaround meant that any last slim hopes of a recall for the final Test had vanished.

Carling was made British Lions captain at last – for the final midweek game against provincial champions Waikato. It was an afternoon of humiliation for the second-string outfit. Carling, who scored his first try of the trip, and Barnes battled as best they could, but the Lions forwards were as poor as they had been the week before and the tourists suffered a heavy 38–10 defeat. McGeechan was especially disappointed in the forwards, many of whom he knew intimately from the Scottish national squad. 'I can't explain it. But mentally it's very different to the Five Nations. You have to be very hard to keep performing.'

Carling had shown a lot of character in defeat. He was rewarded with promotion to the Lions bench. The tourists could not have made a better start in the final Test. Scott Gibbs snapped up an opportunist try to help them to a 10–0 lead. The game and the series appeared theirs for the taking. Then the Lions faltered. New Zealand won 30–13, although the contest was not decided until scrum half Jon Preston dummied his way over on the blindside with a quarter of an hour remaining. All three New Zealand tries were soft, the Lions losing that 10-point lead to touchdowns by Bunce and Fitzpatrick in a four-minute spell towards the end of the first half.

The Lions won seven matches and lost six, scoring 33 tries and conceding 31. The Wellington Test victory was the undoubted highlight of the visit, but they could have left with so much more.

WILL CARLING
I had let myself down. I had injury problems, but they were just excuses. I

wasn't concentrating on my rugby. I was missing Julia. There was no edge to my play. I wasn't making things happen. I wondered if I'd been around too long. The 1991 England World Cup side was breaking up. Did I really want to stay and remodel a new team? If I gave up the England job, that would be it. No England. No Quins. No rugby of any sort. Getting dropped focused my mind. Did I want to carry on? I asked Geoff if we could have a chat. He'd been thinking along the same lines. 'Don't you want to do the England job any more?' I told Geoff that the answer was 'yes'. It still is. I was pleased with the way I came through the toughest period of my life because I had to fight. That had never really happened to me before. My silver spoon image took a real battering in 1993. I didn't mind. I learnt a lot and that would help me in the years ahead. The year certainly hadn't gone according to plan, but what does in this life? There were no complaints from me.

I had an interesting Test series – played in the first, commentated on the second and sat on the bench for the third. The bench was easily the hardest. In the commentary box, I knew that I could not get involved, whatever happened. The bench is limbo-land. I hadn't expected to get called up for that job. Now I know what it's like for players such as John Olver, who've spent season after season picking splinters out of their backsides. I've a lot more sympathy now that I've been through the ordeal myself. I still don't understand how we could be so focused for the Tests – and so out of sorts in midweek. I know the Tests are the thing, the only results people remember. But I was shocked to find out that guys who played international rugby were not mentally strong enough. I don't think I've ever been in a side that hasn't competed before. People let themselves down, and that's always sad. It was about character more than ability. Waikato were a good side, but Hawke's Bay were not.

Once my Test chance had gone, it was down to personal pride. The results might have been disastrous, but I got a lot from the last two midweek games. My game was back. My enthusiasm was back. I had solved a lot in my mind. I was under immense pressure. I had to show what I was made of. Everyone's dropped at some stage of his career. It did me no harm to see life from the downside and it gave me the incentive I needed to want to play again. Just being one of the players on the tour took a lot of pressure off me. I could pick and choose my interviews. I think the other players saw a different side of me. I believe many of them thought I'd always had it easy. I'm sure the England boys could see I was a lot more relaxed by the end of the trip. I did miss having an input. I was so used to being involved. I tried to find a balance of not butting in or treading on anyone's toes. Gavin had his own style. He played well, too. That's the most important thing in New Zealand – to be at the top of your game. Gavin left a lot to McGeechan. Cookie found that hard. McGeechan thinks long and hard about his rugby. I admired the amount of work he did. Most of his spare time was spent preparing or studying. We didn't see a lot of him outside the sessions. He was rarely about for a drink. It was very much his tour. He was the driving force in 1989 and the same in 1993. He tried to show the same intensity as the All Blacks. I think Dick Best found it tough, too. He had no defined role.

I'm sure Dick and Geoff looked at me half-way through the tour and wondered what was going on. They must have thought I'd had enough. That my England days were numbered. I felt I had let Geoff down. I hope the final two displays went some way to repairing the damage. A tour like this allows you a lot more time to think about yourself if you're not captain. It was the wrong time for me to be doing that. It was no secret that I missed Julia terribly. I had never been in that situation before. The hotel phone bills were horrendous. From a playing point of view, I was glad I sorted my problems out in New Zealand, instead of giving it away and waiting until I got home. Before I flew back I was determined to prove that Will Carling was not finished – far from it.

Carling's worst fears for 1993 had become a reality. Yet the experience helped make him stronger. It also dispelled much of the mythology surrounding Darling Carling. His critics argued that he had ridden to the top on the back of England's power pack, that the captaincy had provided him with protection and camouflage. Could the bustling centre cut it without all the trappings? The rugby world found out the answer to that in the final fortnight of the Lions tour. Carling, out of favour with the Test selectors, had nothing to play for in the last two weeks of the tour. The easy option would have been to throw in the towel, settle in the midweek side, pretend it was just a bad experience or find a niggling injury that might save face. Others took that route. The press, especially, watched and waited for his reaction. Many of them had been waiting for this moment for five years. Would their theories hold water? The character, courage and class of Carling, which some doubted existed, were never more necessary. They were never more evident than when the northern hemisphere's most famous player played his heart out as a 'dirt-tracker' in those two final games. Carling knew it would not win him back a Test place. Yet he came home a winner. His reputation was restored, even enhanced. Now nobody could doubt that the England captain had what it takes to stand on his own two feet.

# CHAPTER 11

# ROWELL ENTERS THE COMFORT ZONE – 1994

Carling was more positive about his future than he had been for a long time. England, too, he felt, had the potential to regain their position as the northern hemisphere's top side. England's players had taken full advantage of the Lions tour, as they had done in 1989. Lions coach Ian McGeechan recognised that progress: 'Well, that helped England sort out her pack problems for 1994.' The staggering progress of Ben Clarke, the emergence of Martin Johnson and the switching of Jason Leonard to tight-head opened up all sorts of options for Cooke and Best. Dooley and Winterbottom joined Ackford in retirement. Probyn and Teague were near the end of a long hard road. Carling remembers how the other Lions players sensed England stealing a march. 'It was Welsh coach Alan Davies who first described it as the "England Development Tour". There was a joke among the dirt-trackers that they would be terribly honoured to play for the England tour team.'

England's new stars were to be given the sternest test on their return. The All Blacks came to England on tour for the first time in a decade. The post-Lions, early-season optimism had vanished by the time New Zealand came to Twickenham at the end of November. The tourists had travelled without Grant Fox (retired after 645 points), John Kirwan (dropped) and Michael Jones (broken jaw). The All Blacks had played some marvellous rugby, culminating in a 50-point thrashing of Scotland the week before. Yet they faced England under a cloud. The stamping of Phil de Glanville's face in the South-West game at Redruth was bad enough; the reaction and lack of action by the New Zealand management compounded the offence. The intensity and siege mentality of touring teams must be guarded against. Neil Gray, the manager, stated: 'After viewing the passage of play several times on video, it is clear to us that the injury was an unfortunate accident.' Gray also personally apologised to de Glanville. Cooke said at the time: 'I find it hard to understand that a New Zealand forward does not know when he is treading on someone's face.' Upon his return, Gray was sacked. The touring skipper Sean Fitzpatrick, the alleged assailant, kept quiet. The stamping on de Glanville only came to light on the BBC's *Rugby Special* the day after the match. Despite receiving 15 stitches very close to his left eye, de Glanville recovered to take his place alongside Carling. Guscott was having problems with a groin injury that eventually kept him out of the rest of the season and the tour to South Africa. Nigel Redman replaced

Phil de Glanville, his eye bandaged after a stamping incident, sits out the rest of the South-West's game against the All Blacks. *(Colorsport)*

Bayfield, still suffering from the Lions injury. Jonathan Callard took over at full back from the retired Jon Webb. England's plans were further disrupted when Morris dropped out two days before the match with influenza. Bristol's 22-year-old law student scrum half Kyran Bracken was launched into the big time.

Bracken was not overawed. He had a dream debut in England's 15–9 victory. Bracken's performance was all the more remarkable because All Black flanker Jamie Joseph had stamped on his ankle early on, long after the scrum half had got rid of the ball. This time the New Zealand management did take firm action and Joseph missed the Barbarians game. The afternoon was the first occasion on which Twickenham's new East Stand was full, and the crowd and players alike gave the modern structure a baptism to remember. Callard kicked four penalties, backed up by Andrew's dropped goal. The noise and tension in the final moments surpassed even the World Cup final. In 80 minutes of whole-hearted commitment, all doubts about England's capabilities were swept away. Here were the firm favourites for the 1994 Five Nations Championship. Carling had maintained the recovery begun towards the end of the Lions tour. This defeat of the All Blacks gave him his full set of victories over the rugby-playing countries. Carling had always been impressed by the New Zealanders' commitment and power. It meant a lot to him that England had outlasted them at Twickenham. This scalp is the one he treasures most. Yet England's captain felt it necessary to question the All Blacks' over-physical approach.

Brian Moore leads the celebrations after England beat the All Blacks 15–9 at Twickenham. *(Colorsport)*

## WILL CARLING

Beating New Zealand is the highlight of my career. No question. However exhilarating that victory over Australia was in my first game as captain, that All Black win was much better. We had been written off. They just demolished Scotland. It looked like nothing could stop them. While they were doing the *haka*, I was convinced we would win. There was a great desire to beat them. They are a great rugby nation. That's why I was disappointed to see their standards drop on the tour. I got into hot water when I questioned their behaviour. I was only voicing the views of Twickenham, who didn't have the courage to speak out. Some of their players went beyond the conventions we obey. I felt sad about the damage they had done to rugby's image. They were quite ready to be underhand if they thought it would serve their cause. Two England players were badly stamped that season – de Glanville against the All Blacks and Callard in South Africa. What happened? Precious little. The state of our shirts after the second Test in South Africa gave evidence of one of the main culprits – illegal studs. Referees have got to start checking them in the tunnel. I know players who have two sets of studs. One for the referee. The other for the game. The marks on Paul Hull's head after that Cape Town Test showed how they can be speared into flesh. It's a major problem. The authorities know about it. What are they doing?

Carling took things easy before the Five Nations Championship. A bout of influenza, his annual holiday and a shoulder injury kept him out of action until early January. Carling has always looked on the plus side of such enforced periods of inactivity. 'There is going to be no break between now and the tour of South Africa. I'll end up playing 25 games which I think is the maximum. As captain my first loyalty is to country rather than club and I have always appreciated how much Harlequins have helped me. As Geoff Cooke says, you've got to think of yourself as an international player who happens to play club rugby.' There was no need for Carling to hurry back. England sat out the first championship weekend. France thrashed Ireland, while Wales beat Scotland in the wet at Cardiff. Wales had not made the best of starts to the season as Canada recorded a first win at the National Stadium. Much of the Welsh recovery was due to the emergence of Scott Quinnell, son of three-time British Lion Derek, as a world-class forward.

The two victories on that opening Saturday were predictable. However, England's hopes did suffer a setback that day when Dean Richards damaged his elbow. That injury was to keep him out until the final match against Wales. Ben Clarke moved across to No. 8 with Neil Back making his long-awaited debut. England's back row suffered further disruption when Tim Rodber dropped out and veteran John Hall returned for the Calcutta Cup, a decade after making his England debut at Murrayfield as replacement. This trip to Scotland was Carling's 37th international in charge, taking him ahead of Australian Nick Farr-Jones. Carling had led his country's rugby side more often than anyone in rugby history. England celebrated that landmark with a win in one of the most frantic finishes seen in the Five Nations. It left Scotland captain Gavin Hastings in tears. Hastings thought Scotland had grabbed the Calcutta Cup back when Gregor Townsend dropped a goal on the stroke of full-time. Fortunately for England, there was enough time for a stray Scottish hand to give Jonathan Callard a final penalty chance which he took to secure a 15–14 victory.

That narrow escape began a torrid month for England and Carling. The first shock was a home defeat at Twickenham – the first in the championship in the six years of Carling's captaincy. Ireland came away with the spoils in a 13–12 triumph as England played as badly as they did at Murrayfield, failing for the fourth successive match to score a try. That surprise was nothing compared to what followed. To everyone's amazement, including Carling's, Geoff Cooke announced he was quitting. The man who gave Carling the captaincy in 1988, had helped England to enjoy one of its golden eras and was scheduled to stay until the 1995 World Cup, was stepping down after the 1994 Five Nations Championship. Cooke had already hit the headlines the day before by dropping a third of the side for the game in France. Callard, Tony Underwood, Back, Bayfield and Bracken were the five casualties. The clash in Paris was always going to be England's crunch game. Now it was even more important. The future of Carling's new England was on the line, along with its World Cup aspirations. Even three consecutive wins in Paris

Jonathan Callard's last-minute penalty that snatched the Calcutta Cup from Scotland's grasp in 1994. *(Colorsport)*

did not seem that comforting a statistic. England dug deep to extend that winning run. Rob Andrew took over the goal-kicking duties and scored all 18 points as the visiting defence stood firm against a fierce French onslaught. This was the first England appearance of the new Andrew goal-kicking style, which was to serve the national side so well in the year ahead. Andrew had gone to see kicking guru David Alred on the advice of Dick Best. Andrew was an experienced goal-kicker at international level and had been England's first choice at various times in his career, though often it was a role he avoided as he fought to hang on to the No. 10 jersey. Alred went back to scratch and Andrew emerged as a world-class kicker with a brand new technique. Paris was a tough test for him, but Andrew kept his nerve and was hailed the hero. It was another try-less display, but few were complaining. Although the win was recognised as a tribute to Cooke, it was a victory more for the future than the past.

Even before going to Paris, England knew they were the only obstacle between Wales and a first Grand Slam for 16 years. After the previous year's defeat in Cardiff, England needed no motivating to deny the Welshmen that prize. Also up for grabs was the championship. For the second year running England went into the final round of matches knowing that a win was not enough to take the title. The championship would be decided on points if

England beat Wales. Unlike 1993, England did finish with a win. It should have given them the title. Wales were not in England's class. But, after a promising start, the home side could not get the 15 point margin necessary and were forced to settle for a 15–8 victory and second place in the championship behind Wales. It was Welsh skipper Ieuan Evans who went up to receive the Five Nations trophy, although those claims looked rather false after England's obvious superiority.

WILL CARLING
It was a strange championship. After beating the All Blacks we prepared very thoroughly. I think Geoff and I forgot how inexperienced the side was. There were only a few survivors from Murrayfield 1990. I was convinced there was no way back after that last-minute dropped goal went over. I daren't even ask the referee how long there was to go. Then we were given that penalty. I couldn't help noticing how incredibly pale JC [Jonathan Callard] was as he was lining up the kick. After all that had happened, I didn't really expect that penalty to go over. I'd prepared myself for defeat. It was an enormous relief when it went over. Unfortunately, having escaped against Scotland, we failed to learn the lesson of that afternoon for the Irish match. There was almost the feeling that lightning couldn't strike twice. That we couldn't play that badly again. Well, we certainly did. This time we paid the penalty and lost. I accept at times that I wasn't in control. There were some things I tried to change when it was not going our way, but the players continued to do their own thing in the heat of the moment. Great sides don't just have one leader. After six years of not losing at home in the championship, it was hard to take. Not because it was my first defeat there to another Home Country, but because I don't like losing at Twickenham. France had always been billed as the crunch game. After those two opening displays, there was no way we could leave the side as it was. There were a lot of careers on the line that day in Paris. I was confident that we would win. I dread to think what would have happened had we lost.

I am not happy that the championship is now decided on points differ-ence. That's not just because England suffered the first two seasons it was introduced, 1993 and 1994. Points difference is irrelevant over four games. The Establishment keeps telling us that winning is not everything. If they need a winner, why not have a play-off between the two nations at a neutral venue? The receipts, which would be millions, could go to charity or to help look after injured players. I certainly wasn't dwelling on the points needed when we went into the Welsh game. I had one thing on my mind and one thing only. There was no way we were going to let Wales win the Grand Slam at Twickenham. They were not a great side. There were areas of weakness, although as usual they are a different prospect in Cardiff. The recent successes following that Canada defeat had done wonders for their confidence. I don't think that Wales felt like champions that day. There's not much satisfaction in receiving a trophy when you know you've been out-played and beaten convincingly.

I was totally taken aback by Geoff's quitting. I didn't know a thing about it or see it coming. I knew there were problems. I always thought he would see it through to the World Cup, despite the battles with the media and the RFU committees. I've still no real idea why Geoff chose that moment to call it a day. We had a selection meeting in his room for the French game. As we got up to leave, he just said: 'I'd better tell you that I am finishing after the Welsh game.' I wandered down the corridor in a daze wondering why and what the implications were. I turned to him and asked: 'Is that it? Is there no way I can persuade you to change your mind?' I don't know exactly what I meant by that. But it didn't matter. Geoff had made up his mind. I didn't feel let down. Why should I? Geoff was the man who had made me captain. I owed him, not the other way around. Geoff was like me. He kept things to himself, made up his own mind.

We have never been as close as I think some people imagined. He and I knew that it was very likely that at some stage he would have to drop me, either as captain or player or both. He didn't owe me anything, not even an explanation. I honestly think the continual back-biting and the continual questioning from the media eventually took their toll. He was fed up with the slog. I think he would have carried on if he had enjoyed the full support of the Union. Geoff was sacrificing a lot and still getting sniped at. The Lions tour also took a lot out of him. He did not enjoy the experience at all. His main job seemed to be making speeches and handing out ties. Geoff was used to calling the shots. Ian McGeechan did not call on his expertise or knowledge at all. Ian does everything himself. That's his style. As far as I'm concerned that was a poor use of resources on the Lions tour. Geoff was very down after the Lions tour. When Geoff took over, we were a 50–50 side, middle-of-the-road achievers in the northern hemisphere. The southern hemisphere boys didn't bother with England. We didn't have the confidence or the mental hardness to compete on a regular basis. With Geoff's guidance and strength, England have been the best side in the northern hemisphere in recent times. On our day, we can challenge and beat the best in the world. We are still not there. Yet Geoff's achievements are remarkable. The turnaround is unbelievable.

Carling did not dwell on the disappointments of the championship. He felt the side had come through stronger. England won three games out of four, finishing with wins in Paris and against the champions. If the displays against Scotland and Ireland had been second-rate, the team had responded well to the pressure those poor performances had created.

The departure of Cooke created much speculation about Carling and his future position within the England set-up. The man chosen to take over was Jack Rowell, who had spent 17 years transforming Bath into the premier rugby side in the land. Former England fly half Les Cusworth was brought in to assist Dick Best. Rowell said goodbye to Bath as they celebrated another league and cup double. Two Bath forwards were named 'Player of the Year': Nigel Redman was the recipient of the RFU's new award, while Ben Clarke picked up the Whitbread/*Rugby World* trophy.

WILL CARLING

Jack was the first choice. He was the only choice. I had had very little contact with him. I have a close friend who knows some of the Bath boys. The word came back very quickly that my days were over. 'Jack wants Stuart Barnes as fly half and captain.' I think a lot of people reacted the same way – Carling will go. Jack told me that 90 per cent of the press told him: 'You've got to get rid of Carling.' Fortunately for me, Jack makes up his own mind.

Rowell's first job was to pick an England party to tour South Africa in May and June. There were no surprises, although Neil Back missed out. It was difficult to imagine Cooke selecting a different squad. Rowell was to use the trip to examine England's strengths and weaknesses and judge what needed to be done if England were to win the 1995 World Cup. Rowell's plans were disrupted when Bracken and Hunter pulled out. So did Guscott on the morning of the Pilkington final, which the Quins failed to reach for the first time in three years.

England's tour started in Durban, where they would be based in the pool games the following year. They arrived in time to watch Queensland beat Natal in the final of the 'Super Ten'. It was high-class rugby, organised and unrelenting. The 'Super Ten' competition was playing a big part in rugby's growing commercial success in the southern hemisphere. In the weeks ahead England's rugby players were to find out just how far behind the north was. Defeat has never been a way of life for Carling in an England jersey. England lost four of the opening five tour games. The local referees were not helping, but England failed to find any authority or control. The pace and the power of the South Africans were causing England real problems and the tourists approached the first Test in seeming disarray. Another problem was the many outbreaks of violence. Martin Johnson was put out of the tour with concussion after being punched by Transvaal's prop Johan le Roux. Much of the refereeing was second-rate. England lost 24–21 to Transvaal, a game in which Carling had been denied a try when the referee missed his touchdown. The official later admitted his mistake.

England had given little hint of what was to happen in the first Test. Andrew turned his and England's tour on its head with an opening burst that left South Africa 23–0 down after less than a quarter of the match. South Africa never recovered. Andrew had been struggling, although the expected challenge from Stuart Barnes for the fly half spot never materialised and he announced his retirement at the end of the tour. Andrew contributed a record 27 points in England's 32–15 win, including the second try. It was a stunning team performance, from debut full back Paul Hull right through to loose-head Jason Leonard. All the pressure was now on the home side, trying to establish a unit that would challenge strongly for the World Cup. The South African selectors did not muck about. Six changes were made for the second Test in Cape Town.

Unfortunately for the tourists, they were distracted by a violent encounter against Eastern Province in midweek. Callard, a tour replacement for David Pears, needed 26 stitches after being stamped on the face. Then Tim Rodber became only the second England player to be sent off in an international. Carling watched from the relative safety of the sidelines. He has no doubt it is the most violent game he has witnessed. The South African referee gave four separate warnings for stamping. The two players sent off, Rodber and Simon Tremain, son of All Black Kel, went for fighting. The referee was widely acknowledged as one of the country's weaker officials. He offered prostrate players no protection. The tension between the players and the travelling committee members increased

Carling celebrates Ben Clarke's try during England's astonishing 32–15 victory at Pretoria. *(Colorsport)*

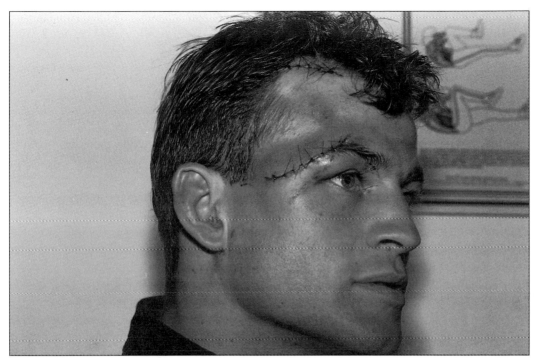

Jonathan Callard, with 26 stitches in his face, after being stamped on during England's midweek game against Eastern Province. *(Colorsport)*

when Rodber was not suspended. The three-man disciplinary committee, which included Rowell, regarded the sending-off as sufficient punishment. England's minds were focused away from the second Test as the row rumbled on all week. That was not all Carling had to deal with. The president of the South Africa Rugby Board, Dr Louis Luyt, made remarks about how much money Carling was making out of rugby. These snide comments were his only response to the growing criticism from visiting rugby officials and media about how far down the professional road South African rugby had gone.

The violence and the sniping conspired to take England's eye off the ball. Just as there had seemed no way England could win at Pretoria, there appeared no way the tourists could lose at Newlands. Carling did not share such optimism. England's captain had learnt a healthy respect for South African rugby in his month there. Pride and passion carries their rugby a long way. Carling was right. The home side came out of the traps like England had done the previous week. The touring defence was more solid and stood firm. That the sides were level, 3–3, at the interval was testimony to England's remarkable tackling and covering. Andrew kicked a penalty that reduced South Africa's lead to 12–9 with 12 minutes remaining. Andrew's delight turned to despair a minute later when he took his eye off a simple pass-back inside his own '22'. Hennie Muller went over on the blindside from the scrum and the contest was decided. A share of the series looked a good result, but Carling was disappointed after such an impressive display in the first Test.

## WILL CARLING

This tour was always going to be difficult. It was the first chance for Jack to make an assessment of us, as well as South Africa. And vice versa. This was an ideal tour a year before the World Cup. We certainly would not have been as well prepared if we hadn't gone. It was important for our players to see their style of rugby, the conditions, the effects of altitude and the size of the task ahead. It confirmed what we already suspected. You can't play conservative Five Nations rugby and expect to win against the big teams. Outside the national team, we don't have anything like Queensland, Natal, Transvaal or Auckland. The divisions in England are not the answer. Establishing five or six 'super' clubs is the only way it will work in England. The players' workload certainly must be cut. Every year I make the same plea – yet each year the demands increase. Twenty games is about right a season. England players are expected to play nearly double that. Bath are already a super club. The process has begun in England. Unfortunately, other countries are moving ahead quicker. It appears that some Establishment figures are trying to halt that natural process. If you want a good national team, you have got to compete.

The year after the Lions tour was hard. I had to prove myself to a lot of people, not least Geoff. He had seen me shot to pieces on the Lions tour. Then Geoff went and Jack Rowell took over. My role has been questioned so often. No matter what England or I achieve, there are still doubts. And then there is the money issue. Why should the president of another Union make a statement that I've made £1 million out of rugby? My accountant was on the phone wanting to know where it was. It was interesting to watch our hangers-on in South Africa trying to come to terms with the game in South Africa and how the top players are treated. It was obvious that England's 'amateur' game was not going to compete with professionals in the long term. After the Lions tour, the All Blacks was my crunch game. We won. Then England lost to Ireland and everything hinged on the French game. And we won. After a bad start to the South African tour, the first Test was another crisis point for me. Again we won. That's the way it is. I've had to live with that for a long time now.

Jack spent most of the tour watching, deciding what he liked and didn't like. He was very much the observer. Geoff was a very organised manager. I knew what was happening all the time. Jack is different. The level of communication is not as high. I felt on trial. That's Jack's way. Part of me likes that challenge. We've had our disagreements and heated arguments about how we go about things. But I have a very healthy respect for him. The bottom line is that it's all about England winning. Jack doesn't go in for the sort of detail that Geoff did. He's much more a delegater.

# CHAPTER 12

# HAT-TRICK OF TWICKENHAM GRAND SLAMS – 1995

Carling was back in action the Saturday after the second South African Test. This time there were no dejected faces or upsets. Carling married Julia Smith, with a star-studded reception at Castle Ashby. The honeymoon took him straight back to southern Africa. The couple spent time in Zimbabwe, Mozambique and at the Victoria Falls. Julia has never been star-struck or over-awed by Will's world. She runs her own successful business and has become a celebrity in her own right. 'Jules' Smith is one of the presenters on VH-1, the new all-music video channel. She outstrips her husband in one department: Julia is more adept and happier at handling the press. She does not find them as much of an intrusion. For the first time in a Carling relationship, England's rugby captain had an equal. Julia is someone who casts her own shadow and tells him what she thinks, not what she thinks he wants to hear. The fact that the pair were friends first has given the partnership a solid base. That helped the couple cope when Carling's friendship with Princess Diana hit the headlines in 1995. Carling has never hidden the fact that he is a 'man's man'. It's been his friends and family to whom he has turned with his real thoughts and worries, not his partners.

England's captain has never been totally at ease with the 'sex symbol' role. At the start such attention flattered and amused him. As English rugby became more successful and his own profile mushroomed, he became embarrassed. Carling positively squirmed when *Good Morning*'s Judy Finnegan and Richard Madeley interviewed him to discuss rugby's growing sex appeal before the 1991 World Cup. The best Carling could do was admit he was 'fanciable'. He knew the problem was partly self-inflicted. He had, after all, appeared oiled up with his shirt off in a Sunday colour magazine. Such shots gave Carling's team-mates plenty of ammunition, as did headlines that asked 'Will Carling ever find a girl to make him happy?' That brought this response from one unnamed Harlequins colleague: 'Will is too intelligent and conscious of press interest in him to be caught with some old boiler of a barmaid in his hotel room.' Rob Andrew and the England squad were amused by his repeated 'I'm in love. This is the big one' statements, and there has always been a big dressing-room interest in Carling's fan-mail.

Carling and his bride Julia on their wedding day in June 1994. Their honeymoon saw Will returning to southern Africa soon after the England tour to that region.

WILL CARLING

There were married women, enclosing pictures and saying please call this number and come round when my husband is out. I used to open all my mail in the early days, even the letters that had been sent care of Harlequins and Twickenham. I became so shocked at some of the explicit things I read, I asked for them to be opened first. I never accepted any of the inducements the lads offered me to pass on the best ones. I've never been a great flirt. I can't handle women coming on. It's not just women who have a perceived idea of what I'm like. It's an effort to break that down. Often, I don't bother. Hero worship from kids I understand, but it seems such adulation has no age boundaries. I find it hard to handle when grown-ups approach me in the same manner. The people who don't push themselves forward are probably the types I would get on with best. If a woman did the running and tried to corner me I was out the door. I can't stand being crowded. I'm rather traditional that way. Basically, I'm an out-and-out man's man. I'm not uneasy with women, but I'm more comfortable in men's company.

I have a great respect for the guys who play rugby, but not when it comes to rugby coupled with beer, dirty songs and abusing women. You can leave me out. I know that some of the older brigade are sad that this way of life has ceased to exist. It doesn't matter. I would never have fitted into that mould. I find it mindless. I'm not comfortable in a big rugby environment among large groups of people. I don't like standing around in the Harlequins clubhouse because I don't get a chance to talk to the people I want to. That's a problem for me. Wives and girlfriends of players are very loyal. I've had a few words said in my direction when they've not been happy. Geoff involved the families more and that continued with the wives coming out to South Africa during the World Cup. I don't disagree with that. The support from home is vital, especially given all the time the players are away. But you can't include them in everything. Wives can never be involved in team matters. A few question selection. It's human nature. They want their man to be successful. I understand that. I would never discuss those sort of decisions with them. It's never become a problem. Susie Ackford, Sara Andrew and Karen Hill liked to talk about matches with me. I find the safest thing is to agree with them. I'm pleased that they enjoy rugby, but discussing selection with them is the last thing I want.

Carling is not one of rugby's legendary drinkers. During the 1992 summer split from Victoria, Carling would accompany Peter Winterbottom and Jason Leonard on a 'mission to get drunk'. Regular outside contact with his team-mates was not normal Carling behaviour and tended to occur only when he was unattached. That was just as well. Carling rarely lasted the pace. More often than not he would be sent home tired and emotional to allow the serious drinkers to get on with the serious business. Carling is not a big drinker or a frequent one. He sees no point in wasting hard-earned fitness. Drink can be a release, often after a tough international. Occasionally it allows Carling to get something off his chest, as with his clash with Eddie Butler after the Barbarians game in 1992. Carling is aware that he has to be careful, even in the relaxed atmosphere of post-match celebrations. There are eavesdropping ears or eyes for the indiscreet word or deed as the press continue to probe, or committee men give Carling the benefit of their thoughts on the day's proceedings or rugby's changing ways. Everyone wants to talk to Will Carling.

The growing influence of the World Cup was never more evident than during the 1994–95 season. All roads, selections and strategy led to South Africa. Those who feared that these changes might diminish the Five Nations Championship have not been proved right. If anything, World Cup objectives have heightened the interest in the northern hemisphere's dress rehearsal. Coaches find tolerance for World Cup objectives in short supply after two championship defeats. The season started with the leading players still unsure about their club and country requirements. The national squad had been planning meticulously for this World Cup for a long time. The RFU organisers of the Courage Leagues had not reacted in any way. England players could be involved in key club matches right up to the World Cup. When Courage launched the new season, Carling was there to ask the powers that be how many matches an England squad member should play. He did not get an answer. 'The pressure of club versus country – and the World Cup – is something the England squad are talking about all the time. It's unfair on the likes of Dewi Morris, captain of Orrell, and Tim Rodber, Brian Moore and Dean Richards, all of whom are captains of their clubs, to leave them in a situation in which they are having to decide where their loyalties lie. We must accept the World Cup is incredibly powerful as a marketing tool. The effect after the 1991 World Cup was quite staggering. A flop in South Africa in 1995 would have a detrimental effect on English rugby. We must be really fresh when we go out there. I believe that means playing no more than 22–24 games.'

The aftermath of the summer tour lingered on. A month after England came home Elandre van der Berg was cleared of deliberately raking Callard. The scarred Englishman was not alone in stating: 'It's a bloody disgrace.' South Africa were on tour in New Zealand at the time. Less than a fortnight after van der Berg's exoneration, prop Johan le Roux, who had laid out Martin Johnson during England's tour, was sent home and given a 19-month ban after biting All Black captain Sean Fitzpatrick's ear. South Africa lost two Tests and drew the other. When manager Janie Engelbrecht and coach Ian McIntosh were not removed on their return, Louis Luyt, the SARB president, resigned. 'I said that unless the Springboks' team management was changed, I would stand down and that is what I'm doing.' Two days later Luyt was back after intervention by South Africa's sports minister, Steve Tshwete. Luyt got his way: McIntosh was dismissed a fortnight later, with Kitch Christie taking over. Engelbrecht was also replaced before the World Cup by Morne du Plessis.

England made changes, too. Dick Best was surplus to Rowell's requirements and was sacked after three years. His record of 13 wins in 17 matches had been impressive. His dismissal once again cast doubts over Carling's future as captain. These were removed in late September when Rowell announced that Carling would be carrying on. Tim Rodber had been mooted as a likely successor, but his sending-off in South Africa delayed any thoughts in that direction. Rowell's 'hands-on' approach was confirmed when it was announced that he was leaving his employers, Dalgety, at the end of the year to concentrate on his rugby commitments. Eventually, some agreement was reached about the players' club responsibilities. Squad members would play two games in April. This was billed as a 'voluntary arrangement depending solely on the players'. Already Carling's club was struggling. After beating Sale by a point, the Quins lost to Wasps and Bristol. Home defeats by Leicester and Orrell on successive Saturdays in October made the situation worse.

Carling made his 50th full appearance for England against Romania in November, his 43rd in charge. The good news was that Jeremy Guscott was back, 20 months after his last England cap. Stuart Barnes felt that Carling should have been the centre to make way for him. 'Even Carling's most loyal supporters would find it hard to refute that Jerry Guscott's return should have been at Carling's expense, not de Glanville's.' The other change saw Johnson return for Redman. Dean Richards's absence led some to believe that Clarke was now the likely World Cup No. 8. Nothing could be further from the truth. Rowell was not happy with Clarke's form and this was his chance to impress. Once again the players' battles with the RFU flared up just as they were trying to concentrate their minds on international rugby. An advertisement for a medical insurance scheme, the Hospital Saving Association from Andover, featuring the England captain in a dark suit, plain shirt and coloured tie, was twice rejected from the match programme. Carling was not distracted on the day as England triumphed 54–3, scoring six tries, one of them by the skipper as he celebrated becoming the sixth England member of the 50 cap club. England's pack had learnt some of their lessons from South Africa. Romania went long periods

Carling became the sixth England player to reach a half-century of caps in the November 1994 match against Romania at Twickenham. *(Colorsport)*

without the ball and only determined defence kept England from leading a real rout. Scotland and Wales faced stiffer tests with the visit of South Africa. Scotland were given a hiding, while Wales led before losing 20–12. England were given a far closer contest by Canada than the 60–19 scoreline suggested. Richards and Bracken had been restored to the side, while Bath's Mike Catt replaced Paul Hull at full back after 25 minutes. All three remained for the rest of the season. Andrew's new kicking technique gave him a 100 per cent record, 12 kicks out of 12, equalling Didier Camberabero's world record 30 points. His five penalties in the first half gave England the platform to score six tries, all from the backs, after the interval.

WILL CARLING

It always amuses me when people look at those sort of margins against teams like Romania and Canada and think they're a doddle. Nothing could be further from the truth. You're in a no-win situation. Anything less than a runaway win is regarded as failure. Romania and especially Canada were tough opposition. Look how hard they made Australia and South Africa work in the World Cup. Our support play was very good against Canada. Putting 60 points on them was an achievement. The first half was very tough, then we broke free. Those games are very hard mentally. You daren't relax. It was in the Canada game that I first thought about Rob's new style goal-kicking: 'This is a different ball game.' His confidence was different and it also helped make him confident in other areas. Rob's improvement with the boot allowed us to play an attacking full back and that gave us many more options. It's a mark of Rob the man that he went away with David Alred and started all over again. It's so important to have a world-class goal-kicker in your side, especially when sides are trying to stifle you. You must punish them for the morale of your side. Canada was a classic case. Rob gave us the cushion that allowed us to play more expansively. It's important too for the opposition to be made aware that they can't kill the ball and get away with it.

England headed for Lanzarote for their traditional New Year break. At least the World Cup organisers could not tamper with those arrangements. The England tour management had scouted around South Africa during the summer tour to find the best places for their campaign the following year. England's pool base was in Durban. Rowell wanted the best. The choice was the five-star Beverley Hills resort outside the city. The organisers decided differently. Chairman Sir Ewart Bell declared: 'We want a level playing field. It's fair and proper.' England now found themselves staying at the three-star Marine Parade in the centre of town. Even Rowell's appearance at the Managers' Meeting in South Africa at the end of November failed to sway the organisers, although England did move half a mile up the road, to the three-star North Beach. Worse was to follow when it was decided that the last eight teams would fly to Johannesburg, irrespective of where their quarter-final matches were. Carling found these changes annoying, especially as England had worked so hard to get things right.

Left to their own devices, the England team's session in Lanzarote went well, despite injury scares to Leonard, Clarke and Ubogu. Carling proved he was at the top of his form as Harlequins drew at home to Sale. The XV to travel to Dublin was named two days later. Catt's promotion was confirmed. Ireland had beaten England in two successive championships, something none of the other countries had managed while Carling was in charge. The England captain woke on the morning of the match to a gale, conditions tailor-made for the rampaging Irish. Players had to jog around during breaks in play to keep warm. The 20–8 victory confirmed England's progress and yet another bid for a Grand Slam and World Cup. Carling was outstanding in defence and attack, scoring England's first try after six minutes. The heroes of Dublin were the England forwards, with the only arguments about whether the man of the match was Richards, Clarke or Rodber. Unlike previous dominating displays by the England pack, this was one of pace as well as power. The tour of South Africa had taught them that one was no good without the other. A rare blemish was the yellow card, the first in the championship, shown to Clarke for over-vigorous rucking near his Bath team-mate, Irish wing Simon Geoghegan.

Carling charges past Brendan Mullin in Dublin in 1995 with Ben Clarke in support. The pair had clashed over a decade earlier when Blackrock College visited Sedbergh. *(Colorsport)*

No one was surprised when Rowell named an unchanged side to face France, who had also got off to a winning start. The French, who had won two Tests in New Zealand in the summer, were once again rated the most serious threat to England. The French coach Pierre Berbizier dropped lock Olivier Merle for disciplinary reasons after Welsh prop Ricky Evans was head-butted just before he fell and broke his leg in two places. The old Anglo-French hostility surfaced when Berbizier reacted angrily to former England manager Cooke describing Merle as a 'hit man'. At Twickenham, the French forwards had too much to do coping with the English pack to worry about getting involved in anything underhand. Rodber, Richards and company were even more awesome than they had been in Dublin and gave the Twickenham faithful another afternoon to remember. The home side led 13–3 at the interval after Guscott's first international try since his return. France fought back at the start of the second half with a typical try from deep in their own territory, but two more penalties for Andrew restored England's advantage. England finished in style with a brace of tries from Tony Underwood, who ignored some barging from Saint-André in the chase for the first. The injection of pace from Catt, who had a marvellous afternoon, created the second for the 31–10 victory. The talk was now not just of a Grand Slam, but about England being favourites for the World Cup.

WILL CARLING

I can't argue that the World Cup didn't dominate everything last season. That's a fact of life from now on. Selection and style of play are geared towards the next World Cup, whether it's three years or one year away. That's what all the countries are building towards – not the next Five Nations or the Lions tour, which I don't think will take place. It's always in the back of your mind. Every performance is assessed in relation to the World Cup. Despite those victories over Ireland and France, I still feel we are too conservative in the Five Nations.

We had planned a fast, direct game in Dublin. I couldn't believe it when I woke up to that gale. It couldn't have been worse. My first real problem was winning the toss. Should I play into the wind or not? The lads were very keyed up, but if I gave Ireland the wind and they went nine points up, it might just be the lift they needed. I decided to do that. That first half was our best 40 minutes of the championship. We did a professional job. In a way it looked much easier than it was. People underestimate year-in, year-out what it means to the other countries to beat England. When you look in rugby's *Who's Who*, you will find that the highlight of most careers is the last time they beat England – or the first. That says it all. By and large, the England game is the most important match for everyone else. Dublin was our best half. France was our best game. Our concentration and lineout was very good. Strangely, that night afterwards was the best that we have ever had with the French team. There has been a lot of trial and tension between the teams in my time. Sella said afterwards that it was the first time the French had felt they had been beaten fair and square by the better English side.

There was little doubt that influence of Rowell was being strongly felt, and was working. Carling had responded to the presence of a new face in charge. Rowell had his suspicions confirmed in South Africa that too many senior England players were enjoying the benefits of the 'comfort zone'. That may not have been their fault. Cooke had been in charge for six seasons. As Carling knows, it's not easy or always possible to come up with something new every time. The players in South Africa also showed Rowell that they were prepared to listen and change and respond to a new challenge. The new coach was impressed, especially with the extra time they agreed to put in at squad sessions through-out the season in search of the ultimate prize.

So far, so good. Almost too good. Rowell had got England's static power pack moving, and moving at pace. Ireland and France had not been able to contain the momentum created. Neither could Wales. This was the least impressive of the three championship outings so far, but it was still too good for a Welsh scrum still struggling to come to terms with the loss of Scott Quinnell, who had joined Wigan early in the season. Again, England's support play was mightily impressive, though Bracken and Andrew had a hesitant day at half back. The papers focused on the opening try by Victor Ubogo. The Bath prop had backed himself to score the first at odds of 14–1 – or so he thought. It transpired the bet was not laid. The other tries came from Rory Underwood, who has not always

Victor Ubogu's 14–1 try against Wales in 1995. Unfortunately, so the story goes, the friend delegated to put on the £100 bet for the Bath prop kept the money in his pocket. *(Colorsport)*

found Cardiff a happy hunting ground. Underwood showed clinical efficiency in touching down twice in the left corner. Wales prop John Davies was sent off after an hour after kicking Clarke on the head. It was not a typical moment. Davies' red card earned him a 60-day suspension. For safety reasons, his dismissal meant back-row forward Hemi Taylor also left the field to allow prop Huw Williams-Jones to come on and shore up the scrum. There was no provision for this in the laws, but Carling happily agreed with Ieuan Evans' request. This time there was no deafening silence from Carling and England in victory at the National Stadium.

Only Scotland stood between England and a third Grand Slam in five years. Only Scotland! Gavin Hastings and his team had looked washed up when South Africa hammered them at Murrayfield. Yet Scotland stole much of England's Cardiff thunder that weekend by recording their first win in Paris for 26 years and their first ever at the Parc des Princes. As in 1990, England had a month off. As in 1990, Scotland had to beat Wales to set up another 'all-or-nothing' Grand Slam decider, this time at Twickenham.

WILL CARLING
There was certainly a change in Cardiff. I went out for a walk on the Friday with Ben Clarke and Phil de Glanville. Normally, we put on our caps and turn the collars up. When the usual taunts start, we smile and keep moving. This was strange. 'Have a good game tomorrow, lads,' greeted us. It was rather unsettling. For the first time in Cardiff, the singing before the game was not as intimidating. Ieuan Evans mentioned it in his speech afterwards. Maybe Wales have a little bit more respect for English rugby these days. Maybe they believe the English aren't as arrogant as they thought. The Lions tours of 1989 and 1993 helped the relationships between the two teams. I enjoyed my time with the Welsh boys in New Zealand. That's not to say we weren't tense. You never know at Cardiff. There's still an aura about the place, although the edge has gone for the moment. It was our second win there in three trips. Before the game we were reminded that we had only won once there since 1963. I'm sure when the side goes down in 1997, the telling statistic for Wales will be that England have only won twice in Cardiff in 34 years. There's huge hype every time we go down there. Rory worked hard for those two tries. I was pleased for him after all the stick he took in 1993. He didn't lose that game. No one person loses a match. Anyway, if that's the case, then Rory Underwood has won more games for England than anyone else.

Scotland overcame Wales and the 1990 Grand Slam hype started up all over again. As five years earlier, England had been in outstanding form, while Scotland were the surprise package. This time England had the home advantage. The Scots had only ever won four matches at Twickenham. Before the match Carling announced that he would not be retiring after the World Cup.

Rowell had told Carling that he wanted him to lead England to that tournament before the Five Nations. Carling has always been sensible about not being too definite about his future plans. Experience has taught him how quickly the tide can turn after one or two bad results.

Expectations were now sky-high for the World Cup. England's barnstorming championship made it difficult to feel otherwise. Carling was careful not to be distracted. The pain of 1990 was still there. Ticket prices defied the recession with the top pairs going for £5,000. The arguments about the merits of Hastings and Carling as captains resurfaced, as did their rivalry with revelations that the pair had not spoken since the Lions tour. Carling was well used to the hype. He knows there are some arguments that he will never win. Scotland proved to be as much of a problem on the park as they had been throughout Carling's eight-year England career. The home side could not breach the Scotland try-line and had to rely on the boot of Rob Andrew to produce another 24 points. It was enough to complete Carling's third Grand Slam in charge. Andrew became England's leading point-scorer of all time with 317, taking him ahead of Webb. England were never clear, but were never threatened.

Moore, never short of words, put the blame for the lack of spectacle firmly at the door of the Tartan Army: 'We were wilfully prevented from playing as we would have liked by a team that was intent on killing the ball – and the game – at all costs. They spent the whole game offside, killing the ball or preventing its quick release. At every ruck they were at it – offside, over the top, hands

Carling in possession against the Scots at Twickenham in 1995 in another all-or-nothing Grand Slam battle against the 'auld enemy'. This time there was no mistake. (Colorsport)

England have owed much to Rob Andrew's new goal-kicking style over the past 18 months. The Scots suffer on this occasion as England's fly half contributes all 24 points in this 1995 Grand Slam victory. *(Colorsport)*

scooping the ball back. You name it, they did it. It was a disgrace and made you want to turn around and kick them. A pity you can't. They came to do very little and did it superbly. I am disappointed for the supporters.' The contents of his mailbag were something to behold over the next week or so. Some of those from over the Border were so incensed that they even invested in first-class stamps.

Carling had personal experience of Scotland's indiscipline when prop Peter Wright was shown a yellow card for trampling on England's captain.

## WILL CARLING

I wasn't sure that Grand Slam game would be on. I thought Wales would cause them problems. I don't think that the most ardent Scottish supporter in his wildest dreams would have imagined that his side would be travelling to Twickenham in search of a Grand Slam. I was glad they were on a high. Had they carried on the season like they started, they might not have been perceived as a big threat. Although the hype was similar to 1990, the situation was not. I was certainly much older and wiser. That Grand Slam defeat didn't play a big part in our preparations. Not that many of the side had been there. We did underestimate them that day five years ago. We were not going to make the same mistake again. Basically I saw no way the Scots could ambush on our home patch at Twickenham.

I always felt in control, but it was a frustrating match. We weren't fluent.

England's 1995 Grand Slam success was based largely on the dynamic form of the back row – Ben Clarke, Dean Richards and Tim Rodber. Here Clarke takes on the Scots. *(Colorsport)*

We were too powerful in the end, although we couldn't really overcome their tactics. When you look at the two teams, there was no contest. But every year the Scots cause us problems. England is a huge challenge for them. Three Grand Slams. The first in 1991 was brilliant because it was the first. The second in 1992 just seemed to happen. We were still on a high from the World Cup and scored 30 points each game. The following two seasons were frustrating because we were good enough to do it. I really wanted another Grand Slam. So did the lads. So did Jack. He's used to success. It took a bit of pressure off. He was looking to develop a style for the World Cup, but we couldn't afford a poor Five Nations. Jack's arrival was a bit like Geoff's style in the early days. Jack gets all the players to think what and why they are doing things. Jack paints a broad picture of what he wants. He leaves it to the players to sort it out. I felt sorry for Dick Best. He had done a good job. But I've seen a lot of players dropped. You can't cry in your beer and say 'that's unfair'. I'm not being ruthless or heartless. You've got to get on with the job. If the situation had been the other way around, I would have expected Dick to react the same way.

Jack had wandered down to the Petersham before one of the pre-championship games. 'By the way, I want you to captain in the World Cup.' That's Jack's way. People always made a lot of how, as long as Geoff was there, I would be captain. I've never gone along with that. Geoff was a realist. I'm sure he was close to getting rid of me in 1993.

One of the advantages of the Five Nations Championship having a trophy these days is that it allows the victorious skipper and his team to drink out of it. *(Colorsport)*

No sooner had the Grand Slam celebrations died down than England announced their World Cup squad. The trio of unlucky players were Hull, Redman and John Hall. Hull was particularly unlucky after his magnificent form in the two Tests in South Africa. Catt had come in and revelled in the space at full back, giving England extra attacking options. England felt the need for goal-kicking back-up for Andrew, so Callard was given the job as the number two full back. Redman had been the 'Player of the Year' the previous May. Unfortunately, however the Bath lock worked, there was no way he could grow half a dozen inches. With Simon Shaw ruled out by injury, the third second-row spot went to Gloucester's 6ft 10in Richard West. Size had often counted against Neil Back, but he was given the nod ahead of the veteran Hall. Rowell had plenty of No. 8 and blindside options with Richards, Clarke, Rodber and Ojomoh. He needed cover for a tearaway flanker. Rowell explained: 'The most difficult responsibility for a coach or chairman of selectors is to tell a player that he is not required. I've made those calls to Hall, Redman and Hull, a charming young man. Upset as they are, their bitter disappointment is for the right reasons. It would be professional suicide not to go into a match with a "professional" goal-kicker – or not to have one in reserve. In the present set-up that means Jonathan Callard, a proven kicker at international and club level, must be the reserve.'

While all thoughts should have been turned towards that departure date in the middle of May, the England players got caught up in crunch relegation battles, just as Rowell and the squad had feared and predicted at the start of the season. There was no escape for Carling as Harlequins and Northampton battled to avoid the one relegation place. Quins' fears were eased the week after the Grand Slam with a 10–9 victory at the Stoop over their rivals. Seven days later Bath again ended their Pilkington Cup hopes at the semi-final stage at the Stoop. Carling thought his interest was over in that competition as Bath lined up to meet Wasps in the final. Yet the date of that final, 6 May, was to have particular significance in the Will Carling story.

April was fairly hectic, too. Quins, without their England stars, lost to Leicester, while Northampton won. The Saints now had eight points, with Quins and West Hartlepool level on nine. The internationals returned for the trip to Orrell, where the London club had never won in the 21 years of travelling up the M6. Both Quins and West Hartlepool eased relegation worries with wins. Northampton lost by a point at Gloucester. West Hartlepool moved clear the following Saturday, but Northampton moved to within a point of Quins. The Quins, who let a 19–3 lead slip against Bath, were not happy that Wasps kept electing not to kick penalties against the Saints. Moore, Leonard and Carling returned for the final League Saturday at Gloucester. Quins needed to win to make sure of staying up. Moore, who was relinquishing the captaincy, announced his retirement from first-class rugby. 'I don't want to be seen to be jumping the sinking ship if we go down,' was the reason from England's hooker. Quins did escape, despite Northampton's win at West Hartlepool. It was an emotional day for Moore and Mike Teague, who was also calling it a day. In fact, it was a mentally draining month for many of England's World Cup stars. Dean Richards recovered from his rib injury sustained in the Grand Slam game to lead Leicester to the Courage title. It was a special moment for a special servant of Welford Road. Now all Jack Rowell had to do was get his Bath and Wasps players safely through the Pilkington Cup final, and England were South-Africa bound. Or so he thought.

# CHAPTER 13

# LOMU LOOMS LARGE – 1995 WORLD CUP

The World Cup has become the biggest event in a modern rugby player's career. In three tournaments going back to 1987, it has established itself as one of the major sporting events, alongside the Olympics and the soccer World Cup. Its success is staggering considering the 'amateur' standards that have been maintained in organisation and commercial dealings. There is little doubt that the Rugby World Cup has been sold drastically short. Its finances are shrouded in secrecy, but too much of the revenue generated goes in non-rugby directions. The organisers proudly announced projected profits of £20 million in South Africa the day before the final. A month later the Wimbledon fortnight topped that by £10 million. The profits should be ten times that. Not that the players benefit, anyway. The rugby stars gather together not only to find the best team in the world, but to compare notes about growing professionalism in the game. It has done little for Carling's and England's tolerance levels to see themselves lagging way behind the southern hemisphere in money matters as well as rugby affairs.

There was little doubt as England set off to South Africa in May that rugby life would never be the same after the third World Cup. The tournament had come a long way in eight years. The first, won convincingly by New Zealand, produced profits of only £1.5 million, way below the total predicted. England received only £46,000 as their share and found themselves out of pocket to the tune of £79,000. That inaugural event had been played in Australia and New Zealand. The strongest subsequent recommendation was that one country only should organise the tournament and travelling should be kept to a minimum. So, naturally, Rugby World Cup 1991 was held in five countries, the Five Nations, with the final at Twickenham. The RFU put up a marketing package for the event in 1988 with £20 million worth of deals in the bag. But a Scotland-led objection put paid to that offer and the marketing arrangements were offered outside. That has caused problems Rugby World Cup has yet to solve. Despite the trouble with sponsorship, promotion and marketing, the event was a great popular success, thanks to England's appearance in the final and tremendous support from the print media and ITV.

South Africa had been awarded the 1995 tournament with almost indecent haste. Nelson Mandela had hardly appeared before the world's TV cameras after being freed before the Republic was being touted as a possible venue. Part of the problem was that the organisers had used up seven major countries in the first two World Cups. France had not been scheduled to host a group in 1991, but did in the end. The same has happened with the 1999 tournament, which will be hosted by Wales, but will involve four other nations. South Africa certainly had the rugby grounds and facilities to host a World Cup, but the hotel and airline infrastructure was rather lacking. Problems with match tickets and travel packages were also evident in South Africa, with ticket prices so high as to leave many grounds half empty.

The players are only too aware of the money the Rugby World Cup makes. The teams had to make do with three-star hotels, while the officials spent most of the month holed up in the lavish luxury of the Sandton Sun, in one of Johannesburg's exclusive suburbs. The England players have been involved in a constant battle with the RFU over money in recent times. World Cups tend to prove the players' case. While the Union can sell the jersey, the match and the players, the players cannot sell themselves. It was way back in 1989 that it appeared the International Rugby Board would introduce trust funds for players. But with Dudley Wood, secretary of the RFU, in pole position to defend 'amateurism', the die-hards had no worries. Even when the IRB allowed players to cash in on non-rugby-related matters, the RFU stood firm. Appearing in a Twickenham programme was 'rugby-related', even if the players were advertising soap, sandals or sacks of sugar. Every time the players believed progress was being made, the RFU and Wood would slam the door in their faces.

Wood, after his attempt to remove Carling, was in his final days of office as England flew out to South Africa. His imminent retirement gave the players a glimmer of hope for the future. Kerry Packer had already announced details of his Super Rugby League to be played in the summer months. All through the World Cup and in the weeks that followed rarely a day passed without stories, some even genuine, of massive deals for rugby unions and players. The first sign the players got that little had changed was a flight to Cape Town from Durban and back again in a day for a World Cup Opening luncheon. The England team had to get up at six in the morning. They were amazed to find the Welsh squad on the plane when they boarded. The Welsh players had got up even earlier in Bloemfontein for a round trip that was to take all of the day and most of the night, and was certainly round the houses. When the players sat down for lunch, the heavens opened and the giant marquee leaked all over. Most of the England squad wondered what they were doing there. Dean Richards had escaped, staying in Durban for treatment on his damaged hamstring.

Carling and the squad quickly settled into their Durban surroundings, eager for their opening game against Argentina. There were 10 days to wait before the off. The biggest interruption to England's careful plans came in the opening game between the holders and the hosts. The losers were almost certain to face England in Cape Town at the quarter-final stage. Whatever the outcome of that first match, England were not going to have an easy game. It was just they expected that opposition to be South Africa. It was Australia. All over South

Carling decides to go topless in the warm waters around Durban as he waits for the 1995 World Cup to kick off. *(Colorsport)*

The worried faces of the England management team as Carling's side struggles to beat Argentina in the first match. From the left: Les Cusworth, John Elliott and Jack Rowell. *(Colorsport)*

Africa were posters of the one coloured player in the national squad, Chester Williams, with the message: 'The waiting is over.' Unfortunately, injury had forced Williams to withdraw a few days earlier. After a lavish opening ceremony and an emotional welcome speech from President Mandela, South Africa defeated the World Cup holders fairly convincingly. Joel Stransky, whose kicking was also to play a vital role in the final, contributed 22 points including a try. The other South African try came from Pieter Hendriks, who left David Campese for dead, though Hendriks' World Cup was not to have the happy ending of Stransky's. The holders looked sluggish. They had lost their direct route to the final. 'Forget the rhino, save the Wallaby' proclaimed one banner. Carling would now be facing the old enemy, Campo and Australia, in the quarter-final. One of the 1991 World Cup finalists was going home early in 1995. Friday's results were more predictable, with wins for Canada, France and Scotland, whose captain Gavin Hastings scored 44 points.

England had already selected the side for the Argentina clash. The change of emphasis saw the inclusion of Dewi Morris at Kyran Bracken's expense. Morris had spent the entire 1991 campaign on the replacements' bench. He was quitting after this World Cup and must have worried that the same could happen again. The hamstring injury to Richards was still a problem, giving Steve Ojomoh a chance at No. 8. England, after two sessions a day early in the week, eased up as the match approached and even gave themselves a day off. Just as well. England gave one of their most lethargic displays in recent years and were lucky to beat

Argentina 24–18, despite the appearance of rain which should have made them feel at home. That man Andrew and his boot was again the saviour who produced all the points, England's forwards showing none of the momentum that had made them such a potent force in Europe the previous winter. England led 15–0 early in the second half, but the power of the Argentina scrum unsettled them as defensive mistakes let in two tries. The final try came after Carling had left the field: England's skipper had damaged his ankle and was out of Wednesday's match against Italy, ending a run of 44 consecutive matches as captain. England's poor performance on that opening Saturday was rather overshadowed by the dramatic emergence of 19st 7lb All Black wing Jonah Lomu, who had battered and bulldozed the Irish all over Ellis Park. Lomu was still on the horizon for England – if they ever got that far.

The Italians were rated England's easiest opponents. This was the game in which the second string would have expected a run-out. Rowell now had a problem. It was blatantly obvious that his big guns were short of more than just a gallop and needed match experience. Graham Rowntree and Neil Back came into the scrum, while Bracken replaced Morris. De Glanville took Carling's place in the centre and Andrew led England for the second time. Western Samoa's spirited recovery over Argentina did not bode well for England's final pool match. Neither did the Italy game. Rowell rated England's 27–20 victory a step up from Argentina. All things are relative. Once again 17 points from the boot of Andrew was the difference between the sides. England led 16–0, but gifted two tries just before the interval. They restored their advantage, but once again failed to show any real control in the wet. Rowell was running out of time to get England's act in gear. He was not the only one. Australia had yet to discover anything like 1991 form.

The two play-off games on that second weekend were Scotland against France to see who avoided new favourites New Zealand, and Wales versus Ireland to see who would meet the winners of that first match. Wales failed to make the last eight for the second tournament in a row, while the Scots lost to a last-minute try by Emile Ntamack after leading throughout. England's side for the last pool game was no dress rehearsal for the quarter-final. The good news was that Richards was back. So was Carling, and Graham Dawe, whose last cap had been in the first World Cup. Richard West was to make his debut. Callard was named full back, with Catt moving to fly half. One-time England full back Ian Hunter came in on the wing. This was very much a damage-limitation side. Should Rowell give his first choice one last run or allow the understudies a chance to move up? It was a bit of both. England's 44–24 win did allow all members of the squad a game as John Mallett and Damien Hopley came on for their first caps. By the final whistle Back, Richards, Carling, Rowntree and Rodber had retired from the fray. To Carling's relief, the England juggernaut was moving at last. There was no danger that Rowell's charges had peaked too soon or left their best rugby in the pool games.

The highlights from the 24 pool matches were South Africa's victory over Australia, France's fightback against Scotland and the All Blacks' 21-try annihilation of Japan. The lowlight was the South Africa–Canada battle that saw three players sent off and Springboks James Dalton and Pieter Hendriks banned from the tournament – Hendriks' exit allowing Chester Williams back into the host squad. The saddest incident was the spinal injury to Ivory Coast wing Max Brito that left him paralysed. Brito's condition was in everyone's minds for the remainder of the World Cup.

WILL CARLING

The Australians didn't look charged up in that opening game. I was surprised that the South Africans played so well in such an emotional environment. It was a warning for all their opponents. It was a bad result for Australia. It was a bad result for England. That was where our minds went straight to – the quarter-final against the holders – even before we had kicked a ball in anger. It was as if the pool games didn't matter. It was probably subconscious, but that's the explanation for our form in pool B. Don't get me wrong. Our preparation went well, always a worrying sign. There was a great spirit and we worked tremendously hard. But that vanished on the field. There wasn't 100 per cent commitment and concentration in the actual matches. It was as if we were going to win those games by divine right and it didn't matter how we won – wrong. I understand that winning the World Cup is not a sprint. It's a hard four or five weeks. You can't go flat out every day.

We hadn't played Argentina for a while. But all the info we needed about them was available. We knew exactly what was coming our way. It was a bad performance. No excuses. It rained. So what. We are more used to that than most. There was no continuity in our play, almost as though everything was done in slow motion. It might have been tough watching, it was even worse playing. It was obvious that we hadn't been together for a while. Just when it looked as if we might build on the platform Rob had given us, we made mistakes in the second half and it was game on again. There was little urgency in our rugby. I won't say we should have lost, but we easily could have. World Cup winners? Not on that showing. The dressing-room was a pretty shocked place afterwards. My ankle was pretty sore. But the plan was that I wasn't going to play all three pool games. Italy is the one I would probably have sat out anyway. Rob's kicking against Italy was just as vital as it had been against Argentina. There were a few glimpses that we were starting to put it together.

Sitting in selection with Jack is very similar to Geoff. The manager has the final say. We had the dilemma in the final game you don't want before the quarter-final. Do you give the second-string a run-out, or do you give those who are going to be needed for the last eight another chance to get it right?

Carling is led off towards the end of the Argentina match and his run of 44 con- secutive matches as England captain comes to an end. *(Colorsport)*

We went for the first option. I was delighted with the way they played, especially when everyone got a game eventually. That was it for a third of the squad. They didn't get another chance. They played well. It was the established players who didn't reach their potential. There was never any intention of us trying to come second to avoid Australia. You can't think or play big-time rugby like that. I would have worried how we lost. Poor Argentina. They went home without a win. But they played good rugby that would have seen them qualifying in another group. Pool B was tough. There was no easy team, like Ivory Coast or Japan.

England's tie with Australia was the clash of the quarter-finals. It was difficult to see Western Samoa, Ireland or Scotland stopping South Africa, France or New Zealand. England's quarter-final was in Cape Town, but they were sent first to Johannesburg to satisfy the requirements of the organisers. The officials relented a little, allowing England three nights in Cape Town, not just one. Cape Town certainly missed out on the pre-match hype. Nobody could call with any certainty this repeat of the 1991 final. Neither side had done itself justice so far. Yet both teams contained world class performers who could turn a match in a moment of brilliance. The only certainty was that one of the favourites for this World Cup was going home early as a failure. Not surpris- ingly, Carling's old adversary Campese had plenty to say for himself. 'I would hate to pay to watch England. I can't see how people enjoy it. They are boring as a team and they would rather kick goals than score tries.' Carling claimed he had heard it all before. There was nothing new to respond to.

The first good news of the week was that the injuries to Rowntree and Back were not as serious as had been first feared. Slight worries about Bracken persisted, so Wasps scrum half Andy Gomarsall was diverted from England's A tour of Australia as precautionary cover. Rowell offered few surprises in the side to meet Australia, with Morris at scrum half the only change from the Grand Slam team. This was Carling's 51st game in charge. Most of the England sessions were played out behind closed doors. The tension around the Sunnyside Hotel was all too apparent. Carling found it difficult to walk into the public areas without a microphone or a notebook being shoved under his nose. His reaction to such intrusions got less friendly as the match day approached. The daily press conferences weren't so bad. Carling was obviously amused as the journalists searched for a new line after six days of previews. It was almost as if the other three quarter-finals were sideshows, although the return of Chester Williams at least gave the new South Africa one representative in the Springbok side. Moore and Morris, possibly playing their last internationals, were asked about their retirement plans. Morris stuck to his guns, while Moore conceded that there were serious second thoughts after talking with Rowell and Carling.

England played on the second day of the quarter-finals. On the Saturday, South Africa, after the brawl against Canada, were forced to turn the other cheek to some dangerous tackles by the Western Samoans. Chester Williams rode his luck to score four tries as the host side went through. France and Ireland were level at half-time, but the French scored 24 points unopposed after the break against a strangely subdued Irish challenge. The first semi-final pairing was decided: South Africa versus France in a week's time in Durban. But the World Cup was waiting for the England–Australia match. This was going to be the game that put the 1995 tournament on the map. 'It is an enormous match. It is death or glory,' predicted Jack Rowell. Nobody quite knew what to expect as both sides had shown so little. As the newspapers declared: 'Now the talking stops!'

The talking stopped. Cape Town stopped. The whole of England stopped to watch the most pulsating match ever played in the World Cup. The two old warriors fought each other to a standstill. Just when it looked as if the extra time that no one wanted was inevitable, Rob Andrew dropped a goal that soared into rugby legend. The tie was not a great spectacle. But for sheer raw, nail-biting, nerve-jangling, stomach-churning, heart-stopping tension, the world of rugby has never seen anything like it.

England could not have started better, despite an early penalty from Michael Lynagh. Andrew kicked two penalties before counter-attacking when Lynagh dropped the ball just outside the England '22'. Carling and Guscott put Tony Underwood clear. The younger brother raced half the length of the field to score. Andrew's conversion made it 13–3 with a quarter of the match gone. One more score and the Aussies were finished. England, with Dewi Morris bustling everywhere, were on song. Unfortunately, the daring of the Underwood try vanished as quickly as it had appeared. Carling was as guilty as anyone of wasting opportunities of extending that lead. England paid the penalty. Lynagh reduced the deficit with his second penalty just before the interval. Then his towering kick to the corner at the start of the second half found Catt and Tony Underwood wanting and Damian Smith hanging to take a marvellous catch and crash over the line. Lynagh's conversion left this quarter-final all square again even before Rowell was back in his seat after his half-time team talk.

Neither side was going to run away with this one. Three times in the second half Lynagh put Australia in front; three times Andrew levelled the scores. That last penalty went over with four minutes of normal time remaining. Both sides looked out on their feet, yet there appeared no way of avoiding extra time. Australia won a scrum not far out and a Lynagh dropped goal looked inevitable. The Aussie captain ran the ball and the dropped goal opportunity fell to Campese, who hooked his kick. Catt cleared the danger with a penalty that found touch on Australia's 10 metre line. Too far for Andrew. Bayfield jumped and England's forwards drove. Then the ball was fed back to Andrew who took aim for glory. The ball soared high and true. Australia remembered their 1991 quarter-final against Ireland and took a quick kick-off. England never let them get close and Morris rolled the ball in touch to end a titanic struggle and begin a night of celebration. Many of the England players' wives and

Rob Andrew keeps his nerve and his head down as he strikes the sensational dropped goal in the dying moments of the Australian tie that takes England into the World Cup semi-finals. *(Colorsport)*

girl friends had watched from the stands. With England losing to Brazil at soccer and to the West Indies in the cricket Test, there was no arguments about who were England's heroes that Sunday night.

WILL CARLING

Australia were not firing. That didn't instil me with any relief before the game. They had lost to South Africa. I didn't think they would have two bad games. It's strange when you move from the pool matches. Suddenly, there was no room for mistakes. This was do or die. I felt the situation was very similar to our 1991 quarter-final in Paris. Again, that was the tie of that round. Again, it was an almost impossible result to predict. The Aussies had a side similar to ours. Players of real calibre who had not been performing. I knew with Campo and Lynagh, they had players who could win the game with one movement. They had so much experience.

We made the classic mistake. At 13–3 up, we gave away a penalty and a try either side of half-time and our lead was wiped out. You couldn't relax for a second. It was the most draining game I've ever played in emotionally. It was so close. Every bit as hard as that French quarter-final. As always, we were a bit conservative and predictable. We should have tried to extend our lead. We are good enough to use the ball in different ways. I know our forwards were criticised for losing their way after a great start. The biggest problem was that the Aussies had cracked our lineout code. I don't know how they did it. All the years I've been playing, we've never cracked anyone else's. When they got level, I told the lads that we had to regain our impetus and concentrate on what we'd done at the start. It's all about being mentally strong. You can't massively alter tactics at that stage. But you must be in a positive frame of mind. It turned into a war of attrition. We showed great resilience. Of course, it was vitally important that Rob kept kicking those catch-up penalties. If either side had gone six points behind in the later stages, that would have been it. I couldn't believe it was still all square with a couple of minutes to go. Nobody wanted extra time. The concern was just to stay out of our half and not give Lynagh a chance. We failed to do that. When they lined up for that scrum, I thought it was all over. I was on the floor when Campo took that dropped goal. I didn't see what was happening. I'm glad I didn't know it was him going for the winner. If that had gone over? I still can't think of anything worse happening. After Cattie found touch, Deano ran past Rob: 'What do you need?' 'Take it further' was Rob's reply. And they did. It was a fantastic catch and drive. Everything was working according to plan. But even when Rob hit it from that range, I had no great expectations of it going over. It was an unbelievable feeling. Unfortunately, it only lasted a few seconds as I saw the Aussies take that quick kick-off. I don't know how long the game lasted after that. It seemed ages. I couldn't believe it when Dewi didn't hoist that ball in the stand. It was a great kick. I didn't want a great kick. I wanted the ball off the park. It was an absolutely unbelievable game to win.

Those were Michael Lynagh's final moments on an international rugby field. A couple of hours later, Scotland's Gavin Hastings also bowed out. The Scots did not have enough firepower to cope with Lomu and the All Blacks, although they scored as many points against New Zealand as anyone had in history. Carling's opponents in the semi-final were the hot favourites for the 1995 World Cup, New Zealand. That game was also in Cape Town, but England once again had to make the trek back to Johannesburg. Carling's squad was allowed some rest and recreation, heading off to Sun City. There was also the odd thought drifting towards the most burning question ever to hit a Rugby World Cup: 'How do you stop Jonah Lomu?' Carling knew that New Zealand were no one-man band. The emergence of Andrew Mehrtens, Glen Osborne and Josh Kronfeld in this World Cup had given the All Blacks a cutting edge that had been missing in recent years.

Not surprisingly, all England's quarter-final heroes were given the nod for the semi-final. The All Blacks made four changes. There was much discussion of the likely conditions; if it rained, this would suit England. The organisers again relented, allowing both teams to fly down to Cape Town on Friday. But they had to be back on a plane three hours after the final whistle; Cape Town had no hotel rooms left. England's squad got a boost when Andrew received an MBE in the Queen's Birthday honours. It led to the usual mickey-taking, helping to ease the tension. The wives and girlfriends had nearly all gone home. They had not seen much of their other halves while they had been there, but at least they had not been forgotten. England's Cape Town hotel resembled the All Blacks' supporters headquarters when they arrived, with flags draped over most balconies. The team very quickly decided to keep out of the public areas and stay on their particular floor, which was out of bounds to the rest of the guests.

All the players noticed the change from the previous World Cup and even from the trip to South Africa the summer before. They were left in no doubt that this was a tournament, not a tour. There was hardly any time for the normal niceties of touring. World Cup business has become very serious. In the press conferences, the same players were asked the same questions they had been before the quarter-final, except that now the name Lomu appeared rather frequently. Sun City had given them a chance to muck around down water slides and jet skis. Other recreational activities included go-karting and war games with paint guns. Usually teams were divided into forwards versus backs. Everyone turned on Victor Ubogu when he was caught on his mobile phone in the middle of one battle.

England went into their semi-final knowing who their next opponents would be. South Africa beat France 19–15 in atrociously wet conditions in Durban. Their match started 90 minutes late. Had it not been the World Cup semi-final, it is doubtful whether it would have started at all. France thought they had

Carling and Jack Rowell face yet another barrage of questions in Johannesburg as they prepare to face the All Blacks. *(Colorsport)*

stolen the tie at the death when Benazzi drove for the line, but Welsh referee Derek Bevan adjudged he was short by inches. The hosts were through to guarantee that the final was going to be an even more emotional day for South Africa than the opening match.

While the first semi-final was in doubt right up to the final whistle, the second was over before it had begun. Lomu scored after 70 seconds. England were history. It was the very thing England had dreaded happening all week. The fact that it happened so quickly and in such a devastating and comprehensive manner destroyed England's spirit. The Kiwis had involved Lomu straight from the reverse kick-off, which left England exposed and Tony Underwood hesitant. A minute later Lomu received the ball in space. Tony Underwood tried the traditional side-on tackle and bounced off. Then Carling attempted the tap tackle with some success. As Lomu stumbled, Catt attempted to drag him down from head-on. Remarkably, Lomu kept his balance and trampled over Catt as if he were not there. The All Blacks celebrated with three England backs lying scattered around the battlefield. 'How to stop Jonah Lomu?' England had tried three ways and all had failed. A couple of minutes later Lomu was at it again. This time he failed to reach the line. Kronfeld didn't. He had spent most of the World Cup on Lomu's shoulder. 'I just hang around behind the truck and wait for it to drop his load,' explained the All Black flanker. The crowd knew they were watching something very special. They

Carling led England's brave second-half fightback after New Zealand threatened to bury the Red Rose in the World Cup semi-final. *(Colorsport)*

were also well aware that the contest was over. If there was ever a sign that this was not going to be England's day it came when Zinzan Brooke dropped the first Test goal ever by an All Black forward. After that early Lomu blow, England needed to hang on for a while, to get their head clear and steady their nerves. The All Blacks gave them no chance as they went for the kill. If it had been a boxing match, referee Stephen Hilditch would have stopped the contest. After 52 minutes of the semi-final, the side that many thought would win the World Cup were 35–3 down and facing the biggest hiding in their history. England fought back and together matched Lomu's individual four tries. Carling scored twice as England's backs showed what they are capable of. Some dismissed the fightback, claiming the semi-final was lost and New Zealand were conserving their energies for the final in six days' time. That was unkind and unfair. As the All Blacks emphatically proved in the Japan massacre, sentiment has no place in their rugby.

The contrast with the previous Sunday in Cape Town could not have been greater. Nor could the journey back on the same plane with the All Blacks. The victors travelled Club class. 'We were in cattle class at the back,' reflected England prop Jason Leonard.

## WILL CARLING

I was convinced we would beat the All Blacks. That might look mad now in light of the result. I thought we could tie them up in the lineout, deny them the ball and keep it away from Lomu and put Mehrtens and Osborne under pressure. They were reasonably inexperienced. You could say our game plan failed. Lomu was not a distraction in our build-up. Obviously, we didn't pay him enough attention. He'd been outstanding in the World Cup, but was brilliant against us. That was his best performance by far. It was also the best game New Zealand played. People rated him another Tuigamala, but there is so much more to Lomu. He's got the build of a 15 stone winger. Somewhere in there hiding is nearly another five stone – most of it is around his thighs. Lomu had balance and speed. He takes no time to get into his stride. When he is that big and fast, you have to hit him spot on. Any slight error of judgement and you bounce off. Teams will work out how to deal with him. That was even noticeable in the Bledisloe Cup that followed. But another thing in his favour at the World Cup was that he was new. We gave the All Blacks, not just him, far too much space. Those opening minutes were extraordinary. I accept they started very well. But we started very badly. They were 10–0 up straight away. We missed a couple of kicks at goal. We weren't giving ourselves a chance of getting back into the game. Then we made defensive errors and the game was over. It was like being on the receiving end of our start at Pretoria the previous year. Game over. As captain you've got to block those thoughts. This wasn't a two-Test series. This was the World Cup semi-final. But somewhere deep inside was the realisation that the dream had gone. We showed a lot of pride. Don't forget, we were over 30 points adrift at one stage. It is still staggering to think that one of the best sides in the world can be on the receiving end of that. It hasn't fully sunk in, even now, that there could be no World Cup for Will Carling. The minute we lost the 1991 final, that was the hope. For the past couple of years, I thought we were capable of winning. Those hopes were gone in 10 minutes, blown away by a devastating hurricane called Lomu.

The biggest downside of losing a World Cup semi-final is the third place play-off. England had to play France in Pretoria two days before the final. The organisers tried to justify this money-raising exercise by allowing the winner automatic qualification for the 1999 tournament. Tony Underwood made way for Ian Hunter, while Dean Richards' shoulder problems gave Steve Ojomoh another chance at No. 8. Rowell used the phrase 'rested', not 'dropped', regarding Underwood's omission. It appeared England's right wing was shouldering much of the blame for Lomu's rampaging. Rowell intimated he would like Carling to carry on after the World Cup: 'If Mr Carling is fit and fresh next season and is available, he might be difficult to replace. What I do know is that

Carling's
World Cup
dream has
gone and,
unlike 1991,
there might not
be another
chance for
England's
record-
breaking
captain in four
years' time.
*(Colorsport)*

the 50 plus cap brigade are not surplus baggage.' Rowell's biggest problem regarding Carling's successor was that Rodber had had such a poor World Cup. After his towering displays the previous winter, the Northampton skipper had never got into his stride. The talk about the long-term prospect to replace Carling moved to someone not even in the side. Phil de Glanville takes over as Bath captain in the 1995–96 season and his progress will be monitored closely.

England's 19–9 defeat in the play-off was as depressing as the score-line. Midway through the game, it was announced that John Major had resigned as leader of the Conservative Party. It was suggested that the reason was his embarrassment over giving Andrew the MBE. England meekly surrendered their eight-match winning streak over the French going back to Carling's debut in 1988. On his final day in an England jersey Dewi Morris, as ever, bust a gut. The rest were nowhere. Carling refused to discuss his future afterwards: 'I'm in no fit state to make that sort of decision. You can throw up any number of excuses, but excuses are not important. By having to pre-qualify, we have let down the people who are going to be around in the squad for the next World Cup.' England drowned their sorrows with a French team not used to such celebrations after playing England. The French had acquitted themselves well and had come within a whisker of the final. Now they can leave qualifying for 1999 to all the other northern hemisphere countries apart from the hosts, Wales.

The focus was firmly on the southern hemisphere the morning after the play-off as the Rupert Murdoch $550 million TV deal with South Africa, New Zealand and Australia was announced. Europe and the Home Countries were looking more and more the poor relations on the world circuit. Murdoch's 10-year contract was to begin a busy few months of massive-money rugby union deals.

New Zealand were 2–7 on favourites to take the World Cup final. Lomu mania had reached epidemic proportions. His Mum, Dad and two brothers jetted in to walk the edges of Ellis Park early on Friday, where their son was going to destroy South Africa the next day. It did not happen. The All Blacks were in trouble the minute President Mandela met the teams wearing François Pienaar's No. 6 jersey and waving a Springbok cap. That must have been unsettling, although not as frightening as when a Jumbo flew a few feet over the top of the stands. Many of the crowd ducked. The South Africans had obtained no permission for the stunt and every car alarm for a mile around the ground went off. Carling watched from ITV's commentary box. He wondered if there would have been a fuss if the Queen had come out in his No. 13 England shirt before the final at Twickenham in 1991.

It soon became obvious that the Lomu factor was more of a problem for the All Blacks than for the South Africans. The favourites were trying too hard to bring him into the game. For the first time in the World Cup, the All Blacks' machine stuttered. Mehrtens and Osborne lost their composure. Kronfeld was running with the pack, not in front. The All Blacks were indecisive, hesitant, definitely off their game. Afterwards, it transpired the New Zealanders had been off their food after 18 of them had gone down with various degrees of food poisoning on Thursday night. Eventually, Jeff Wilson left the field feeling unwell. The All Blacks did not make excuses. They never do. But it was a plausible explanation for what happened in the final.

That should not detract from the courage and commitment of the Springboks. A month after playing the most important rugby match in the history of the new nation, Pienaar's team had to do it all over again in the final. The bookies might not have given the Springboks a chance, but the whole Republic demanded the World Cup. South Africa led 9–6 at the interval. Mehrtens' dropped goal was the only score of the second half as the final went into extra time. There was a sting in the tail for the hosts. If the score remained the same, the cup would go to New Zealand, because of the sending-off of Hendriks. Not that the South Africans felt bounded by the host nation tag. In the final, the Springboks were the home side. Mandela's performance could be excused, but the playing of patriotic songs during the game to lift the home side's spirits could not. Mehrtens put the All Blacks in front. South Africa needed to score twice. Joel Stransky levelled the score at the end of the first

The star of the World Cup and the single biggest reason for England's semi-final defeat, New Zealand's wing Jonah Lomu. *(Colorsport)*

period of extra time. The crowd sensed the World Cup was South Africa's, despite the fact that New Zealand would win if the score remained unchanged. Eight minutes before the end, Stransky dropped a goal that sent a nation even more frantic than Andrew had done a fortnight earlier. Shortly afterwards, President Mandela, waving his Springbok cap in jubilation, stood alongside

Pienaar, who was holding the cup aloft. The old and the new South Africa together on top of the world. It ended for all time the arguments about sport and politics not mixing. It was impossible to deny either his moment of triumph. There were not too many blacks faces in the crowd; yet the biggest smiles at Ellis Park belonged to the two black men on the field, Mandela and Chester Williams.

Nothing could spoil South Africa's great day, though the Rugby Union president, Dr Louis Luyt, did his best at the official dinner. He managed to upset the All Blacks, England, the referees and even his own team in his speech, the thrust of which was that the first two World Cups did not count because South Africa was missing. He left referee Derek Bevan in tears after a special presentation of a watch, thanking him for getting South Africa to the final. All Black Mike Brewer had to be restrained from attacking Luyt. As it was, the All Blacks, England and many others walked out. It was a sad, sour note on which to end the World Cup. Luyt was right in many ways. It was the first real World Cup; but not only because of South Africa's presence. This was big-time, money rugby. And that is the future.

## WILL CARLING

I didn't pick South Africa to win the opening game. I got it wrong again in the final. The All Blacks were the best side overall. But they didn't win all their games. South Africa did. Their commitment in the final was just staggering. You can see why the Springboks and the All Blacks are the great rugby rivals. They are so similar in many ways. I've always thought the All Blacks were the realists, with the South Africans slightly more romantic about the way they play their rugby. That was reversed in the World Cup. South Africa knew what was required and did it. There's a mental hardness about both that I admire. You don't just find that on the rugby field.

Being in the commentary box was a disappointing way to finish the World Cup. I thought we had a side that could win. Despite being frustrated in the pool games, I was convinced we could pull it off. When you know you are good enough to beat anyone on your day, it's all the more disappointing when you don't. Beating Australia was an emotional high. We couldn't get back up there for the All Blacks. Looking back, that quarterfinal was the problem. It had dominated our thoughts for two years when we believed it would be South Africa. None of the other favourites had to worry about that stage of the competition. Their big time started at the semi-final. By the time we got there, the quarter-final had taken too much out of us, mentally and physically. The third-place game is pointless. Every side who's played one thinks the same way. I was disappointed with the way we played. I was disappointed to lose our unbeaten run against France. The qualifying aspect doesn't worry me too much. At the end of the day it was an international match. That should be enough of a challenge.

# CHAPTER 14

# PACKER, DIANA AND THE WIND OF CHANGE – 1995

Carling returned from the World Cup determined to take England forward. For all England's rugby talent, Five Nations success and hard work, the southern hemisphere still ruled the roost. That was merely confirmed by events in South Africa. The announcement of the Murdoch TV deal suggested that England was losing ground again. Carling wants a structure along 'Super Ten' lines, with England competing with South Africa, Australia and New Zealand on a regular basis. He wants it now. His sense of urgency is not down to personal reasons, as his distinguished rugby career nears its end. It is because that is the only way forward. The International Board and the Rugby Football Union have never acted hastily, but the business moguls getting involved in rugby union do not hang around. They are not used to committees and do not expect general approval or consensus for their decisions. Even the IB caught that mood in late August when they announced that rugby union would be a totally professional sport from now on.

England's World Cup squad had been offered huge sums to join Kerry Packer's World Rugby Corporation. The WRC proposed more than an international rugby circus. To have satisfied Packer's needs, 100-plus players would have disappeared from the Courage First Division. Carling knows that most sportsmen struggle to see beyond the pound signs when a fat contract is laid on the table. Throughout July, Carling joined Andrew, Moore, Catt and Rodber in meetings with the RFU. The replacement of Dudley Wood with Tony Hallett as RFU secretary gave the talks some prospect of success. The discussions centred on money and a new structure. As ever, the RFU were offering too little, too late. Carling knew the seriousness of the Packer threat. The England captain at first hoped that the visit of the World Cup champions to Twickenham in November would stem the tide. The eventual collapse of the Packer deal allowed all parties breathing space. Carling knows how easily outside influences can distract the most successful of sides. This season remains, for him, crunch time for the England rugby team as well as English rugby as they enter this new professional era.

WILL CARLING
This is a very important year for this side. If it goes well, it might be regarded as a great side. But not yet. Too many of the experienced players

who came into the side after the 1991 World Cup did not perform in South Africa. The Rodbers, Clarkes and Bayfields must provide the nucleus of the next World Cup challenge. To do that, they must start becoming serious internationals, must start taking control. The mental hard core has to come from those players. They have to change. The World Cup was a watershed for them. It was a big test and they can't have been happy with the results.

This current side is more athletic and flexible than the 1991/1992 Grand Slam team. But they are not as hard. I don't think any of the newcomers can match the hardness of Peter Winterbottom, Wade Dooley, Mike Teague and or even my old mate, Jeff Probyn. I suppose I will always be biased towards that first team because half of them had been my heroes when I was at school. They looked after me. Looking back, it's staggering how little I did know in those early days. The team had weaknesses, but it was the best set-piece outfit in world rugby. Jack talked about the 'comfort zone' when he took over from Geoff. I had to agree. Some players were collecting caps at an alarming rate without doing too much. One of the advantages of a tougher, more elite structure is that it would weed those blokes out – or force them into action. Players respond to the environment around them. They should never feel that their places are safe or guaranteed.

On top of Carling's rugby commitments, there is the small matter of business and home life, both of which took centre stage in late summer. His company, Insights, which organises management seminars and talks, enjoys a high profile in a growing marketplace. After his time at Mobil, Carling wanted to run his own business, with the freedom to expand and develop in other areas. That has allowed him also to organise his work around his sporting life.

WILL CARLING
My time with Mobil allowed me to find out certain things. I enjoyed working from home. Office life would not have suited me. With my rugby commitments, it would not have been fair to others to see how often I was away. I started up my own business just before we went to Argentina in 1990 with an office in Piccadilly. It was tough at first, but it was what I wanted to do. I had realised that sportsmen were the best way of getting management messages over. Not only did the audience relate to the sporting person, but a famous name added star quality. Eventually, I wanted to expand the presentations into a more interactive service. I was basically concerned with where I'd be in five years' time. We are in a niche market and it's a quality product. Sportsmen we use include Gary Lineker, Mike Brearley, Sebastian Coe and Tracey Edwards. The actions of the individual have got to benefit the company. The great weakness is the lack of communication. There's not enough delegation.

We discuss how you cope with disappointment. When someone in a job is patently not good enough, it's demoralising not only for him, but for others. You have to find him another job, whether it's sideways or down-wards. You don't need to disguise it. People know when they are out of their depth. We tell the story of a company in Japan. When they find someone is not capable, they promote him. I don't think much of that as a solution. Yet it's probably a policy many of our sporting bodies have employed for years.

During the summer of 1995 Carling brought out a new book, *The Way to Win*, subtitled 'Strategies for Success in Business and Sport'. He wrote it with Robert Heller, the founder of *Management Today*. Carling does not find 'change' is such a dirty word in his business career. But then he does not often have to deal with '57 old farts'. New challenges are what keeps Carling fresh. Yet, as he enters his eighth season as England captain, he is acutely conscious of outstaying his welcome.

WILL CARLING

I will know when it's time to go. If I don't, I'm sure Jack will tell me. South Africa's visit is a huge incentive for me and everyone else. There couldn't have been a better game. It's a chance to take away a small piece of the frus-tration caused by the World Cup. It would mean a lot to beat them. I'm taking it one season at a time. It would be stupid to say I'm definitely going to play for two years. Too much can happen. And has! Already, I've gone further than I thought I might a few years ago. Jack's arrival couldn't have come at a better time for me. I played better last season than I've done for a few years. I was back to running at people again. That's always a good sign.

As Carling enters the 1995–96 season, he has 40 victories and 12 defeats in his 53 matches as England captain. Australia, Wales, Ireland, New Zealand have triumphed twice each, with single victories for Scotland, Argentina, South Africa and France. England have lost only one championship game at Twickenham during his seven years in charge. As well as those three Grand Slams, England have entered the final round of championship matches in every one of those seven years with a chance of the title. The key to England's contin-uing Five Nations success in 1996 will be the trip to Paris on the first Saturday of the championship.

However, Carling had not even packed his boots for the new campaign before the uncertain world of today's sporting stars homed in on England's rugby captain. Rugby, even with the Packer Circus at full throttle, was forced to take a back seat in August when the closeness of his relationship with the Princess of Wales was revealed on the front page of the *News of the World*. The friendship was no secret, but it was the detailed testimony of Hilary Ryan, Carling's former personal assistant at Insights, that allowed the paper to devote its first five pages to the story. The front page headline 'Di's Secret Trysts With Carling' was careful not to suggest intimacy, but it was obvious from the alleged long personal phone calls and secret assignations that this was a close relationship. Flattered by the attentions of one of the most desirable women in the world, Carling seemed oblivious to the consequences and dangers of any liaison with the lady who was still married to the heir to the British throne.

It quickly became obvious that England's rugby captain was in trouble at home. Julia was not aware of the extent to which her husband had been enticed into Princess Diana's phone circle. However hard Carling protested his innocence, there was little doubt that he had been speaking and seeing the Princess of Wales behind Julia's back. Carling went from the edge of the Packer Circus into the middle of a media one. This time public support was not unanimous. Carling was not censured as much as Princess Diana, but England's captain was criticised for being naive and for putting his new marriage at risk. The silliness of a dalliance that was going nowhere became all too apparent when it fell under the public gaze. Although Carling rightly felt aggrieved that a former employee should break her contract of confidentiality, it quickly dawned on him that he was primarily to blame. He should not have allowed himself to be seduced by Diana's position and personality. Hilary Ryan gave details of the couple's pet names for each other – 'Boss' and 'Captain' – and of gifts swapped – the Princess received a two-inch china pig in shorts and she responded with a two-foot troll in an England rugby jersey. The pair had met at the Harbour Club, a gym in Chelsea Harbour, 18 months earlier. After a while, they started having coffee together and later Carling would visit Kensington Palace for lunch. England's rugby captain may have felt safe in such a public friendship, but previous experiences of Princess Diana's male friends should have warned him that he was playing with fire. Hilary Ryan described Carling as 'running around after her like a puppy'. Ryan was Carling's personal assistant who worked for Insights for just over a year on a salary of £22,000. She had been dismissed from the company a few weeks earlier. Carling must have regretted giving her the following reference: 'Hilary Ryan worked as my personal assistant from May 1994 to July 1995. During this time she not only organised my personal diary, but she co-ordinated all the organisation involved in setting up and running our seminars. She liaised with all our major clients as well as dealing efficiently with the media. During her time here I have always found Hilary to be highly efficient, very reliable and totally dedicated to the company. Yours sincerely, Will Carling.'

The glowing reference was some way off the truth. Why would someone that valuable and high-class be asked to leave? It was also clear that Carling had absolutely no inkling that she would go public on her time at Insights. Carling's hand-written statement, read out to the waiting press on the Sunday the story broke, clarified Hilary Ryan's position, if nothing else: 'It is no secret that I know Princess Diana. Our acquaintance has not in any way affected the priority I have always given to Julia and my rugby. Hilary Ryan was employed by my company for 14 months after she approached us showing interest in a job. She claimed she had worked in management training for a firm of accountants and should therefore be well aware of the meaning of confidentiality. As Hilary is correctly reported as saying, she was dismissed because of her habit of making waves in the office and inventing and initiating confrontations when none existed. She told me she wanted another job in a similarly confidential post in management training. She asked me to sign a reference which she wrote herself. I'm afraid that she might find it rather hard to get that job now.'

For the second weekend that summer, the mass forces of the press corps laid siege to the Carlings' Barnes home. Julia was on her own that Saturday night, but her husband returned to join her just before midnight as they realised the story would be front-page news the next day. The reporters had kindly pushed an early edition of the *News of the World* through their letterbox. The Carlings' discussions also involved Jon Holmes. He helped prepare the statement that Carling read out the following morning. The most revealing words came, though, when he was asked how his wife was. 'Well, you know,' was all he said. Carling drove off on his own. He returned later and the pair went shopping at Sainsbury's.

The papers were full of revelations the following morning, with much made of the fact that Carling was the latest in a long line of relationships Princess Diana had carried out on the telephone. The extent of Carling's telephone involvement came as a shock to Julia. It reminded her that she had carried on a phone relationship with her future husband while he had been involved with others. For all her glitzy pop background, Julia is a very down-to-earth character and much less impressed than her husband by the ephemeral attractions of the world of glamour and fame.

## JULIA CARLING

I'm a country lass who quit university after a term of history. I then had a six-year relationship with a man who didn't want me to work. I got into pop PR in 1989, working with the Rolling Stones on tour. The most important thing then was to make sure that Mick and Charlie got the faxes letting them know what was happening with the England cricket team. I met Will through Nikki, his girlfriend at the time. I'd heard of him. I'd seen a few rugby internationals on TV. I'd been one of the few girls in an all-male school, so I'd learnt the normal rugby chants. I suppose I was expecting someone who was brash and arrogant. At that first dinner party, he was desperately uncomfortable. Will didn't say a word. He felt on show. I couldn't believe how incredibly shy he was.

I used to go with Nikki to watch him play at Twickenham. Then Nikki headed for Australia after they finally split. Will and I always had a phone relationship, abusing each other and I went out with him a couple of times

Carling is presented to the Princess of Wales at a Help the Aged charity awards night in 1993. But it was the extent of their relationship since then which hit the headlines in August 1995 and put a strain on Carling's year-long marriage to Julia in the weeks ahead. *(Express Newspapers)*

as an escort. I suppose we always knew there was something there, but it took him four years to ask me out. It was pathetic really. He said he was waiting for me, but I would never have asked him. When he was first asked about us, Will insisted that we were just friends. That annoyed me. You can't handle the press that way. He gets very protective and doesn't want me bothered. Dealing with the media is my job. I was half Jeff Beck's age when I went to live with him. He had another girlfriend and family, so I know what the press can be like. I handle the press better than Will. He sometimes doesn't understand that you can't muck them around, although he's learning. Will Carling, the rugby hero, thinks he can be a private person in public. It's not on. You just have to accept it and get on with it. He doesn't like to give too much away in interviews but the less you give a journalist, the more he's going to have an input.

I know when Victoria went public, after Will's relationship with me became known, it annoyed him. Often I was piggy-in-the-middle when Will and Nikki, then Victoria, were having problems. That was difficult for me because nothing could happen with me while they were together. I had been potty about Jeff, but I knew it wasn't love. Will is the first person I've been in love with.

It was a crisis in our marriage. We had been married for just over a year, which made things difficult enough, but then it's made public so you have to deal with the publicity as well. It is how you handle things that really counts. You can make a big scene out of it, but at the end of the day does that help? Will and I are straight with each other. We know what is going on in each other's lives. Diana's business is her business and she has to leave Will and I to get on with ours.

This was an unexpected early test of their marriage, and a serious one. It quickly became clear in the days that followed that Julia was now the key figure. She decided not to go the Elizabeth Hurley way. There was no pouting and public condemnation of her partner's behaviour. This was something Julia was going to sort out in private. So she smiled for the cameras and saved the recriminating looks for behind closed doors. With more revelations promised from the *News of the World*, Mrs Carling wanted to be reassured that there were no more surprises for her. Carling had been guilty of a betrayal of trust. Once trust has been abused, the relationship is never the same again. It can continue and grow, but the ground rules have changed. Carling was going to have to live with that, along with his wife's demands that he left the Harbour Club and never saw Princess Diana again, except in the line of duty. Carling initially felt England's rugby captain should not be dictated to, even by his wife. It was quickly explained to him by Jon Holmes and others that these were not unreasonable requests in the circumstances. As the week progressed, the painful truth dawned on Carling that he might lose Julia, who had no desire to play games with her marriage. Holmes got Carling out of England and the Carlings spent a few days abroad. Carling's exclusive contract with the *Mail on Sunday* meant that paper would announce the outcome of those discussions. Even Holmes was worried.

Saturday's *Daily Mail* ran a full-page advertisement proclaiming: '"I love my wife more than anything" – Will Carling talks exclusively about the relationship at risk. And Julia Carling speaks frankly about her husband and the Princess. Tomorrow – only in the *Mail on Sunday*.' It was a story most of the other Sunday newspapers lifted for their later editions. Most of the words came from Carling, but the headlines focused on Julia's thoughts on Princess Diana. 'I am sad that Will put himself in that position and that the Princess did as well. This has happened to her before and you hope she won't do those things again, but she obviously does. She picked the wrong couple to do it with this time because we can only get stronger from it.'

Carling admitted that he had spoken to the Princess in the past week. 'She says she is sad about it and says it has happened to her time and time again. But it hasn't happened to Julia and me before and I never want it to happen to us again. My main feelings are about what it has done to the people around me, the people I really care about and love, Julia, what it has done to her. That is unforgivable. It was a perfectly harmless friendship. But, as a high-profile person, I should have thought about it differently. It was flattering that the Princess was interested in me. That is probably where I made my mistake.'

WILL CARLING

I was incredibly naive. That's the start and finish of it. There was so much that was open to misinterpretation. Yes, I had been to Kensington Palace, but nowhere as often as was said. Yes, I saw the Princess the day England flew off to the World Cup, but for 20 minutes, not three hours. Of course, I have a private line in my office, but it wasn't installed for the Princess. But, at the end of the day, arguing about bits and pieces was pointless. It just fanned the flames. I wanted the episode closed as quickly as possible. So I held my hand up, admitted I was stupid to let myself get in that position and promised that it would never happen again. I could handle the sacking and 'old farts' affair because that was just me. But the Princess Diana story affected Julia. The person who had stood by me most when I lost the captaincy was now suffering because of my carelessness. When Hilary was sacked, it crossed my mind that she might go to the papers and do a 'Will Carling sacked me' story. I never expected anything like this. It makes me wonder just how long this had been in her mind. She was dismissed when I returned from the World Cup. I trusted her as a member of my team, but quickly she started coming to me with information about other staff. She wanted to be in control. If anyone came up with an idea I liked, she would try and drive a wedge between me and them. After the World Cup, she told me to get rid of two members of staff and put her in charge. I sat down with her and Jon. The outcome was her dismissal. I couldn't believe it when she wrote a week later for a good reference. I didn't want to be vindictive, so I gave her one. I've always been wary of people in the past. Obviously, I wasn't wary enough. All it means is that those who complained about Will Carling being cold, arrogant and aloof in the past will have more to moan about in the future. I find it very sad that you have to be on your guard, even in your own office.

The Carlings' problems continued to be public property. Princess Diana was featured on the cover of *Private Eye* with the caption: 'There's only one Willy in my life.' The roles of all three main participants were analysed repeatedly in the press. Even personal letters Carling had written to Victoria Jackson during England's tour of Australia four years earlier found their way into print. It was a humiliating time for someone who had always enjoyed great loyalty among his small close-knit band of friends and was ultra-sensitive about any intrusion into his private life. One article even conducted a 'Battle of Will' with the Princess and Julia matched like boxers over Body, Brains, Clothes, Track Record, Sex Appeal, Hair and Diet with marks out of 10 in each category. For the record the *Sun*'s assessment gave Julia victory by 62 points out of 70 to Princess Diana's 53. Julia Carling hoped to clear the air once and for all a few days later when she announced: 'There is no animosity between Princess Diana and myself. I have no feelings about her. The whole thing is over and I want to forget about it. I am not asking for an apology from her. I never have.'

Any hopes of Carling stepping out of the public gaze vanished the very same day when Rob Andrew and Brian Moore resigned from the England players' negotiating team, leaving Carling, Mike Catt and Tim Rodber to continue. The departing duo had been the ones most closely associated with Packer's rebel World Rugby Corporation, which had become a non-starter after the three big southern hemisphere Unions settled with their leading players. Moore and Andrew sent letters to their England colleagues, explaining why they had stood down after only 10 players had turned up for a meeting the previous weekend: 'As all our success in recent years has been due to team-work, on and off the field, we hope we are not entering into an era of prima donnas who expect everything to happen for them without putting in too much. To say we were disappointed that so many of the squad chose not to attend is an under-statement. It was a very important meeting, especially for the younger players whose long-term future is directly affected by developments, and particularly in the light of frequent requests by the same people for repeated updates in the last few weeks on all issues. Any success which we have had has been due squarely to the squad sticking together in any negotiations and under any form of pressure. It was always a probability that when individual agents became involved there would be conflicting demands, loyalties and priorities. Events of the past few weeks seem to have proved this to be the case.'

The start of the new English season and beginning of rugby's professional era. The man not identified by his name-badge is Mike Humphreys, who handles the PR for Courage. *(Colorsport)*

There was little doubt that England had missed the money boat again. The whole saga had been played out on the other side of the equator. The England supporting act became a cheap side-show once Australia, South Africa and New Zealand got their act together. The new secretary of the RFU, Tony Hallett, phoned Carling in the hope that England's captain would lead the new players' committee and use his stature to resolve the situation amicably. It had been five years since Carling had made a conscious decision to stand back in the money battle. There would have been no such offer, or acceptance, if Dudley Wood had still been in office. Hallett gave Carling hope, not only of a breakthrough on the money front, but also in giving England's players a structure that would allow them to compete with the best. That means emulating the southern hemisphere playing structure, where the top players are virtually free of club commitments. England's stars want regular competition against the best in Europe and the best in the world.

Every new season brings Carling a new challenge, especially as he approaches his thirtieth birthday. The 1995–96 season is no different. On the playing side, Carling will take on the new World Cup champions South Africa before seeking a fourth Grand Slam, to match the achievement of the England side of the 1920s. His progress will be watched just as closely away from the action.

England's captain has a vital part to play as the oldest Union attempts to find its place in the rugby revolution, money and otherwise. His marriage will be studied, too. His 'golden boy' image has taken a battering, much worse than in 1993 when he was dropped by the British Lions. Errors of judgement on the playing field are one thing, blunders of the Princess Diana type are another.

That particular problem flared up again with the new season only a few days old. Carling was spotted in his new Range Rover entering Kensington Palace. Carling was delivering rugby jerseys that had been promised to the princes. Carling felt he was honouring a commitment and Princess Diana was not at home. Yet, not even Jon Holmes could believe his client's action. Again, innocent or not, it publicly opened up old wounds that had hardly begun to heal. It merely increased the pressure on Carling and his marriage, although no one appeared sure about who had tipped off the papers. England's captain might have been set up, but he walked into the trap like a lamb to the slaughter. His reactions will now be studied under the media microscope.

Carling still has plenty to prove, especially after a summer of discontent on all fronts – his 'old farts' sacking, England's World Cup failure, England's continuance as the poor rugby relation after the collapse of the Packer Circus, and then the right royal row over his marriage. It would be easy to give it away. Carling's place as the most successful captain in rugby history is already assured. But the challenges are still there. Perhaps more than ever this season.

# CARLING'S CAREER STATISTICS

## (to 1 November 1995)

### Carling's England career

| | |
|---|---|
| 16.01.88 | France 10, England 9 (Parc des Princes) |
| 06.02.88 | England 3, Wales 11 (Twickenham) |
| 05.03.88 | Scotland 6, England 9 (Murrayfield) |
| 19.03.88 | England 35, Ireland 3 (Twickenham) |
| 23.04.88 | *Ireland 10, England 21 (Lansdowne Road) |
| 12.06.88 | Australia 28, England 8 (Concord Oval, Sydney) |
| 17.06.88 | Fiji 12, England 25 (Suva) |
| 05.11.88† | England 28, Australia 19 (Twickenham) |
| 04.02.89† | England 12, Scotland 12 (Twickenham) |
| 18.02.89† | Ireland 3, England 16 (Lansdowne Road) |
| 04.03.89† | England 11, France 0 (Twickenham) |
| 18.03.89† | Wales 12, England 9 (National Stadium) |
| 04.11.89† | England 58, Fiji 23 (Twickenham) |
| 20.01.90† | England 23, Ireland 0 (Twickenham) |
| 03.02.90† | France 7, England 26 (Parc des Princes) |
| 17.02.90† | England 34, Wales 6 (Twickenham) |
| 17.03.90† | Scotland 13, England 7 (Murrayfield) |
| 28.07.90† | Argentina 12, England 25 (Buenos Aires) |
| 04.08.90† | Argentina 15, England 13 (Buenos Aires) |
| 03.11.90† | England 51, Argentina 0 (Twickenham) |
| 19.01.91† | Wales 6, England 25 (National Stadium) |
| 16.02.91† | England 21, Scotland 12 (Twickenham) |
| 02.03.91† | Ireland 7, England 16 (Lansdowne Road) |
| 16.03.91† | England 21, France 19 (Twickenham) |
| 20.07.91† | Fiji 12, England 28 (Suva) |
| 27.07.91† | Australia 40, England 15 (Sydney Football Stadium) |

#### World Cup

| | |
|---|---|
| 03.10.91† | Group A  England 12, New Zealand 18 (Twickenham) |
| 08.10.91† | Group A  England 36, Italy 6 (Twickenham) |
| 11.10.91† | Group A  England 37, USA 9 (Twickenham) |
| 19.10.91† | Quarter-final  France 10, England 19 (Parc des Princes) |
| 26.10.91† | Semi-final  Scotland 6, England 9 (Murrayfield) |
| 02.11.91† | Final  England 6, Australia 12 (Twickenham) |
| 18.01.92† | Scotland 7, England 25 (Murrayfield) |
| 01.02.92† | England 38, Ireland 9 (Twickenham) |
| 15.02.92† | France 13, England 31 (Parc des Princes) |
| 07.03.92† | England 24, Wales 0 (Twickenham) |
| 17.10.92† | England 26, Canada 13 (Wembley) |
| 14.11.92† | England 33, South Africa 16 (Twickenham) |
| 16.01.93† | England 16, France 15 (Twickenham) |
| 06.02.93† | Wales 10, England 9 (National Stadium) |
| 06.03.93† | England 26, Scotland 12 (Twickenham) |
| 20.03.93† | Ireland 17, England 3 (Lansdowne Road) |

| | |
|---|---|
| 27.11.93† | England 15, New Zealand 9 (Twickenham) |
| 05.02.94† | Scotland 14, England 15 (Murrayfield) |
| 19.02.94† | England 12, Ireland 13 (Twickenham) |
| 05.03.94† | France 14, England 18 (Parc des Princes) |
| 19.03.94† | England 15, Wales 8 (Twickenham) |
| 04.06.94† | South Africa 15, England 32 (Pretoria) |
| 11.06.94† | South Africa 27, England 9 (Cape Town) |
| 12.11.94† | England 54, Romania 3 (Twickenham) |
| 10.12.94† | England 60, Canada 19 (Twickenham) |
| 21.01.95† | Ireland 8, England 20 (Lansdowne Road) |
| 04.02.95† | England 31, France 10 (Twickenham) |
| 18.02.95† | Wales 9, England 23 (National Stadium) |
| 18.03.95† | England 24, Scotland 12 (Twickenham) |

#### World Cup

| | |
|---|---|
| 27.05.95† | Pool B  England 24, Argentina 18 (Durban) |
| 04.06.95† | Pool B  England 44, Western Samoa 22 (Durban) |
| 11.06.95† | Quarter-final  England 25, Australia 22 (Cape Town) |
| 18.06.95† | Semi-final  England 29, New Zealand 45 (Cape Town) |
| 22.06.95† | Play-off  England 9, France 19 (Pretoria) |

†Captain
*Millennium Match

### Other England matches

| | |
|---|---|
| 08.06.88 | NSW B 9, England 25 (Wollongong) |
| 01.05.90 | Italy 15, England XV 33 (Rovigo) |
| 14.07.90† | Banco Nacion 29, England 21 (Buenos Aires) |
| 21.07.90† | Buenos Aires 26, England 23 (Buenos Aires) |
| 29.09.90† | England XV 18, Barbarians 16 (Twickenham) |
| 07.07.91† | NSW 21, England 19 (Waratah Rugby Park, Sydney) |
| 14.07.91† | Queensland 20, England 14 (Ballymore, Brisbane) |
| 07.09.91† | England 53, USSR 0 (Twickenham) |
| 21.05.94† | Natal 21, England 6 (Durban) |
| 25.05.94† | Western Transvaal 24, England 26 (Potchefstroom) |
| 28.05.94† | Transvaal 24, England 21 (Johannesburg) |

### England tries

| | |
|---|---|
| v | France, Twickenham, 1989 |
| v | France, Parc des Princes 1990 |
| v | Wales, Twickenham, 1990 |
| v | USA, Twickenham, 1991 |
| v | France, Parc des Princes, 1991 |
| v | Wales, Twickenham, 1992 |
| v | South Africa, Twickenham, 1992 |
| v | Romania, Twickenham, 1994 |
| v | Ireland, Dublin, 1995 |
| v | New Zealand, Cape Town, 1995 |
| v | New Zealand, Cape Town, 1995 |

**England matches missed**

| | |
|---|---|
| 05.06.88 | Australia 22, England 16 (Ballymore, Brisbane) (Sitting university exams) |
| 13.05.89 | Romania 3, England 58 (August Stadium, Bucharest) (Injured, shin splints) |
| 31.05.95 | Pool B England 27, Italy 20 (Durban) (Injured, ankle) |

**Carling's England record**

| Career | P | W | L | D | For | Agst | % |
|---|---|---|---|---|---|---|---|
| England | 60 | 44 | 15 | 1 | 1351 | 760 | 74.16 |
| England captain | 53 | 40 | 12 | 1 | 1241 | 679 | 76.41 |

**Five Nations Championships**

| Year | P | W | L | D | For | Agst | Pts | Pos |
|---|---|---|---|---|---|---|---|---|
| 1988 | 4 | 2 | 2 | 0 | 56 | 30 | 4 | 3rd |
| 1989† | 4 | 2 | 1 | 1 | 48 | 27 | 5 | 2nd |
| 1990† | 4 | 3 | 1 | 0 | 90 | 26 | 6 | 2nd |
| 1991† | 4 | 4 | 0 | 0 | 83 | 44 | 8 | 1st |
| 1992† | 4 | 4 | 0 | 0 | 118 | 29 | 8 | 1st |
| 1993† | 4 | 2 | 2 | 0 | 54 | 54 | 4 | 2nd= |
| 1994† | 4 | 3 | 1 | 0 | 60 | 49 | 6 | 2nd |
| 1995† | 4 | 4 | 0 | 0 | 98 | 39 | 8 | 1st |
| Total | 32 | 24 | 7 | 1 | 607 | 298 | 49 | 76.56% |

| Opponents | P | W | L | D | For | Agst | % |
|---|---|---|---|---|---|---|---|
| France | 10 | 8 | 2 | 0 | 191 | 117 | 80.00 |
| Wales | 8 | 5 | 3 | 0 | 142 | 63 | 62.50 |
| Scotland | 9 | 7 | 1 | 1 | 148 | 94 | 83.33 |
| Ireland | 9 | 7 | 2 | 0 | 184 | 70 | 77.77 |
| Australia | 5 | 2 | 3 | 0 | 82 | 121 | 40.00 |
| Fiji | 3 | 3 | 0 | 0 | 111 | 47 | 100.00 |
| Argentina | 4 | 3 | 1 | 0 | 113 | 45 | 75.00 |
| New Zealand | 3 | 1 | 2 | 0 | 56 | 72 | 33.33 |
| Italy | 1 | 1 | 0 | 0 | 36 | 6 | 100.00 |
| USA | 1 | 1 | 0 | 0 | 37 | 9 | 100.00 |
| Canada | 2 | 2 | 0 | 0 | 86 | 32 | 100.00 |
| South Africa | 3 | 2 | 1 | 0 | 74 | 58 | 66.66 |
| Romania | 1 | 1 | 0 | 0 | 54 | 3 | 100.00 |
| Western Samoa | 1 | 1 | 0 | 0 | 44 | 24 | 100.00 |

| Venue | P | W | L | D | For | Agst | % |
|---|---|---|---|---|---|---|---|
| Twickenham | 27 | 22 | 4 | 1 | 736 | 277 | 83.33 |
| Paris | 5 | 4 | 1 | 0 | 103 | 54 | 80.00 |
| Edinburgh | 5 | 4 | 1 | 0 | 65 | 46 | 80.00 |
| Dublin | 5 | 4 | 1 | 0 | 76 | 45 | 80.00 |
| Cardiff | 4 | 2 | 2 | 0 | 66 | 37 | 50.00 |
| Sydney | 2 | 0 | 2 | 0 | 23 | 68 | 0.00 |
| Suva | 2 | 2 | 0 | 0 | 53 | 24 | 100.00 |
| Buenos Aires | 2 | 1 | 1 | 0 | 38 | 27 | 50.00 |
| Wembley | 1 | 1 | 0 | 0 | 26 | 13 | 100.00 |
| Pretoria | 2 | 1 | 1 | 0 | 41 | 34 | 50.00 |
| Cape Town | 3 | 1 | 2 | 0 | 63 | 94 | 33.33 |
| Durban | 2 | 2 | 0 | 0 | 68 | 42 | 100.00 |